Sto
BORC

BLACKSTONE'S GUIDE TO
The Identity Cards Act 2006

BLACKSTONE'S GUIDE TO

The Identity Cards Act 2006

John Wadham
Caoilfhionn Gallagher
Nicole Chrolavicius

OXFORD
UNIVERSITY PRESS

OXFORD

UNIVERSITY PRESS

Great Clarendon Street, Oxford OX2 6DP

Oxford University Press is a department of the University of Oxford.
It furthers the University's objective of excellence in research, scholarship,
and education by publishing worldwide in

Oxford New York

Auckland Cape Town Dar es Salaam Hong Kong Karachi
Kuala Lumpur Madrid Melbourne Mexico City Nairobi
New Delhi Shanghai Taipei Toronto

With offices in

Argentina Austria Brazil Chile Czech Republic France Greece
Guatemala Hungary Italy Japan Poland Portugal Singapore
South Korea Switzerland Thailand Turkey Ukraine Vietnam

Oxford is a registered trade mark of Oxford University Press
in the UK and in certain other countries

Published in the United States
by Oxford University Press Inc., New York

British Library Cataloguing in Publication Data

Data available

Library of Congress Cataloging in Publication Data

Data available

Typeset by RefineCatch Limited, Bungay, Suffolk
Printed in Great Britain
on acid-free paper by
Biddles Ltd, King's Lynn

ISBN 0–19–928606–X (Pbk)   978–0–19–928606–5 (Pbk)

1 3 5 7 9 10 8 6 4 2

Foreword from Richard Thomas, Information Commissioner

The controversy stirred up by the identity card debate came as no surprise to anyone giving serious thought to data protection issues. A national ID system goes to the heart of the relationship between government and its citizens. The legislation may say 'Identity Cards Act 2006' on the front cover, but the substance deals with the National Identity Register. The Act deals with its compilation and maintenance, the circumstances where these details can be accessed by others and what it records about the circumstances where individuals produce their ID cards.

Much of this raises questions about benefits and risks. Will the ID system introduce a secure and reliable way for identity to be authenticated to the advantage of citizens and service providers alike? Or will the main focus be increased—and perhaps excessive—governmental information about citizens and their activities?

The answers will largely flow from how the scheme is operated in practice. There is much detail still to be established, not only in terms of the extensive range of matters left to secondary legislation, but also the actual systems of work that will be deployed. For example, the unique National Identity Registration Number could be used to link together many different records about individuals to their potential detriment. And any wide availability of the number itself could undermine security of personal information.

Addressing practical issues like these in ways that secure proper respect for individuals' data protection and privacy rights will be essential if public trust in the ID cards scheme is to be established and maintained. This book is a thorough analysis of the Identity Cards Act 2006 and provides comprehensive insights for all who will be grappling with what the legislation will mean in practice.

Contents—Summary

Contents

Contents

Contents

Preface

Identity cards generally, and this Act in particular, are controversial. People's views on the virtues or otherwise vary quite considerably. It will not be difficult for people to predict that, given that we have all worked for Liberty (the National Council for Civil Liberties), the three of us were not happy to see Royal Assent (and not just because of the hard work that lay ahead). However, we have tried to do our best to analyse and describe the legislation in a fair-minded way.

Given that we have now made clear our position on this, we would like to acknowledge the very significant contribution that Lord Phillips of Sudbury made during the passage of this Bill. He and his colleagues nearly stopped the legislation in its tracks. He certainly put off the most significant effects of compulsion until after the next election and, from the perspective of those who will be subject to the Act, he has clearly improved their remedies and their rights. There has been a lot of recent criticism of appointed peers in the House of Lords but he is an example of the necessary constitutional protection that members of the second chamber provide.

Acknowledgements

Although a significant number of people have contributed to our thinking about identity cards generally and this Act specifically, all three of us have a very significant debt to Greg Ó Ceallaigh and Emily Coates. They were there in the last week or two before our deadline to bail us out from meltdown. They specifically drafted the incredibly helpful Parliamentary Status Table setting out the very confusing parliamentary progress for this Bill. They were also there late at night on a couple of weekends doing the less glamorous and more tedious work of checking and double checking. Nevertheless, it was not just this that they helped with, and all of us learnt new things about the Act from their contributions. We would also like to thank others who helped us, including Ian Brown from the London School of Economics, Stephen Harrison from the Home Office, Guy Herbert from No2ID and Martin Westgate, Phil Haywood and Edward Fitzgerald QC from Doughty Street Chambers. The availability of the computer systems, the library and photocopies and tea and coffee, plus the administrative support provided by the other staff kept us going when we thought it was time to give up. If there are any mistakes they are ours alone.

Lastly, we would like to record our thanks to Annabel Moss who waited whilst we tried to read between the lines of the *Hansard* debates to predict whether this Bill would ever be an Act, what its content would be and when it would finally finish.

To the extent that any of this legislation has an immediate effect, the law is stated as at 7 June 2006.

John Wadham
Caoilfhionn Gallagher
Nicole Chrolavicius
June 2006

Table of Cases

References are to Paragraph Numbers

Table of Legislation, Treaties and Conventions

References are to Paragraph Numbers

1

INTRODUCTION

A. OVERVIEW

The Identity Cards Act 2006 puts in place the first national ID card scheme in **1.01** Britain since 1952. The scheme will, eventually, directly affect the daily lives of millions of people, and routinely involve sensitive and often highly personal information. The new system will, undoubtedly, fundamentally alter the relationship between the individual and the state—its most ardent supporters and its staunchest critics alike agree on that much. Whether this alteration will be for better or worse is a far more contentious question.

Grand rhetoric on either side of the debate has variously claimed that the ID **1.02** card itself will be a badge of citizenship for those entitled to be part of UK society, thus 'asserting our sense of identity and belonging'[1] and providing a means to tackle xenophobia and racism,[2] or an 'internal passport—don't leave home without it'[3] which treats the public as 'suspects, not citizens'.[4]

The constitutional significance of the Identity Cards Act 2006 is threefold: **1.03** what it creates in itself; what may follow, in a second Identity Cards Act; and, also, how it came into being.

The Act puts in place the infrastructure for a compulsory national ID scheme, **1.04**

---

[1] Statement by the Home Secretary to the House of Commons on Identity Cards, 11 November 2003, available at http://www.identitycards.gov.uk/downloads/statement_non-braille031111.pdf.
[2] Speech by the Home Secretary to the Institute of Public Policy Research (IPPR), 18 November 2004, available at http://www.identitycards.gov.uk/news-publications-general-speech.asp.
[3] Home Affairs Select Committee, Written Evidence, 38. Memorandum submitted by Privacy International (20 July 2004).
[4] 'Universal entitlement cards are compulsory IDs: the government does not trust its citizens', Liberty press release, 3 July 2002.

but it will not become compulsory to obtain a card without a new Act of Parliament. As it stands, the scheme may affect all those over the age of 16 residing in the UK for more than three months, of any nationality. All such individuals will be 'eligible' for an ID card.

1.05　　From late 2008, eligible individuals will be able to obtain a stand-alone ID card. Before that, individuals applying for certain documents which are 'designated' will be issued with an ID card, whether they want one or not. The government has indicated that it intends eventually to designate passports, immigration documents and biometric residence permits, although those applying for passports will be able to 'opt out' from obtaining an ID card until 2010 under a compromise agreed by the government and opposition to save the Act itself. Further documents, such as Criminal Records Bureau checks, may be designated at a later date.

1.06　　The Act introduces a complex range of new civil and criminal penalties, a new Commissioner's Office, and new ways of working for those providing public services (including the police, the National Health Service, passport office and benefit workers). This will also impact on the private sector, including retailers, banks and employers. Since April 2006 a new executive agency of the Home Office has been created as a result of the Act, the Identity and Passport Service (IPS). The Act will affect the operation of other legislation, such as the Data Protection Act 1998, the Police and Criminal Evidence Act 1984, the Regulation of Investigatory Powers Act 2000, the Race Relations Act 1976, the Immigration Acts (in particular, the Asylum and Immigration (Treatment of Claimants, etc) Act 2004 and the Immigration, Asylum and Nationality Act 2006), and the Terrorism Act 2006.

1.07　　There is very little information on the face of the Identity Cards Act 2006 concerning the ID card itself. Then Home Secretary, Charles Clarke, explained this absence to the Joint Committee on Human Rights during the passage of the Bill through Parliament:

> I must stress that the Identity Cards Bill is *enabling* legislation. Many of the precise details relating to the application process, the format of the ID card itself and the arrangements for the provision of information from the National Identity Register have yet to be decided. We have therefore not spelt out all the details on the face of the Bill and many of these can only be set out later in secondary legislation which will also have to be compatible with our ECHR obligations.[5]

1.08　　As the Act is enabling legislation only, and includes 60 regulation-making powers for the Secretary of State,[6] it is difficult to predict precisely how the scheme will operate in practice.

1.09　　During the passage of the Identity Cards Bill through Parliament a central

---

[5] Letter to the Joint Committee on Human Rights (JCHR), Appendix 1 to the JCHR's Eighth Report of Session 2004–05 (HL 60/HC 388).
[6] *Hansard*, HC col 152 (11 July 2005).

part of the Act, clause 6, which would have enabled compulsion to be 'rolled out' gradually to certain groups of individuals by regulation, was removed. The result is that ID cards and entry on the Register cannot be made compulsory, in the full sense of the word, without another Act of Parliament.

The Act is also constitutionally significant because of how it came about. The **1.10** Act eventually limped its way onto the statute book, minus many of its original crucial provisions, following a protracted Parliamentary stand-off between the House of Commons and the House of Lords. The Shadow Home Secretary said it was 'just about' acceptable in this form, and the Conservatives vowed to reverse the Act if they were to be elected at the next general election. The government accused the House of Lords of getting above their station as the unelected House, and ignoring the Salisbury Convention, the unwritten gentlemen's agreement that suggests the Lords should not block legislation based on the government's manifesto promises. The Bill's passage through Parliament reveals much about the interaction of the two Houses, and the ability of the legislature to oversee the executive.

There has been much sound and fury in delivering the Act to the statute book. **1.11** Quite what it signifies is, as yet, difficult to quantify fully. This text attempts to set out the immediate and likely effect of this Act, but also to predict future developments—in particular, what the consequences of a second Identity Cards Act could be.

B. IDENTIFICATION SYSTEMS

1. Overview

Systems of human identification are not new. Handwriting, dog tracking, ear **1.12** prints and fingerprinting have long been relied upon by law enforcement agencies as means of identifying individuals. Visual identification has long been relied upon by law enforcement agencies and the courts, but it is notoriously fallible. In 1976 the Devlin Committee (set up to propose reforms for the avoidance of miscarriages of justice in eyewitness cases) concluded that such identification evidence should be regarded with caution as it was unreliable.[7]

Less than a decade later, however, Alec Jeffreys discovered 'DNA fingerprint- **1.13** ing', and since then identification technologies have rapidly developed. They are now widely used within the UK, and provide a far more accurate and reliable method of identification than those the Devlin Committee examined 30 years ago.

Human identification is the association of data with a particular human **1.14** being. It may be used in relation to historical data already held on files, and to

---

[7] Report of the Committee on Evidence of Identification in Criminal Cases, Cmnd 338, 1976.

new transaction data that captures continuing aspects of that person's life or behaviour.

1.15　A number of bases are available to assist in formal identification. None of them is foolproof, and so identification usually operates through using a combination of identification techniques in order to achieve an appropriate balance between the harm arising from false inclusions or false positives (ie associating data with the wrong person) and from false exclusions or false negatives (ie failing to associate data with the right person).

1.16　A common approach when the state or another organization first establishes a relationship with a person is to seek a variety of information about them, from a variety of sources. In the absence of inconsistencies or 'bad' references the person is accepted as being identified by that loose set of data.

1.17　To facilitate identification during subsequent interactions between the organization and the individual, a token—usually a card—is issued to the individual. Filed information may then be linked to the individual through requiring them to produce the token/card. An additional 'real-time' identification technique may also be required when the card is produced to verify the individual's identity, such as requesting knowledge that the individual would be expected to have (such as a password or 'personal identification number', a PIN) or analyzing or measuring a physical characteristic recorded at the time of initial identification (such as fingerprints).

1.18　Technology may assist at each stage of the identification process.

2. Database Linking

1.19　In many countries worldwide, a national identifier, contained in an ID card, enables disparate information about a person that is stored in different databases to be easily linked and analyzed through 'data mining' techniques. On the face of the card only a certain amount of basic information may be displayed, but the card links to 'hidden' information stored on various databases.

3. Smart Cards

1.20　ID cards have become 'smarter' due to the availability and lowered cost of tiny micro-processors suitable for wallet-sized cards which can store a large amount of data. This technology allows multiple applications to be stored on the same national ID along with a personal identifier (such as a password or biometric identifier).

1.21　A smart card is a portable, hand-held card, usually the size of a credit card, containing an embedded computer microchip. Early generation smart cards contained only a memory function and some security protection. The most common application for such cards was as disposable stored value cards, eg as telephone cards in France, one of the earliest applications.

1.22　Smart card technology has actually existed for over 20 years, and has been considered for much of that time to be a technology in search of an application. Renewed interest in the technology is largely attributable to recent reductions in production costs, and the end of the period in which a licence fee had to be paid to the holder of the US smart card patent (1997). In 1995, there were only eight licensed smart card production plants in the world; a decade later there are over 3,000, each producing smart cards in their millions.

The modern smart card is essentially a stand-alone computer, much like a personal computer without a screen or a keyboard. Smart cards carry in-built microprocessors, enabling them to carry out intelligent functions. They have their own operating systems, temporary memory and file storage memory. In contrast with a PC, the operating system for a smart card is usually installed on the card by the manufacturer and cannot be changed. The existence of this operating system gives the card enormous flexibility. The smart card is self-sufficient, can follow its own programs and organize its own memory independent from an online network. At the time of manufacture, a unique serial number is programmed into each card, along with codes which allow the card to interact with other system components such as card readers and automatic teller machines. **1.23**

'Contact' smart cards use electrical contacts, placed on the cards in accordance with international standards, to allow them to be read by purpose-built smart card readers. 'Contactless' smart cards use low frequency radio waves to provide power and to communicate with smart card readers. Most contactless smart cards can be read from a distance of about six inches, and can be read without being removed from a wallet or purse, making them easier and faster to use for some applications. Both types of smart cards offer multi-functionality. The storage and processing capacities of smart cards are impressive, and it is not unusual to find a smart card that is capable of performing up to 50 different functions. **1.24**

Smart cards are already used by many private organizations in the UK for specific purposes, such as supermarket loyalty cards and travel cards for public transport (including Oyster cards on the London Underground network). **1.25**

4. Biometrics

'Biometrics' is a term which refers to the identification or verification of someone's identity on the basis of physiological or behavioural characteristics. Fingerprinting has long been used for a variety of governmental purposes, but newer forms of biometric identifiers include retina or iris scans, hand geometry, voice, facial and gait recognition, and digitized (electronically stored) images. **1.26**

A biometric system involves comparing a previously captured unique characteristic of a person to a new sample provided by the person. This information is used to authenticate or verify that a person is who they said they were (a one-to-one match) by comparing the stored characteristic to the fresh characteristic. It can also be used for identification purposes where the fresh characteristic is compared to all the stored characteristics (a one-to-many match). **1.27**

1.28   Biometric verification of identity, linked to a national ID card scheme, is popular in Asia and the Gulf States. The US government's requirement that countries with which it has visa waiver arrangements introduce biometric passports by 2006 has led a number of European countries, including the UK, to consider combining biometric technology for passport and national ID use.

C. STATE IDENTIFICATION SYSTEMS IN BRITAIN

1. Overview

1.29   Britain has introduced national ID card schemes twice in the past, both during the 20th century, and both at the outbreak of a World War. The first scheme was in place from 1915–1919, and the second from 1939–1952. During the passage of the Identity Cards Act 2006 through Parliament, the second scheme was repeatedly referred to by lobby groups and during debates, but the earlier scheme was largely ignored.

1.30   There are two general lessons to be learnt from the UK's historical experience: first, the cards were relatively popular; and secondly, 'function creep' appears to have been an issue.

1.31   In general, the cards tended to be popular—or certainly not unpopular—when introduced. This may, in part, have been due to a renewed sense of patriotism associated with the fighting of a major war abroad.

1.32   The experience of both schemes indicates that, although introduced for specific reasons connected to national security and the existing state of emergency, eventually the cards became used or demanded in a far wider range of situations. Indeed, this is how the World War II scheme eventually became unstuck.

2. The First National ID Card

1.33   In 1915, at the beginning of World War I, the National Registration Bill was before the House of Commons. It would require every person between the ages of 15 and 65 to register in a national register for the purposes, so it was said, of using the workforce to the best effect.

1.34   The Labour Party was against the Bill in principle. Philip Snowden, later to be Chancellor of the Exchequer in the first two Labour governments, said that the hidden purpose was to aid conscription. He said:

> I submit that the ulterior purpose of this Bill has not been disclosed, because if there was no motive behind the Bill than that which is disclosed in it, then such a Bill could not possibly have emanated from any other source than Bedlam.[8]

1.35   The government denied that the register was to aid conscription. The Bill

---

[8] Cited by Lord Thomas of Gresford, *Hansard*, HL col 1009 (15 November 2005).

passed. However, six months later the then National Registration Act was used to aid conscription. It is unclear whether the government's intention, from the outset, had been to use the card for conscription, or whether its intentions changed following the passing of the Act.

When the Act was passed there was no requirement to carry the identity certificate or produce it on demand. During Parliamentary debates the government explicitly criticized such a power and denied that such a power would be introduced. In early 1918, however, the Act was amended to permit a constable to demand sight of the identity certificate on pain of criminal sanctions.   1.36

When hostilities ceased in November 1918, the 1915 Act expired.   1.37

3. The Second National ID Card

On 5 September 1939, at the outbreak of World War II, another Emergency Registration Act was passed. It was passed for three stated reasons: first, the dislocation of the population caused by mobilization and mass evacuation; secondly, the likelihood of rationing; and, thirdly, the need for recent statistics because there had been no census since 1931.   1.38

That Act did not cease at the end of that war. By the time of its abolition in 1952 it was used not for three purposes but for 32, the most bizarre of which was to trace who was guilty of bigamy. Nye Bevan said of it: 1.39

I believe the requirement of an internal passport is more objectionable than an external passport, and that citizens ought to be allowed to move about freely, without running the risks of being accosted by a policeman or anyone else, and asked to produce proof of identity.[9]

In the post-war years there were protests against the continuation of the ID card scheme, often from unexpected quarters. The British Housewives' League assembled outside Parliament in April 1951 to burn their ID cards and ration-books. Rain almost destroyed their protest, but a number of the women found inventive ways to burn their cards regardless. Mrs Palmer of Sidcup managed to destroy her card by setting fire to it in a coffee tin, and Mrs Irene Lovelock of Denton was, *The Times* reported, 'partly successful with a frying pan'.[10] Mrs Lovelock, President of the League, was a rector's wife and she became something of a national celebrity after her protest. Her gesture of defiance earned her front-page coverage and police attention: 'two six foot policemen knocked the pan out of her hands and wrote her name and address in their notebooks'. She reportedly received hundreds of supportive letters and telegrams and became 'a folk hero'.[11]   1.40

---

[9] Cited by Lord Thomas of Gresford, *Hansard*, HL col 1010 (15 November 2005).

[10] *The Times*, April 1951, cited by G Stewart, 'Identity Cards and the Ghost of Mr Willcock', *The Times*, 1 April 2006.

[11] B Paine (ed), G Ward and P Francis (compilers), *Kent—Our Century, by the People who Lived it: A record of 100 years' history as reported by newspapers of the Kent Messenger Group* (Kent: privately published, 1999, funded by the Unseen History Project Millennium Festival).

1.41   Clarence Henry Willcock also became a national celebrity when in 1950 he refused a police officer's demand to stop his car and show his national ID card, stating 'I am a Liberal'. He was arrested. His case reached the High Court in June 1951: *Willcock v Muckle*. Mr Willcock challenged the obligation imposed on him by the National Registration Act 1939 to produce his national ID card to a police officer during a routine driving violation. In granting Mr Willcock an absolute discharge, Lord Goddard CJ noted that the original purpose of the national identity scheme, national security, had given way to numerous other functions which the ID card scheme was never meant to address. Lord Goddard CJ stated:

> This Act was passed for security purposes; it was never passed for the purposes for which it is now apparently being used. To use Acts of Parliament passed for particular purposes in wartime when the war is a thing of the past—except for the technicality that a state of war exists—tends to turn law-abiding subjects into lawbreakers, which is a most undesirable state of affairs.[12]

1.42   The Tories won the next general election, in October 1951. The new Minister for Health, Harry Crookshank, was greeted with cheers when he announced in the House of Commons in February 1952 that national ID cards were to be scrapped.[13]

4. Subsequent Attempts to Introduce a National ID Card

1.43   ID cards have been proposed a number of times since their abolition in 1952. In the past decade, both the Conservatives and Labour have, on occasion, advocated their use.

1.44   Prior to the election of the Labour government in May 1997, the Conservatives had considered introducing a national ID card. The then Home Secretary, Michael Howard, told the Tory Party Conference in 1994 that, 'in time, carrying your ID card would seem as natural as carrying a credit card is at the moment'.[14] In August 1996 he announced that, after a considerable period of consultation, he had concluded that the benefits outweighed any disadvantages. His key argument was that if one had nothing to hide, there was nothing to fear from the scheme. He argued that ID cards would cut crime and foil benefit cheats (so eager was his audience at one event that they booed him for daring to suggest that his scheme might be voluntary and not compulsory). The decent, law-abiding citizen would have nothing to fear from his proposals, he promised. Later, however, the Conservatives changed their position and decided that they would not introduce ID cards, either on a voluntary or compulsory basis.

1.45   Labour's recent history also includes consideration of compulsory ID cards. As Home Secretary, Jack Straw considered their introduction. He first suggested

---

[12] *Willcock v Muckle* [1951] 2 KB 844.   [13] 21 February 1952, cited by G Stewart (n 10 above).
[14] Home Office Parliamentary Labour Party Briefing, *Identity Cards*, 26 April 2004, 5.

the idea of a 'citizen's access card' shortly after Labour came to power in 1997. The idea never came to fruition, reportedly because it was shelved on the basis that the money could be better spent elsewhere.

D. STRUCTURE OF THE BOOK

The book's structure does not follow the structure of the Act because we have **1.46** based the chapters around the key functions and concepts instead. However, we start with a description and summary of ID card systems in other countries in order to put what is happening in this country into some kind of perspective. This comparative analysis is set out in chapter 2.

For those wanting an overview of the Act itself, we have set this out in sum- **1.47** mary form in chapter 3. Those wanting to know how the Act works in practice should start with chapter 3 and then move onto the specific provision or issue of interest to them.

Bizarrely, chapter 4, about the ID card, is perhaps not as important as other **1.48** chapters. Those who read on will realize that the legislation can make all kinds of documents, items and other things 'cards' for the purposes of the Act, and no one—including the government—is yet quite sure what people will be given when they are issued with an ID card. Will it be a chip in your passport, or look like yet another credit card?

The key structure of the new system is, in practice, not the ID card itself **1.49** but the National Identity Register. The process of how individuals will be entered onto the Register, and the constitutional loss of anonymity, is set out in chapter 5.

Once the system is up and running, one of the bureaucratic tasks for everyone **1.50** in this country will be to notify the Identity and Passport Service of changes of address and other things. 'How the register is maintained' is set out at chapter 6.

What might become in future more than merely an added bit of life's bureau- **1.51** cracy will be a significantly increased number of identity checks, whether those are for the purposes of obtaining public services or for consumer purposes. The extent of this intrusion into all of our lives may not depend so much on this legislation, but the extent to which all and any of those providing services (whether public or private) will impose de facto identity checks, well beyond what might be necessary to prevent crime or protect national security. This is detailed in chapter 7.

Once the Register is established, it will then be a key source of information **1.52** for a significant number of public bodies who will be able, not only to check identity via the Register in order to deliver a service, but also to check it without the consent of the subject and—in some cases—without them even knowing. Chapter 8 sets out how these powers will operate.

In order to ensure that the Register is kept accurate, and in order to deal **1.53** with identity fraud and to protect the Register from unauthorized disclosure, a significant number of criminal offences have been created by the Act. They are listed in chapter 9.

1.54　　In addition to the criminal offences, there is also an administrative penalty regime created by the Act, which will be operated by the Secretary of State. It is described in chapter 10.

1.55　　There are some significant and important protections for the individual in the Act, however. These include a newly created Identity Cards Scheme Commissioner and, of course, Parliament, because significant parts of the details will have to be developed by statutory instrument. One of the key issues for Parliamentarians will be the cost of the scheme, and the 'ping-ponging' between the Lords and the Commons during the final Parliamentary stages of the Bill ensured that the government must regularly report to Parliament on cost.

1.56　　The specific remedies that individuals might have in the case of a complaint relating to how they have been dealt with under the national identity scheme (including complaints to the Information Commissioner in relation to their data protection rights, or appeals to the civil courts following the imposition of a civil penalty by the Secretary of State) are dealt with in chapter 12.

2

NATIONAL IDENTITY SYSTEMS IN OTHER COUNTRIES

A. INTRODUCTION

1. Overview

National ID cards are in use, in some form, in many countries worldwide, **2.01** including most European, Asian and African countries. There are two blocs of countries that have traditionally tended not to have such national ID schemes: those with common law legal systems, and the Nordic countries.

The traditional common law aversion to ID card schemes is readily explicable, **2.02** given the Diceyan notion of 'residual liberty': that everything the citizen does is legal unless explicitly made illegal by government. As David Davis, Shadow Minister for Home Affairs, put it during the Second Reading of the 2005/06 Identity Cards Bill: 'The reason the common law countries are unique in this respect is that they are the countries which presume that the citizen is free to do anything unless there is a law against it. That is rather different from the Napoleonic law countries.'[1]

The legal philosophy of the Nordic countries, or 'Norden', is very different. **2.03** While all European countries may to some extent be described as general welfare states, what is distinctive about the Nordic approach is the dominant role of national governments in the formation of social policy and the development of an extensive public sector for the implementation of that policy. The state and

---

[1] *Hansard*, HC col 1174 (28 June 2005).

civil society are partly superimposed, and the public/private distinction is less clear than in its European neighbours.[2] The Nordic countries, to some common law traditionalists, might be considered to have tendencies indicative of the 'over-mighty state' which Lord Philips of Sudbury warned against in opposing the 2005–06 Identity Cards Bill.[3] Nevertheless, they traditionally have also avoided the use of national ID schemes (although in recent years this traditional aversion has largely dissipated). There is a degree of overlap between the Nordic and the common law countries, as both blocs are traditionally Northern European and they adhere to a basic guiding principle of the liberal rule of law. However, whether the historical absence of Nordic national identity schemes is accidental or principled is unclear.

2.04   In excess of 100 countries worldwide use some form of national ID card system. The type of card, its functions, its purposes, the information it contains, the technology used and the legal framework vary enormously from country to country. Some countries have 'an old-style card with a photograph',[4] others hi-tech 'smart cards' which boast unique, specific personal identifier samples or biometrics (such as an iris scan or fingerprint); some countries have full independent oversight of their national ID scheme, whereas others do not; some cards record sensitive information such as previous convictions, religion and immigration status, others only address, age and physical description; some are compulsory to have and carry at all times, others compulsory to obtain only, and others are voluntary.

2.05   ID cards in the majority of countries predate the 1980s and, in many cases, they were originally introduced when the country was under colonial rule,[5] a dictatorial government,[6] or during a state of emergency or wartime.[7] However, this often controversial history of the systems' introduction does not appear to impact on their current perceived legitimacy or public opinion. The fact that most countries with national ID schemes did not introduce them while independent democracies in peacetime means that their purposes have never been articulated; they are simply an accepted fact of life which remained post-independence, post-dismantling of a dictatorial regime, post-war. This chronology means that there is little precedent in terms of national debate over the aims or purposes of

---

[2] See S Kuhnle, 'Reshaping the Welfare State' in I Budge and K Newton *et al* (eds), *The Politics of the New Europe* (London and New York: Longman, 1997); S Kuhnle and R Ervik, 'The Nordic Welfare Model and the European Union' in B Greve (ed) *Comparative Welfare Systems: The Scandinavian Model in a Period of Change* (Basingstoke: Macmillan Press, 1996).

[3] *Hansard*, HL col 22 (31 October 2005).

[4] David Blunkett, ID Cards Statement to the House of Commons, 11 November 2003, available at http://www.homeoffice.gov.uk/docs2/statement%20non-braille031111.pdf.

[5] eg Cameroon, Rwanda, Democratic Republic of the Congo. Cf Burundi which abolished its national ID card scheme in 1962 following the ending of Belgian colonial rule. The cards had been introduced by the Belgians in the 1930s.

[6] eg Spain, Germany, Italy.

[7] eg Luxembourg, where ID cards have been compulsory for all citizens over the age of 15 since 1939.

ID card schemes, as very few democratic, non-colonial countries have attempted to introduce them during peacetime.[8]

2. Functions of National ID Schemes

Given that most ID card schemes internationally were retained rather than introduced with full public debate, it is often difficult to discern the schemes' purposes. However, it is possible to analyze their functions and the uses to which they are put. Further, in certain instances, public debate and articulation of the purposes of ID cards has occurred when the schemes have changed from paper-based, traditional schemes to electronic or smart card schemes.   **2.06**

Benefits of national ID card schemes are said to include combating various types of crime (including terrorism), improving the efficiency of the police, tackling illegal immigration and maintaining border integrity, preventing benefit and identity fraud, administrative ease, ensuring public services are available and provided to those who are entitled to them, and convenience to the citizen.   **2.07**

3. Objections to National ID Schemes

Long-established national ID card schemes tend to be uncontroversial amongst the general public, although opinion polls show marked differences in attitudes between ethnic, religious and socio-economic groups. In countries without national ID cards, the prospect of their introduction has often proved controversial. Objections raised have focused on privacy, equality and police powers, although cost has also been a key issue.   **2.08**

In many countries these objections have been raised by the public. In Australia in 1987, massive protests against the Australia Card almost brought down the government and led to the hasty withdrawal of the controversial proposals. A national ID card was dubbed a 'licence to live' in New Zealand when proposals there failed due to public opposition in 1992, and in the US a national ID card has long been termed an 'internal passport', a phrase which resonates in a country in which many inhabitants do not hold an actual passport and have never travelled outside their own country. In France, plans for an automated ID card were stalled for five years (1979–1984) due to public and political opposition. As Professor AC Grayling has pointed out, ID checks have recently caused friction amongst minority communities in France, and the catalyst for the French riots of October and November 2005 was the electrocution and death of two black youths who were attempting to escape an ID check.[9]   **2.09**

In other cases national ID systems have stumbled in the courts rather than in the public arena. The Supreme Court of the Philippines, for example, ruled in   **2.10**

---

[8] Examples of democratic peacetime introductions are the Netherlands (1994) and Malaysia (2001).
[9] Letter to *The Times*, 10 November 2005.

1998 that a national ID system violated the constitutional right to privacy.[10] In 1991 the Hungarian Constitutional Court found that a law creating a multi-use personal identification number also violated constitutional privacy.[11] In May 2005 a Japanese court ruled that the government's operation of its national computerized ID system 'seriously violates' citizens' constitutional right to privacy protected by Article 13 of the Japanese Constitution.[12] The decision is currently under appeal.

4. National Single-Purpose Card Schemes

2.11 Certain governments that have not instituted national ID cards nevertheless use cards for single-purpose transactions. Often, smart cards are used, which operate on the same technology as national ID cards in Asia and the Gulf States, but their purposes and functions are strictly limited and they cannot in any sense be considered national identity documents.

2.12 It is notable that the level of public support for the introduction of national ID schemes tends to be in inverse proportion to public knowledge of the details of the proposals. In Australia and New Zealand, for example, opinion polls revealed initially high levels of support when the proposals were first made, coupled with a lack of awareness of the government's plans (how the cards were intended to work, their functions, cost, and what information would be stored and shared). As awareness of the details grew, support decreased, and eventually, when public awareness of the details peaked, a majority of the public opposed the proposals.

2.13 In Norway, for example, smart cards are used to streamline voting administration and to reduce problems of electoral fraud. The system eliminates the need for ballot slips and envelopes and, as the card is difficult to counterfeit, the possibility of fraud is reduced. Voters enter a private booth to load their choice of candidate onto their card and then they use a voting unit to unload their choice from their card into the system. After the closing of the poll, the system automatically calculates the results.

2.14 In Mexico, state social security benefits are issued to over two million people in smart card form instead of cheques or cash. Purchases can only be made for certain goods at certain locations, for example, basic food and clothing purchases from government approved stores.

2.15 In Australia, a system is being developed whereby social security payments

---

[10] *Ople v Torres*, decision of the Supreme Court of the Philippines, GR No 127685, 23 July 1998, available at http://www.supremecourt.gov.ph/jurisprudence/1998/jul1998/127685.htm.

[11] Constitutional Court Decision No 15-AB of 13 April 1991.

[12] Ruling of Judge Kenichi Ido, Kanazawa District Court, Ishikawa, 30 May 2005. See 'Court Rules Resident Registry Network Unconstitutional', *Nihon Keizai Shimbun*, 30 May 2005; 'Court: Juki Net violates privacy', *The Asahi Shimbun*, 31 May 2005. Cf ruling of Nagoya District Court, 31 May 2005.

can be accessed directly using a government-issued card (initially a magnetic stripe card, but subsequently to be reissued as a smart card) at automatic teller machines. This would remove the need for the Department of Social Security to issue cheques.

In the Czech Republic, which also has a national ID card, a separate single- **2.16** purpose smart card for patient data was piloted in 1998. The smart card replaced the paper-based system, as it was considered inaccurate, labour-intensive to maintain and open to widespread abuse.

B. EUROPEAN COUNTRIES

1. Overview

Most continental European countries have long had some form of national ID **2.17** card. This history was one of the reasons why the debates concerning both previous British ID card schemes (1915–1919 and 1939–1952) were framed by notions of national identity. Even the civil servants administering the first card system described it as a 'Prussianising' institution.[13] Public commentators pointed out how the card conflicted with patriotism, describing it as an 'Unbritish' system. Churchill, in a House of Commons debate on 3 September 1939, regretted the trespass made on 'our dearly valued traditional liberties', and looked 'forward to the day, when our liberties and rights will be restored to us, and when we shall be able to share them with the peoples to whom such blessings are unknown'.

In the past two decades, the principles of free movement of goods and persons **2.18** within the EU have inspired much discussion concerning identity documentation. In 1983 the European Council affirmed the principle of harmonization of identity documents and the acceptance of ID cards as an alternative to passports within member states.[14] With the signing of the original Schengen Agreement in 1985, the general goal of abolishing all frontier controls and harmonizing cross-border procedures was established. A total of 26 countries, including all EU states except the Republic of Ireland and the UK, but including non-EU members Iceland, Norway and Switzerland, have signed the Schengen Agreement. The implementing Convention was signed in 1990 detailing measures necessary to achieve those goals. However, the opening of borders for legitimate reasons has raised concerns that this will facilitate an increase in cross-border crime, and in the mid-1990s a European Identity Card was tentatively proposed in order to police a borderless Europe.[15]

---

[13] Dr J Agar, 'Identity Cards in Britain: Past Experience and Policy Implications', paper published by the Cambridge University History and Policy Initiative, 22 November 2005; available at http://www.historyandpolicy.org/archive/policy-paper-33.html.

[14] *International recognition of national identity cards* (Strasbourg: Council of Europe, 1983).

[15] Statewatch, 1995.

2.19   However, until May 2004 there was no discernible trend across EU Member States in relation to national ID card schemes. Of 15 Member States, four countries had no card whatsoever (Britain, Ireland, Sweden and Denmark), five had compulsory schemes (Belgium, Germany, Luxembourg, Spain and Greece) and the remaining six had voluntary schemes (Austria, Finland, France, Italy, Netherlands and Portugal).

2.20   The arrival of 10 new entrants to the Union in May 2004 tipped the balance. Of the 25 current Member States, 10 now have a voluntary scheme and 11 a compulsory scheme. Until the introduction of the Identity Cards Act 2006 Britain was one of four countries without a card (the others being Ireland, Denmark and Latvia, as Sweden introduced a voluntary scheme in October 2005).

2.21   The Identity Cards Act 2006 now leaves Ireland as the only common law country in the EU (of three in total) without a national ID card scheme. The third common law country is Cyprus, and, as the Home Office pointed out during passage of the Identity Cards Bill through Parliament, it has ID cards which all Cypriot citizens over the age of 12 must obtain.[16]

2.22   In July 2005, shortly after the bombings in London, an extraordinary meeting of EU Justice and Home Affairs Ministers was held to discuss tackling terrorism. The meeting was led by the then UK Presidency of the EU.[17] The UK proposed that the Ministers agree common standards for security features (including biometrics) and secure issuing procedures for ID cards by December 2005, with detailed standards agreed as soon as possible thereafter. The Ministers collectively urged the member states to adopt this proposal. A 'collaborative approach to the provision of biometric capacity to visa issuing posts' was urged, along with a call on member states to 'intensify the exchange of police and judicial information'. The Council of Ministers said it would develop further the ability to share visa information (via the VIS) and law-enforcement information (via the SIS-II), and prioritize the rollout of biometrics to immigrants and asylum seekers from 'high-risk regions and countries'.

2.23   In addition, the extraordinary meeting considered other mechanisms to 'build on the existing strong EU framework for pursuing and investigating terrorists across borders, in order to impede terrorists' planning, disrupt supporting networks, cut off any funding and bring terrorists to justice'. In this respect, the Council said it would soon agree the Framework Decisions on the retention of telecommunications data (October 2005), on the European Evidence Warrant (December 2005), and on the exchange of information between law enforcement authorities (December 2005). The Council also said that it would soon adopt the Decision on the exchange of information concerning terrorist offences (September 2005), agree and adopt a number of relevant regulations and directives aimed at preventing terrorism financing, and it urged the European

---

[16] *Hansard*, HC Written Answers, col 1416W (24 May 2004) (Mr Browne to Mr Gibb).
[17] Meeting held 13 July 2005 following the bombings in London on 7 July 2005.

Commission to bring forward the proposal on airline passenger name records by October 2005.

2. Compulsory Schemes

Compulsory national ID card schemes now operate in 11 EU member states. **2.24** However, 'compulsion' is not by any means uniform: although there is, in practice, an obligation to establish identity in certain circumstances in all 11 countries, the countries differ in relation to whether the card is compulsory to *obtain*, compulsory to *carry*, and compulsory to *produce* when requested.

It is compulsory to carry one's ID card at all times in only two EU countries, **2.25** Belgium and Cyprus. In Belgium, the legislation states:

Police officials control the identity of each person whose liberty has been taken or who has committed a crime. Moreover the police official can proceed to identity control whenever there is a reasonable presumption that a person is being tracked down, has tried or is *preparing* to commit a crime, or *might* disturb public order or has already done so.[18]

Failure to prove one's identity immediately can lead to administrative detention for a maximum of 12 hours and a possible fine.

In Germany, Spain, Luxembourg and Lithuania, residents must carry some **2.26** form of identity document or otherwise be able to prove their identity to police if stopped, but the proof need not necessarily be the 'compulsory' ID card.

In Luxembourg, Germany and Spain, inability to prove one's identity satis- **2.27** factorily can lead to a fine. Under the German ID Card Act, last amended in 1987, it is not a criminal offence to fail to carry a card, but it is an offence to fail to obtain an ID card or to refuse to establish one's identity when stopped.[19] The police are entitled to stop and search on the grounds of criminal procedure, the execution of a sentence or in the interest of public safety and, in all of these instances, ID of some kind may be demanded. The police may also demand ID at the border or at a checkpoint installed for reasons such as the prevention or detection of terrorist activity.[20] If an individual is stopped and cannot satisfactorily prove his or her identity, the police are entitled to accompany the individual to his or her address until the card is produced. The individual may also be asked to accompany the police officer to the police station, where identity may be established by other means, such as fingerprinting.[21] Failure to establish identity on the spot may lead to the individual incurring an administrative fine.

In Greece, although it is not legally compulsory to carry the card, the police **2.28**

---

[18] Ministère de l'Interieur, *Loi sur la fonction de police* (Royaume Belgique, 1992) 11 (emphasis added).

[19] D Zimmerman, *Amendment to the Identity Card Act* (Bonn: Ministry for the Interior, 1986).

[20] A Beck and K Broadhurst, 'Compulsion by stealth: lesson from the European Union on the use of national identity cards' (1998) 76 *Public Administration* 779–792, 785.

[21] Bundeskriminalamt, 1995.

are entitled to ask individuals to produce their ID cards in a range of circumstances in order to confirm their identity. In practice this means that the card tends to be carried. Persons who fail to produce an ID card when requested to do so by the police are usually taken to a police station for verification of their identity and status.

2.29   In Luxembourg, the police may demand that a person prove his or her identity if he or she is suspected of having committed or conspired to commit an offence.[22] Individuals wanted by legal or administrative authorities may also be obliged to produce ID. Those who witness a crime may also have to produce ID.

2.30   There are states in which ID cards may not be compulsory, but registration is either required or automatic. In Sweden, for example, although the recently introduced ID card system is voluntary only, it has been long been compulsory to belong to a national register. At birth or when settling in the country everyone receives a personal identity number (*personnummer*) which remains with that person for life. Until 1991 the register was managed by the Swedish church, but it is now administered by the tax authority. Registration through the church has taken place since the 17th century, and the current numbering system dates from 1947.

2.31   The *personnummer* is registered by local authorities but connected to the national register. As a governmentally held document the number is public, but privacy laws prevent certain personal details (such as mental or physical health, family circumstances or ability to work) being revealed to any party other than the individual in question and the relevant public authority. It has been argued that the number is 'part of the cultural heritage' of Sweden, and that it is perceived by some as a right of the citizen rather than an intrusion:

An instrument that (from a British, or indeed an American perspective) could be perceived as a compulsion is in Sweden at least seen as a person's natural right. There is an important contractual, even democratic, element here: some data (like tax returns) has to be provided to state authorities, but citizens also expect the state to automatically provide them with the different type of benefits due to them—including many that are sent automatically and not even applied for.[23]

3. Voluntary Schemes

2.32   Ten EU member states currently operate a 'voluntary' national ID card scheme. As with 'compulsion', 'voluntariness' is a spectrum which includes many different approaches. In some countries, the card is theoretically voluntary but, in practice, it is required for a range of everyday transactions, whereas in other countries the card is genuinely voluntary and has a very low take-up rate. No

---

[22] Beck and Broadhurst (n 20 above) 781.
[23] S Forsstrom, 'Identity Politics', *Open Democracy*, 24 May 2005.

other EU country uses the theoretically 'voluntary' scheme which the UK is using during phase 1 of the roll-out of ID cards, obliging everyone who applies for certain official 'designated' documents to register and obtain a card.

In France, the ID card or other official ID is needed for voting, social security **2.33** and financial transactions. The police have very broad powers to stop and ask an individual to prove his or her identity. If the police feel there is a genuine risk to public order, for example, they are entitled to carry out an identity check on any individuals in the area.[24] In 1993 the French Parliament adopted a Bill designed to reinforce and enlarge the possibility of identity checks. It included a police power to stop and check the ID documentation of those suspected of being in the country illegally. This power may be exercised anywhere in the country, at any time, and not simply at border crossings.

In the Netherlands, every citizen from the age of 12 has a duty to produce **2.34** identification in a range of everyday situations. The Identification Act specifies circumstances in which an individual may be asked to prove their identity immediately. These include, for example, a duty to show ID if asked when attending a professional football game (although the police are not legally entitled to ask a spectator to produce ID without reason); a duty to show ID if asked by police who have a 'genuine suspicion' that he or she may have committed an offence; a duty to show ID if asked by a police officer investigating illegal immigration; a duty to prove identity on public transport if unable to produce a valid ticket to a fare inspector or the police.[25] Since a voluntary national ID scheme was implemented in 1994, many choose to carry their card in order to comply with these duties.

4. Cost

Fourteen EU countries charge for the ID card. The approach to cost for com- **2.35** pulsory cards across the EU has been described by the London School of Economics (LSE) Identity Project as 'remarkably consistent';[26] the charging regime reflects an understanding amongst governments with compulsory schemes that compulsion is particularly divisive if the cost of the card is high. The highest charge for any compulsory card is in Germany, at £6.00; the average charge for a compulsory card across the EU is only £3.90.

The approach to charging for voluntary cards is not consistent across the EU, **2.36** however. In general, voluntary cards are far more expensive. This is explained by the LSE Identity Project as indicating that when the unit charge is high, only a voluntary scheme is deemed acceptable by the public:

Countries that have adopted voluntary cards, such as Austria, Finland and Slovenia, have developed their systems with the aim of delivering proven benefits to the citizen and thus

---

[24] ibid 786.   [25] *Identification Rules*, Ministry of Justice (The Hague, 1994).
[26] LSE Identity Project, *House of Lords: All-Party Briefing for Report Stage*, 23 January 2006.

building a resilient foundation of public trust. This evolution is necessary to make the cards attractive and desirable. Thus the average charge across the EU for a voluntary card can be justified at a higher unit price than a compulsory card, ie £14.40.[27]

The most expensive cards in Europe are the voluntary cards in Austria (£39.00) and Sweden (£30.00).

2.37   However, other countries with voluntary schemes do not follow the LSE logic. In France, for example, the card is currently free. Previously, the government did charge for the card, but the cost was relatively low. This low cost was a means of ensuring the card was popular and to improve the take-up rate. Many French citizens chose to buy a voluntary ID card because it could be used for travel within the EU, and it cost one-third of the price of a passport.[28] The Lithuanian voluntary ID card is also free, and in Hungary, Italy and Portugal the cards cost under £5.00.

5. Types of Card

2.38 The majority of EU countries with national ID schemes have a free-standing ID card, not a card linked to other identity documents, such as passports or driving licences.[29] Most countries have plastic cards bearing photographs, which are in some cases machine-readable. Electronic or 'e-cards' have been introduced in Finland and Spain, and are currently being rolled out in Italy (completion expected by 2008) and Belgium (e-cards will be compulsory by January 2009).

2.39   The US government's requirement that countries with which it has visa waiver arrangements introduce biometric passports by 2006 has led a number of European countries to consider combining biometric technology for passport and national ID use, although only the UK has adopted this approach. The Spanish government has started rolling out biometric cards, although they are not linked to its passport infrastructure. There are also plans to use such technology for French and German cards, but there is, as yet, no specific timetable in place for this.

2.40   Within certain EU countries there are distinctions between types of card. Immigrants or asylum seekers often have a card with different information displayed upon it or with a noticeably different appearance. In Austria citizens with certain criminal convictions (child sexual offences and certain violent offences) are only entitled to hold a red ID card, whereas the standard card is blue. The red ID cards are valid only within Austria in order to prevent the holders from using the card for travelling.

---

[27] ibid 1.   [28] G Stefani and G Levasseur, *Procedure penal* (Paris: Dalloz, 1996).
[29] *Identity Cards*, Government Reply to the Fourth Report from the Home Affairs Committee, Session 2003–04 HC 130, October 2004, col 6359 at 5.

6. Information Retained and Displayed

In all EU countries with ID cards certain basic identificatory information is 2.41 displayed on the card: name, address, date of birth, signature, photograph and card number. Dates of issue and expiry are also noted.

Additional information is included on certain national ID cards. Uniquely, 2.42 Italian ID cards (which are voluntary) state the holder's marital status and profession. In Finland, health insurance data may be added to the face of the ID card if the cardholder so requests. Until 2000, the mandatory ID cards used in Greece included details on religious affiliation. A binding ruling was issued by the Hellenic Data Protection Authority (HDPA) on 15 May 2000 ordering religion, fingerprints, citizenship, spouse's name and profession to be removed from the cards.[30] In June 2000 the European Commission against Racism and Intolerance (ECRI), the Council of Europe's expert body on combating racism, echoed the HDPA's decision. It recommended that 'any reference to religion be removed from identity cards, in order to limit overt or covert discrimination against members of non-Orthodox religions, who may in some cases be considered less "Greek" than Orthodox ethnic Greeks'.[31] The government responded by promising to introduce new identity documents which would not include the offending information. This decision provoked outrage on the part of the Greek Orthodox Church, which organized major demonstrations and a petition in opposition to the government's proposals. However, the HDPA's ruling and the ECRI recommendation were followed, and since 2001 Greek ID cards now omit religious details, even if the holder specifically requests their inclusion.

The main distinction between the different EU schemes relates to the informa- 2.43 tion retained and linked to the card, rather than the information displayed on the card itself. Unlike national ID schemes in Asia and the Gulf States, most European ID cards tend to have very little 'hidden' information and database linking.

Portugal retains no 'hidden' information whatsoever: a single database exists 2.44 which simply reproduces the information listed on the face of the card itself. Portuguese ID cards are thus purely 'on-the-spot' cards—partly due to Article 35(5) of the Portuguese Constitution, which states that 'citizens shall not be given an all-purpose national identity number'.

The same is true of the French, German, Swedish and Dutch cards. In these 2.45 countries the reason for the lack of broader database linkage is specific legislation protecting privacy and freedom of information which guarantees citizens the right to access and modify any governmental records involving them. In Germany in particular, data protection has evolved into a human right, protected as part of the general right to the protection of an individual's personality

---

[30] Decision 510-17-15.05.2000, available at http://www.dpa.gr/Documents/Eng/DEC.Idcards510-17-15.05.2000.doc.
[31] *ECRI's second report on Greece*, 27 June 2000.

and thereby worthy of constitutional protection.[32] The German Federal Constitutional Court declared it incompatible with human dignity if the state were systematically to create a personal profile of extensive information on certain citizens.

2.46   In Belgium and Finland the national ID card can be used to access government services, and so the card number links to various state databases concerning entitlement to those services.

7. Functions of National ID Cards

2.47   The functions to which ID cards are put vary greatly across the EU. There are two common factors. First, all national ID cards within the EU, voluntary or compulsory, may be used for travel within the European Economic Area and to any other countries with which the state has a bilateral agreement. Secondly, all national ID cards are accepted by the state and private sector as official proof of identity.

2.48   Within the EU, Greece has the widest range of purposes for its ID cards. Production of an ID card is required in an extremely wide range of circumstances. It is a prerequisite for receiving state benefits; opening a bank account; being admitted to a university; buying property; and appearing in court.

2.49   An increasing trend in EU countries is for ID cards to be available for accessing online government services. Currently Finland and Belgium are the only EU countries with capacity to do this, but seven further states have plans to introduce new e-cards with this capacity over the next five years.

2.50   Notably, Germany restricts the uses for which information gathered in the German register can be used. Paragraph 2 of the *Personalausweisgesetz* provides that the information provided to the German register can only be used for two limited purposes: first, to issue ID cards and determine their validity and, secondly, to determine the identity of the person holding the card. The function of the information collected for the register is just to facilitate the production of ID cards. In this way, the amount of information held on the German register is less extensive than the amount of information that is anticipated will be collected for the UK National Identity Register.[33]

8. Non-Nationals

2.51   A contentious issue in all EU countries surrounding ID cards, voluntary or compulsory, is how the schemes apply to non-nationals. This is a logical problem as the majority of governments have stated their intention to use the cards to

---

[32] J Fedtke, 'Identity Cards and Data Protection: Security Interests and Individual Freedom in Times of Crisis', Current Legal Problems lecture, delivered at University College London, 3 November 2005.
[33] ibid.

tackle illegal immigration (and have, since 11 September 2001, increasingly linked this issue to terrorism).

Two-tier ID card schemes which distinguish between 'nationals' and other 2.52 EU nationals have been held to breach Community law. Community law does not prevent a member state from carrying out checks on compliance with the obligation to be able to produce a residence permit at all times, but if the same obligation is not imposed on its own nationals as regards their ID card, this will constitute a breach.[34] In the event of failure to comply with an obligation to produce identification, the national authorities are entitled to impose penalties comparable to those attaching to similar offences committed by their own nationals. A further restriction is that even if the sanction is comparable to that imposed upon nationals, it cannot be so disproportionate a penalty that it becomes an obstacle to the free movement of workers.

In 2003, the UK plans outlined by the Home Office in *Identity Cards: the* 2.53 *Next Steps* breached this principle of equal treatment, as the cards were to be compulsory in phase one for non-nationals, including EU citizens, and failure to comply with the obligation to register would give rise to a range of civil and criminal penalties. As UK nationals would not be obliged to register during this phase, they would not be subject to any such sanctions. This discrimination between UK nationals and other EU nationals no longer appears on the face of the Identity Cards Act 2006.

In order to comply with EU law, any regulations must treat EU nationals 2.54 equally.

A number of EU countries do distinguish between EU and non-EU nationals 2.55 in their ID card schemes. Additional information is requested, or added to the database, or appears on the face of the card. Spanish ID cards, for example, have no biometrics for EU nationals, but 'foreign nationals' must provide two finger-prints.[35] The Belgian *carte d'identité* or *identiteitskaart* displays the nationality of non-EU foreigners.

In all EU countries with compulsory schemes, and in those with 'voluntary' 2.56 schemes in which voluntariness is largely illusory, nationality and perceived nationality impact on the operation in practice of powers linked to requests for proof of identification, even if the distinction is not drawn on the card or the database. In France, for example, 1993 legislation introduced a police power to stop and check the identification papers of any individual suspected of being in France illegally. During the passage of the Bill through Parliament, and following its introduction, human rights groups criticized this power, arguing that, in practice, it would open the door to arbitrary, discriminatory and racist practices, often based merely on physical appearance, and that certain groups of

---

[34] Case 321/87 *Commission v Belgium* [1989] ECR 997, para 12; Case C-24/97 *Commission v Germany*, Opinion of Advocate General Jacobs (1998); Case C-24/97 *Commission v Germany* [1998] ECR I-2133.

[35] LSE Identity Project (n 26 above) 2.

young people, non-whites and other marginal groups would be far more likely to be submitted to an identity check. The government has repeatedly stated that the immigration status checks must be carried out in a 'non-discriminatory manner', and assessment of who constitutes a foreign national 'shall be based solely on objective criteria which comply with non-racist and non-xenophobic principles'. However, commentators have claimed that: 'these restrictions are somewhat meaningless and in practice have provided officers with an excuse to harass those of ethnic minority, be they non-French individuals or actual natives of the country'.[36]

2.57 As national ID cards are linked to notions of statehood, nationhood and citizenship, it is unsurprising that they prove particularly controversial in disputed territories. Some Basque nationalist organizations issue para-official ID cards (*Euskal Nortasun Agiria*) as a means of rejecting the nationality notions implied by Spanish compulsory and French voluntary ID documents. They try to use the ENA instead of the official document when ID is requested.

2.58 Since 2005, the EU Council of Ministers has prioritized distinguishing between identification required of EU and non-EU nationals. It intends to develop further the ability to share visa information (via the VIS) and law-enforcement information (via the SIS-II), and prioritize the rollout of biometrics to immigrants and asylum seekers from 'high-risk regions and countries'. These measures are intended to operate at point of entry to the EU, but as the biometric requirements are being linked to ID cards by many countries (including the UK, France, Italy, Spain and Germany) in practice this will also impact on internal identification checks.

C. COMMON LAW COUNTRIES

1. Overview

2.59 No traditionally common law country has ever introduced a national ID card outside the context of war. During the passage of the Identity Cards Act 2006 through Parliament David Davis raised this point:

As yesterday's report from the London School of Economics found—I do not want to give the Home Secretary dyspepsia –

'With the exception of Malaysia, Singapore, Hong Kong and Cyprus, no common law country in the world has ever accepted the idea of a peacetime ID card'.

The Prime Minister has always been concerned about making his mark on history. That is quite a legacy to leave.[37]

2.60 Proposals to introduce such a card have been rejected by Australia (1987),

---

[36] Beck and Broadhurst (n 20 above) 787.   [37] *Hansard*, HC col 1174 (28 June 2005).

New Zealand (1991), the US (most recently in 2002) and Canada (2004). In all cases, it was argued that a national ID card was anathema to the relationship between the individual and the state at common law. In Canada, the Federal Privacy Commissioner submitted to a Parliamentary Committee examining the issue that, 'feeding all our daily transactions into a massive database that could then be mined for signs of potential terrorist activity would be highly invasive and contrary to our common law traditions and long-established civil liberties protections'.[38]

All common law countries without national, universal, multi-purpose ID cards **2.61** do nevertheless have sectoral cards or identifier systems, used for particular purposes, such as health or social security.[39] Examples include the Social Security Number in the US, the National Insurance number in the UK, the Social Insurance Card in Canada, and the Medicare Card in Australia. These were introduced as low-integrity systems designed for a single purpose, although the US and Canadian Social Security numbers did grow from this and have been used for additional public and private sector purposes. Successive Committees established during the 1980s and 1990s to consider whether the US Social Security Number and Card scheme should be replaced, recommended against such a project on the grounds of impracticality and excessive infringement of human rights. Some common law countries also use identifiers for particular groups, for example fingerprint scanning systems for welfare recipients.

It has been suggested that the concept of 'one-person-one-identity' which **2.62** underlies the Identity Cards Act 2006 is dubious in a common law context. It is a concept foreign to traditional English law, because the use of an alias has never been in itself a crime. Many people 'hide behind' more than one name, variously for psychological, security, personal and sometimes criminal reasons. Users of aliases include creative people such as artists, authors and actors, and professional people, particularly females, but also staff at psychiatric and prison institutions, private detectives and intelligence operatives.

2. United States

The US does not have a national ID card as such. When the Social Security **2.63** Number (SSN) was created in 1936, it was intended to be used only as an account number associated with the administration of the Social Security system. Use of the SSN has expanded considerably since its introduction, and it is now widely used. Despite this, it is not a universal identifier and efforts to make it one have been consistently rejected. In 1971, the Social Security

---

[38] Submission of the Office of the Privacy Commissioner of Canada to the Standing Committee on Citizenship and Immigration, 18 September 2003, available at http://www.privcom.gc.ca/media/nr-c/2003/submission_nid_030918_e.pdf.

[39] The reverse is true in a non-common law country, Sweden, which has a multi-purpose number but no ID card.

Administration task force on the SSN rejected the extension of the SSN to the status of an ID card. In 1973, the Health, Education and Welfare Secretary's Advisory Committee on Automated Personal Data Systems concluded that a national identifier was not desirable. In 1976, the Federal Advisory Committee on False Identification rejected the idea of a national, multi-purpose identifier. In 1977, the Carter Administration reiterated that the SSN was not to become an identifier.

2.64   In 1981 the Reagan Administration stated that it was 'explicitly opposed' to the creation of a national ID card.

2.65   The Clinton administration advocated a 'Health Security Card' in 1993 and assured the public that the card, issued to every American, would have 'full protection for privacy and confidentiality'. Still, the idea was rejected and the health security card was never created.

2.66   In 1999 Congress repealed a controversial provision in the Illegal Immigration Reform and Immigrant Responsibility Act 1996 which gave authorization to include SSNs on drivers' licences.

2.67   Following the tragic events of 11 September 2001, there was renewed interest in the creation of national ID cards. Soon after the attacks, Larry Ellison, head of California-based software company Oracle Corporation, called for the development of a national identification system and offered to donate the technology to make this possible. He proposed ID cards with embedded digitized thumbprints and photographs for all legal residents in the US. There was much public debate about the issue, and Congressional hearings were held. Former House Speaker Newt Gingrich testified that he 'would not institute a national ID card because you do get into civil liberties issues'. When it created the Department of Homeland Security (DHS), Congress made clear in the enabling legislation that the agency could not create a national ID system. In September 2004, then DHS Secretary Tom Ridge reiterated that 'the legislation that created the Department of Homeland Security was very specific on the question of a national ID card. They said there will be no national ID card.'[40]

2.68   Since 11 September 2001, Americans have accepted many incursions into their personal privacy in the name of increased security. Airline passengers have removed their shoes and stood with arms outspread as uniformed officials peered into their cabin baggage; the Department of Homeland Security has had mainstream support for its proposal to colour-code all passengers based on the likelihood that they may commit a terrorist act; banks have requested information from new customers which is promptly transferred to federal investigators. In this context, the withdrawal and rejection of these national ID card proposals are extremely significant. The refusal to introduce national ID cards in the US following 11 September was repeatedly commented upon in the Commons and the Lords during the passage of the 2004–05 and 2005–06 Identity Cards Bills:

---

[40] Remarks made at the National Press Club, Washington DC, 7 September 2004.

Patrick Mercer:	Is it not interesting that the country that has been so afflicted by terrorism—so seriously hurt in such a brief time scale—does not have identity cards? Indeed, the introduction of identity cards in that country would be illegal.
Mr Garnier:	President Bush has made it clear that the compulsory introduction of identity cards and a national identity register would be a step too far in the United States, where terrorists have attacked the fabric of the nation and where an attack was carried out with identity documents. The people who committed the attacks on 11 September had passports, and some even had pilot's licences. They certainly had other forms of identification. An identity card system, which the Bill seeks to introduce in this country, would not have prevented that attack and I am not even sure that it would have helped to detect it, not least because all those who took an active part in the outrages were killed—they all committed suicide.

However, there are two caveats to this picture. First, although the US itself has no federal ID card scheme, it has threatened to withdraw the facilities of the visa waiver scheme (under which nationals of favoured countries need not apply for visas to enter the US in advance of travel) from countries that do not introduce digitally readable passports enabling electronic checking of individuals against extensive databases for the purposes of ensuring homeland security. Second, in 2005 Congress passed the Real ID Act. This endorses standardized, electronically readable drivers' licences, and many critics of the Act argue that it ushers in what, in practice, amounts to a national ID card. **2.69**

The Real ID Act was backed by the Republican Party. On 26 January 2005 the House of Representatives Judiciary Committee Chairman introduced the Real ID Act, describing it as 'the first must-pass legislation' of the year, which contained 'common-sense provisions'. He stated: **2.70**

The goal of the Real ID Act is straightforward: it seeks to prevent another 9/11-type attack by disrupting terrorist travel. First, this legislation does not try to set state policy for who may or may not drive a car, but it does address the use of a driver's license as a form of identification to a federal official. American citizens have the right to know who is in their country, that people are who they say they are, and that the name on a driver's license is the holder's real name, not some alias . . .

The Real ID Act will end this by establishing a uniform rule for all states that temporary driver's licenses for foreign visitors expire when their visa terms expire, and establishing tough rules for confirming identity before temporary driver's licenses are issued. The Real ID Act tightens our asylum system that has been abused by terrorists with deadly consequences. It will finish the 3-mile hole in the fortified U.S./Mexico fence near San Diego. And it will protect the American people by ensuring that all terrorism-related grounds for inadmissibility are also grounds for deportation.[41]

---

[41] 'Sensenbrenner introduces terrorist travel legislation: Real ID Act includes provisions dropped from 9/11 legislation,' press release, US House of Representatives Committee on the Judiciary, 26 January 2005.

2.71 The Congressional votes on the Act largely divided along party lines, with the Republicans in favour and the Democrats against. The Act eventually became law on 5 November 2005. It compels states to design their drivers' licences by 2008 to comply with federal anti-terrorism and anti-illegal immigration standards. Federal employees will have the power to reject licences which do not comply, meaning that the Act could 'curb Americans' access to everything from airplanes to national parks and some courthouses'.[42] One of the Republicans who voted against the measure criticized it for its pseudo-voluntary nature: 'Supporters claim it is not a national ID because it is voluntary. However, any state that opts out will automatically make nonpersons out of its citizens. They will not be able to fly or to take a train.'[43]

2.72 Prior to the passing of the Real ID Act, states used 'a hodgepodge' of systems and standards in granting drivers' licences. In some states, a high school yearbook was enough to prove identity.[44]

2.73 The Real ID Act sets minimum security standards with which states must comply, but states are entitled to go beyond these federal requirements. Virginia, for example, is going further. It intends to embed radio-frequency identification (RFID) tags into all its drivers' licences. The US State Department also plans to begin issuing passports embedded with RFID chips.

3. Canada

2.74 Canada has never had a national ID card scheme.

2.75 Since June 2002 a card has been available for immigrants to Canada who have permanent resident status but are not Canadian citizens. The card is referred to as a PR card (Permanent Resident) or the Maple Leaf card. The card has a laser-engraved photograph and signature, it lists physical characteristics of the holder, and it has an optical stripe with encrypted information detailing the circumstances in which the individual was granted PR status.

2.76 It is not compulsory for permanent residents to obtain the Maple Leaf card, but Citizenship and Immigration Canada (CIC) has since 28 June 2002 automatically posted the cards to new permanent residents arriving in Canada. Since 31 December 2003 all Canadian permanent residents arriving back into Canada after travelling have to show their Maple Leaf card if they have travelled by commercial vehicle.

2.77 Following 11 September 2001 a national ID card was suggested as a means of tackling terrorism and illegal immigration. As in the US and UK debates, terrorism and immigration were considered to be inextricably linked. The drive

---

[42] D McCullagh, *CNet News.com*, 10 February 2005.

[43] Representative Ron Paul of Texas, 'HR418—a national ID bill masquerading as immigration reform', speech to the House of Representatives, 9 February 2005.

[44] 'National uniform driver's licence law "nightmare" for states,' Associated Press/*Ashville Citizen Times*, 23 January 2006.

to introduce a card scheme was spearheaded by CIC. In November 2003, Denis Coderre, the Immigration Minister, announced a public consultation on the introduction of a high-tech national ID card. He focused on terrorism and illegal immigration in his announcement, but also suggested that the card could help Canadians avoid delays at the US border. Further, he suggested that the cards could authenticate a person's entitlement to government services, such as welfare payments and healthcare. The card would, he suggested, only be issued to Canadian citizens, as non-citizens would have the Maple Leaf card (the issue of pre-June 2002 permanent resident arrivals was not discussed).

At Minister Coderre's request, the Canadian House of Commons Immigration Committee on Citizenship and Immigration held hearings on the issue. During these hearings, the provincial privacy commissioners wrote to the Committee to express their concerns over the proposals. The Federal Privacy Commissioner's Office agreed. In a submission to the Committee, it stated that: **2.78**

> The debate about the need for a national identification card may be the most significant privacy issue in Canadian society today. The development of a national identification card would require the collection, use and dissemination of the personal information of Canadians on a massive scale. Canadians and Parliamentarians need to consider carefully the privacy risks that this would entail and weigh them against the likely benefits of such a scheme. The debate has to be about more than just cards. A national identification card would require an elaborate and complex national identity system, with a database, communications networks, card readers, millions of identification cards, and policies and procedures to address a myriad of security, privacy, manageability, and human factor considerations. The costs associated with such a system would be enormous. Just creating it could cost between $3 billion and $5 billion, with substantial additional costs to actually operate it. There would also be costs to Canadians' privacy rights, and to the relationship between Canadians and the state.

> Identification cards allow us to be identified when we have every right to remain anonymous, reveal more information about us than is strictly required to establish our identity or authorization in a particular situation, and allow our various activities to be linked together in profiles of our lives. The system would likely entail compulsory participation, massive databases of personal information, serious problems of inaccuracies, and significant disruption and inconvenience to individuals. Are these financial and social costs justified by any significant benefit?

The Committee eventually rejected Minister Coderre's proposals. **2.79**

4. Australia

Australia does not have a national ID card. In 1987 plans to introduce such a card were comprehensively rejected. **2.80**

In July 2005 the idea was briefly revived but the Federal government has ruled out introduction of national ID cards, at least in the short term. Instead, it announced that moves would be made to integrate national databases in order to identify Australians better. The Attorney General told a national security **2.81** conference that the government was trawling through databases, including Medicare and the Australian Tax Office, to cross-reference Australian identities. He said properly identifying Australians was the first step towards creating a national ID card, but promised the government had no plans to do so:

> The real question as far as the government is concerned is to ensure that the data that we have is accurate. That's one of the reasons we want to go through a number of the agency databases because one suspects that there have been creations of false identities and multiple identities over a period of time in some of those agencies. There is a new effort being undertaken to cleanse a lot of those databases. If you were to go down the route of a national identifier with all of the implications that has, all of the work that we're doing now would have to be undertaken before you could believe that you had anything that was anywhere near efficacious. We're putting in place the appropriate strategy and in time we will look to see whether or not we've established that the government databases have been effectively enhanced to the extent to which we can go to the private sector.

> We made it very clear that we're not about establishing a national identity card, but we do want to improve the efficiency of the databases we hold.

D. OTHER JURISDICTIONS

1. Overview

2.82 National ID card schemes are in place throughout Asia, South and Central America, Africa and the Gulf States. The majority of systems in place are voluntary schemes with limited information used and retained. The Gulf States and Asian countries, however, tend to have compulsory schemes using hi-tech 'smart' cards.

2.83 There is no direct link between a country's economic or political development and whether it has a national ID card. The majority of developing countries do have either an ID card system or an identity document system, but Mexico and Bangladesh have no national ID card. India still has no national ID card scheme as such, although it did introduce a national voter registration card in 1995 and is currently piloting a multi-purpose national ID card.

2.84 National ID cards are compulsory in only 14 non-EU countries, including three EU accession states: Slovenia, Romania and Estonia. The other 11 countries with compulsory schemes are Argentina, Brazil, Chile, Egypt, Hong Kong, Indonesia, Israel, Malaysia, Singapore, South Africa and Thailand. Compulsion in South Africa is somewhat illusory, however. The South African ID card (which replaced the old Passbook introduced by the apartheid regime) has been technically compulsory since 1996 but in practice large parts of the population have not obtained this.

2.85 The national ID card schemes in Asia and the Gulf States are markedly different to those in operation within the EU, in terms of the technology used, the purposes to which the cards are put and the information retained.

2. Technology

In many countries, identification documents are being replaced with cards which **2.86** are more durable and harder to forge. Many African nations are currently replacing old documents with magnetic stripe or bar-coded cards. In Asia and the Gulf States plastic cards are now being replaced with 'smart' or e-cards. The change from one form of ID card to another is often accompanied by a change to the nature and content of data on the document and on any accompanying register.

The technology used in Asia and the Gulf States is more sophisticated than **2.87** that in most European countries. There has been a discernible trend towards introducing 'smart' national ID cards over the past five years. The Gulf States agreed amongst themselves to introduce machine-readable ID cards by 2008, and most are choosing also to use biometric identification technology. Malaysia and Hong Kong already have smart national ID card systems, and Thailand, Indonesia, Vietnam, India and China are in the process of planning or piloting similar schemes. South Korea is also considering a smart public ID card. In Taiwan, where there is no compulsory national ID card, there is a voluntary smart health card available for citizens to access the health system.

Smart card technology has actually existed for over 20 years, and has been **2.88** considered for much of that time to be a 'technology in search of an application'.[45] Renewed interest in the technology is largely attributable to recent reductions in production costs, and the end of the period in which a licence fee had to be paid to the holder of the US smart card patent (1997). In 1995, there were only eight licensed smart card production plants in the world; a decade later there are over 3,000, each producing smart cards in their millions. The majority of these plants are based in South-East Asia, which partly explains the recent Asian phenomenon of introducing smart national ID cards.

The Malaysian scheme is the longest established. Since 1999 the government **2.89** has gradually phased in the 'MyKad'—a mandatory, multi-purpose smart card that functions as an ID card, driver's licence, passport, health card and an ATM bank card.

The South African government announced plans for replacement of their **2.90** paper-based national ID system with electronic ID cards. The card will include a chip storing biometric data. The transition is scheduled to begin in April 2006.[46] As with the UK scheme, the South African scheme is linked to the passport-issuing agency.

3. Functions of National ID Cards

The functions of national ID cards vary greatly from country to country. As with **2.91** the EU cards, national ID cards worldwide may be used to satisfy governmental

---

[45] *Smart Cards: Big Brother's Little Helpers*, Privacy Committee of New South Wales, 1995.
[46] 'South Africa Pushes Electronic ID Cards', *The Register*, 26 October 2005.

and private sector identification requirements, and they may be used for travel in certain circumstances in place of passports.

2.92 The smart cards used or being introduced by Asian governments tend to be multi-purpose, incorporating other documents such as driving licences or passports, and acceptable for accessing government services.

2.93 In some cases governments negotiated with private sector businesses when introducing their cards in order either to spread cost, increase take-up rates for the cards, or maximize the information obtained from transaction trails for law enforcement purposes. For example, in Malaysia the MyKad operates as a bank ATM card. The South African government has agreed parameters of its proposed smart ID card with national banks, and it will include a payment application for social grants (pensions and subsidies).

2.94 Crime prevention is regularly claimed as an aim of national ID schemes. In South Africa, the main purpose of the population register and national ID system is said to be to 'curb crime levels'.[47] Despite neither India nor Nepal currently having a mandatory national ID scheme, an identity verification system was introduced at the Indo-Nepal border in 2001 to tackle cross-border smuggling. India's stated aim of its proposed mandatory national ID card scheme is to track down illegal foreign nationals who pose a security risk: illegal immigration and national security.

4. Information Retained and Displayed

2.95 In common with European countries, the majority of cards in use in developed countries worldwide carry certain basic information on their faces: the holder's name, date of birth, sex, signature, photograph and the issuing coordinates of the card. In many cases (such as Brazil, Chile and Korea) a fingerprint is also included.

2.96 Asian countries with ID cards tend to include additional information on the face of the card, such as parents' or father's name, ethnicity and military record. The Malaysian card includes details on religious affiliation.

2.97 In contrast to EU countries, the extent of the 'hidden' information not revealed on the face of the card but retained on governmental databases is huge in the Asian smart card schemes.

2.98 In China, legislation requires national ID cards to include an 18-digit code referencing each person's genetic code. This code is derived from a required sample of the person's blood, tissue or hair.[48] This legislation was to be put into

---

[47] South African Department of Home Affairs, Outline of the Home Affairs National Identification System (HANIS), March 2003. Available at http://home-affairs.pwv.gov.za/projects.asp.

[48] 'La Chine passera à la carte d'identité électronique à partir de janvier 2004' (1 September 2003), http://www.transfert.net, cited by Sabrina Safrin, 'Hyperownership in a time of biotechnological promise: the international conflict to control the building blocks of life' (2004) 98 American J of Intl L 641, 662.

force from 2004, and, once fully implemented, China will have a DNA sample and record of that sample for every citizen. Such samples and records may be cross-referenced on the basis of nationality, family and locality, and potentially alienated by the government.[49]

Further, in most Asian national ID schemes the information retained on **2.99** governmental databases linked to the card is not merely information provided at registration stage; the card's uses are tracked and these details are also retained. These transaction trails reveal information about the uses to which the card is put, and thus information concerning the holder's routine.

The extent of database linking and number of transaction trails recorded **2.100** usually depends on the purpose of the ID card. If the card is multi-purpose, used by the state for a variety of reasons, database linkage will be extensive. This in turn will lead to intensity of transaction trails: whereas a credit card in the UK typically generates an average 'trail' of five transactions per month, multi-purpose national ID cards such as Malaysia's or Thailand's generate five to ten transactions per day.

The Japanese computerized online ID system, Juki Net, was ruled unconsti- **2.101** tutional in May 2005 as it gives citizens no control over their personal data. The system was introduced in August 2002 for administrative convenience and it includes basic identificatory details of all 126 million Japanese nationals. The system is still in place (although the details of the 28 plaintiffs in the lawsuit have been removed) and the ruling is currently the subject of challenge.[50]

5. Non-Nationals

National ID cards often include details on national status, usually on the face of **2.102** the card itself. In some cases resident foreign nationals may obtain an ID card, but their status means their card has a different appearance. In Brazil, for example, cards are available to non-national alien residents. The distinction between Brazilian nationals and alien residents is made on the face of the card. As it is compulsory to carry ID cards at all times in Brazil, and the police are entitled to request proof of identity, this status will be known immediately if the card is requested.

Several nations have been accused of conducting discriminatory practices **2.103** using ID documents. In 1996 the Government of Japan was criticized by the UN Human Rights Committee for this practice. The Committee had expressed concern that Japan had passed a law (the Alien Registration Law) requiring that foreign residents must carry identification cards at all times. Japanese nationals were subject to no such requirement. The Committee found that the statute was not consistent with the Covenant.

Population groups in disputed territories may reject the cards or refuse to **2.104** register, as has happened in the Basque territories in Europe. In the Western

---

[49] ibid.   [50] See n 12 above.

Sahara, there has been an unusual approach to disputed land. Pre-1975 Spanish ID cards are retained by many holders as proof that they were Saharaui citizens rather than Moroccan colonists. The cards are not currently used for any purpose, but they are retained on the basis that they would entitle the holders to vote in an eventual referendum on self-determination.

2.105   In Israel, issues of nationality and religion in relation to the ID card have long been fraught with difficulty. The ID card is compulsory to obtain and carry for all over-18s in Israel. On every ID card issued before April 2002 the card owner's nationality was recorded. The term 'nationality' referred to one's nation as opposed to one's political citizenship. In Hebrew, this is expressed by two different words: *ezrahut*—citizenship; *leom*—nationality. In most countries, nationality is synonymous with citizenship—a person who was born in a country is its citizen and also belongs to its nation. For the majority of Israeli citizens, however, the question of nationality is more complicated.

2.106   The Ministry of the Interior was responsible for assigning nationality to Israeli citizens. The possibilities were Jewish, Arab or Druze. Individuals who did not fall into these three nationalities were registered by their country of origin or, alternatively, the space on the ID card was left blank.

2.107   The nationality section of the ID card proved controversial. Many Israeli Jews objected to being referred to as Israeli rather than Jewish, a term which they considered to define their citizenship and their religion. Non-Jewish family members of Jews who immigrated to Israel under the Law of Return but are not Jewish according to traditional Jewish law (ie they were not born to a Jewish mother) had their nationality defined according to their country of origin, or that section of the card was left blank; many objected as they considered themselves a part of the Jewish people living in Israel and wanted to be defined as such. The inclusion of 'Arab' in the nationality section was intended to suggest that the cardholder was an Arab citizen of Israel, but many holders wanted to be referred to as Palestinian rather than Arab.

2.108   From 1987 groups of academics, lobby groups and politicians in Israel campaigned to have this section of the card removed. In March 2002 the Knesset Committee on Constitution and Law finally passed a regulation ordering the removal of nationality from all newly issued identification cards. There are two caveats: first, the change applies prospectively only, and new cards are not being issued to the six million citizens who received their cards prior to that time; second, nationality continues to be recorded in the Population Registry (*Mirsham Ha-uchlusin*), together with other personal details that do not appear on the identification card.

E. FUTURE DEVELOPMENTS

2.109   There are two likely future developments internationally: first, technology upgrade, and second, multi-national cooperation.

Technology upgrade is likely to incorporate two changes: improved identifica- **2.110** tion technology (such as biometrics) and 'smarter' cards capable of performing multiple functions. In the EU, Asia and the Gulf States in particular, cards with these twin technological changes are gradually being introduced. It is also pos- sible that more countries will follow Finland's lead and move from electronic IDs to mobile telephone-based IDs. Since 1999 the Finnish Population Register (VRK) has issued smart ID cards to Finns. In 2005, in collaboration with a private sector company, VRK created a mobile telephone identification scheme. Government-guaranteed 'citizen certificates' are incorporated into SIM cards for mobile telephones. Subscribers to the scheme are able to use their telephones to identify themselves when electronically filing tax returns, registering for social security, or paying for goods online.

Many of the problems which national identity systems are supposed to **2.111** solve are no longer contained within national borders. It is likely that national identity systems will either begin to interact with other national systems, or that multi-national schemes will be proposed.

Within the EU, harmonization of national ID schemes has been raised, and **2.112** this would be in keeping with harmonization of European arrest procedures, evidence gathering and the retaining of communications data.

In 2004, a campaign was launched by various technology companies based in **2.113** South-East Asia entitled One Card—One Asia.[51] The idea is to standardize ID cards and smartcard readers throughout Asia.

---

[51] 'One card for travel and payment could become reality in Asia', Channel NewsAsia, 14 November 2004.

3

OVERVIEW OF THE IDENTITY CARDS ACT 2006

A. INTRODUCTION

1. Overview

The Identity Cards Act 2006, which obtained Royal Assent on 30 March 2006, **3.01** introduces a national ID card scheme in the UK for the first time since the second wartime scheme was abolished in 1952. A statutory framework is now in place, and the scheme will be introduced on a rolling basis. There are no provisions in the Act to require anyone to carry an ID card. In fact such checks are made unlawful by ss 13(3) and 16(2) of the Act. However it is likely that possession of an ID card will be increasingly necessary to access public services (see below). It is argued by those who oppose them that over time it will become the only acceptable method of establishing identity when individuals are involved in other transactions. Those opposed also argue that once the need to carry an ID card becomes the norm, it is likely that law enforcement bodies such as the police will routinely require them to be produced.[1]

Originally, according to the Home Office's stated timetable, the first ID cards **3.02** would be issued in early 2009.[2] However whilst the Bill was going through Parliament it was subjected to very considerable debate. Versions of the Bill 'ping-ponged' from House to House, and a different version of the Bill was

---

[1] The amendments to the power of arrest in s 110 of the Serious Organised Crime and Police Act 2005 extend the power of arrest to a much wider set of circumstances (amending s 24 of the Police and Criminal Evidence Act 1984). One of the grounds for an arrest relates to the police officer's degree of confidence that the name and address given by the suspect is accurate. An identity card would make it easier for a person in such circumstances to establish this and, as a result, to avoid arrest.

[2] Andy Burnham, Home Office Minister, press statement, 15 February 2006.

enacted by Parliament than was hoped for by the government. In this text we have tried to make clear what has been enacted so far as well as what is likely to be added subsequently by future legislation. It is likely that those original provisions, lost in the tussle between the two Houses, will be reintroduced before the majority of this Act takes effect. It was originally proposed by the government that by 2013 registration on the National Identity Register and possession of a National Identity Card would be compulsory for all those aged 16 or over who are British nationals or are residing in the UK for more than three months, of any nationality.

3.03 There were two key elements to the original proposals: first, to introduce a system of registration for all individuals and second, to require individuals to purchase ID cards based on the identity information set out on that register. The compulsory nature of the original proposal was to be introduced in two ways.

3.04 First, the original Bill would have required those who applied for passports (and probably driving licences) to be registered on the identity registration system and to be supplied with a passport which doubled as an ID card.

3.05 Second, the Bill would have also allowed the government, at some point in the future, to introduce compulsory registration for all those who had not yet obtained an ID card in this way. The method by which the Bill would have introduced compulsory registration for everyone was by regulations which would have been passed into law by Parliament by 'super-affirmative resolution'. Regulations are usually passed by Parliament by a 'negative resolution' procedure; usually there is no debate but if they are opposed they can be subjected to a vote but not amended. Affirmative resolution is used less often because it requires regulations to be subject to greater scrutiny by both Houses of Parliament, including debate and a vote. The super-affirmative process goes further than the affirmative resolution procedure. In this case it would have required the government to publish a report outlining its reasons for wishing to designate a particular group of persons to be subjected to compulsory registration. There would have then had to be a draft order laid before Parliament. This would have allowed a debate and, as a result, modification before implementation.

3.06 The 'super-affirmative' process for agreeing this extension of the Bill's powers did have added constitutional safeguards and protections compared with the procedure for ordinary secondary legislation, but these were not sufficient for the opposition parties in the House of Lords and those particular clauses were removed and not replaced by the House of Commons following a major concession by the government. The opposition parties argued that the House of Lords was entitled to remove these clauses, first, because making the scheme compulsory using secondary legislation was wrong in principle and whatever safeguards would be provided by the 'super-affirmative' procedure were insufficient because they would not allow the detailed consideration that could be given to primary legislation. Second, the opposition in the House of Lords argued that it was entitled to make such a significant change to the Bill because the basis for the legislation in the Labour Party's last election manifesto only referred to a voluntary scheme for ID cards. This analysis of the manifesto was not accepted by ministers, but the 'ambiguity' in the text in the manifesto allowed those in the House of Lords to oppose the will of the elected house.

Given the commitment by ministers to a compulsory scheme it is very likely **3.07** that new primary legislation will be introduced in the future to make it compulsory, and therefore this text sets out both the provisions as finally enacted by Parliament as well as the details of how it is likely to be extended in the future.

The original Bill also made registration and the requirement to acquire an ID **3.08** card compulsory by linking this to any application for a passport. This provision was also debated robustly in both Houses, although ministers for the government argued that the proposals did not make registration compulsory because a person was able to choose whether or not to apply for a passport. Finally, the two Houses agreed on a compromise whereby anyone who renews a passport as of 2008 will be put on a national ID database, but will not be forced to have an ID card until 2010. In effect, people are permitted to opt out of the scheme until 2010. Considering the Conservative opposition has indicated that it would scrap the Act if it were elected in the next general election, this means the Identity Cards Act 2006 is likely to become an election issue.

The Act itself does contain a number of measures which are significant in **3.09** themselves however, and sets up a system remedy for the compulsory provisions which are likely to be enacted in the near future. It introduces a complex range of new civil and criminal penalties, a new Commissioner's Office, and new ways of working for those providing public services (including the police, the National Health Service, passport office and benefit workers).

The Identity Cards Act 2006 is therefore essentially an enabling measure. It **3.10** sets up the framework for the introduction of the national ID card scheme, but it leaves the compulsory 'sting' of the provisions for a future Act and the bulk of the detail for regulations to be issued later.

The Act applies to the whole of the United Kingdom, but certain sections **3.11** grant powers to the devolved assemblies.

A multi-tier system will be initiated by the Act. Central to the Bill (and there- **3.12** fore to a future measure) was the original clause 6, the 'compulsion' clause.[3] At first, registration on the National Identity Register and obtaining an ID card will be 'voluntary' rather than universal or compulsory, but under that provision the Secretary of State could designate certain groups as being subject to compulsion. Individuals within this group would be obliged to register and obtain an ID card, and they would be subject to provisions of the Act inapplicable to those outside the designated group. Although clause 6 has now been removed from the Act, the government has indicated that it intends eventually to reintroduce this multi-tier system via fresh primary legislation. In practice, even under the Identity Cards Act 2006 a distinction will be drawn between different categories of

---

[3] Identity Cards Bill, clause 6 (HL 28, 19 October 2005).

person, as, if residence permits for foreign nationals become 'designated documents', such persons will be obliged to register and obtain an ID card. The government envisages this multi-tier system being temporary, as eventually the scheme will be rolled out and everyone will be subject to it.

2. Parliamentary History of the Identity Cards Act 2006

3.13 In February 2002 the Labour government set out its policies on nationality, immigration and asylum in the White Paper, *Secure Borders, Safe Haven*.[4] In the paper they announced that they would be publishing a full consultation on 'entitlement cards' later in the year.

3.14 A number of different immigration-related rationales for the introduction of entitlement cards were hinted at in the White Paper. First, then Home Secretary, David Blunkett, suggested that there may be a perception that entry to and remaining in Britain was easier than doing so in other European countries, and this led to 'the international "free for all", the so called "asylum shopping" throughout Europe'. He stated that: 'This mistaken perception may arise in part because of the differences between the UK and the rest of Europe in respect of internal identification procedures. That is why a debate around the issue of entitlement cards is so important.'[5]

3.15 Second, the White Paper referred to future consultations with employers and trade unions as to whether entitlement cards could provide a means of identification of potential employees to assist employer compliance with s 8 of the Asylum and Immigration Act 1996 (which made it an offence for employers knowingly or negligently to employ people who have no permission to work). Third, the White Paper referred to entitlement cards in the context of discussing possible general strengthening of the powers possessed by the Immigration and Nationality Directorate (IND) and the Joint Entry Clearance Unit, including in particular greater use of information-sharing. The paper stated that, 'in performing its law enforcement functions, the IND requires information from various other sources to enable it to combat fraud, people trafficking and illegal employment and to locate offenders'. These sources might include 'a broader range of social players' than government sources alone.[6] Finally, the White Paper linked entitlement cards to other proposals, such as citizenship tests, which had the purpose of 'engaging those who seek citizenship so they can enjoy the full benefits of this status and understand the obligations that go with it'.[7]

3.16 In July 2002, as announced in the White Paper, the government launched a consultation entitled *Entitlement Cards and Identity Fraud*, which ran until

---

[4] *Secure Borders, Safe Haven: Integration with Diversity in Modern Britain* (hereafter *Secure Borders, Safe Haven*) col 5387.
[5] ibid, David Blunkett, Ministerial Foreword.   [6] ibid, para 5.18.
[7] ibid, David Blunkett, Ministerial Foreword.

January 2003.[8] Alongside the consultation document the Home Office published a Cabinet Office study on identity fraud.[9]

The consultation document sought views on a voluntary scheme of 'entitle- **3.17** ment cards', which British residents would be 'entitled' to obtain. The cards could be used as formal identity documents in place of passports and driving licences, and they would be accepted as proving entitlement to public services. There were four general aims to the proposal, to:

(i) provide people who are lawfully resident in the UK with a means of confirming their identity to a high degree of assurance;

(ii) establish for official purposes a person's identity so that there is one definitive record of an identity which all government departments can use if they wish;

(iii) help people gain entitlement to products and services provided by both the public and private sectors, particularly those who might find it difficult to so do at present;

(iv) help public and private sector organizations to validate a person's identity, entitlement to products and services and eligibility to work in the UK.[10]

The consultation document explicitly ruled out the introduction of a compul- **3.18** sory scheme, but with a caveat: 'The Government does *not* wish to consult on the introduction of a compulsory scheme, by which it means a card which everyone would have and be required to carry at all times' (emphasis in original).[11]

On 11 November 2003 the Home Office published a summary of the consul- **3.19** tation findings.[12] Critics of the proposals queried how 'voluntary' the cards would be to carry, suggesting the cards would either be compulsory to carry in practice or that, once introduced, there would be 'function creep' and a new criminal offence would eventually be created for not carrying the cards. Critics also queried whether they would tackle identity fraud or the other problems outlined in the consultation paper. However, according to Home Office figures, the majority of responses received were supportive of the idea of a voluntary scheme of entitlement cards. This claim in itself proved controversial, as individuals who had responded to the consultation through a campaign organized by opposition lobby group Privacy International did not have their own responses taken into account, and instead their responses were collectively considered to be a single organizational vote.

At the same time as publication of these findings, the government announced **3.20** its decision to build a base for a compulsory national ID cards scheme. This

---

[8] *Entitlement cards and identity fraud: a consultation*, Cm 5557 (hereafter *Entitlement cards and identity fraud*).
[9] *Identity Fraud: a study*, Cabinet Office, July 2002.
[10] *Entitlement cards and identity fraud*, executive summary, para 1.   [11] ibid, para 2.
[12] *Identity Cards: a Summary of Findings from the Consultation on Entitlement Cards and Identity Fraud* (Cm 6019).

was said to be on foot of the support received during the consultation on entitlement cards.

3.21   *Identity Cards: The Next Steps*[13] set out in more detail how the government would proceed. The scheme would be gradually rolled out, with non-EU foreign nationals being obliged to obtain cards first, followed by non-British EU nationals, and, finally, British nationals.

3.22   Following these Home Office publications, a Bill to introduce ID cards was the Home Office's 'flagship Bill' for the short 2004–05 Parliamentary session. It was first introduced as a draft Bill on 26 April 2004, as part of a larger Home Office consultation document.[14] The Home Affairs Select Committee, which had already begun considering the Home Office's proposals for ID cards in the abstract, announced that it would widen the scope of its inquiry to take account of the draft Bill.[15]

3.23   The Committee published its report into ID cards and the draft Bill on 30 July 2004. While broadly supportive of the idea in principle, and finding that the ID card scheme should certainly go ahead, the Committee was critical of the detail—or lack of it—in the government's proposals:

> The Committee is concerned about the lack of clarity over the scheme's scope and practical operation: the report warns that key elements in the proposal are poorly thought out and that the draft Bill goes far wider than is necessary to introduce a simple scheme to establish and demonstrate identity.
>
> It is unclear how the card and the register will work in practice. The Government should clarify the number, type and costs of card readers and supporting infrastructure required by the scheme. It should also be clear about the number and level of checks on card use that it anticipates.[16]

3.24   The Report made a number of recommendations to strengthen the draft Bill, including clearer statutory aims for the scheme, a 'powerful and independent' regulator, and new primary legislation before a compulsory scheme is introduced for British citizens.

3.25   Two members of the Committee dissented from the report's conclusions. They did not believe that an ID card scheme was needed, nor did they agree with the draft Bill. Their minority report appears as a (rejected) amendment in the published report.[17]

3.26   The government formally replied to the Committee's report in October 2004.[18] They announced certain refinements to the scheme, such as simplifying

---

[13] Cm 6020.   [14] *Legislation on identity cards: a consultation* (Cm 6178).

[15] Home Affairs Committee press notice, 'Home Affairs Committee to scrutinize ID Cards Bill: Denham pledges "thorough examination" ', 26 April 2004.

[16] Home Affairs Committee press notice, 'Committee backs ID cards but criticises implementation and proposed draft legislation', 30 July 2004.

[17] The dissenting members were David Winnick MP (Labour) and Bob Russell MP (Liberal Democrats). Their minority report is available at Home Affairs Committee, *Identity Cards* (HC 130-I 2003–04) 85–92. Their amendment was rejected by a majority of five to two.

[18] Cm 6359.

the scheme's operation by issuing a single, universal ID card for all UK nationals, alongside passports, and a simpler structure to deliver and run the scheme, in the form of a new executive agency incorporating the UK Passport Service.

A substantive Bill was introduced into Parliament on 29 November 2004.[19] It remained very similar to the draft Bill. The Bill cleared its Commons stages on 10 February 2005 and was given a Second Reading in the House of Lords on 21 March 2005. However, the Bill failed to become law before Parliament was dissolved for the general election of May 2005. In the so-called 'wash-up' period before dissolution of Parliament, the opposition parties were not prepared to drop their opposition to the Bill, and the government was unwilling to make concessions which would have satisfied the Conservatives, and so it did not reach the Statute Book in the short Parliamentary time available.[20] **3.27**

In the lead-up to the general election of May 2005, Labour reaffirmed its commitment to the scheme by making the introduction of ID cards a manifesto commitment. The manifesto promised that, if re-elected, a Labour government would 'introduce identity cards, including biometric data like fingerprints, backed up by a national register and rolling out initially on a voluntary basis as people renew their passports'.[21] **3.28**

The Queen's Speech following the general election featured ID cards, and the Identity Cards Bill was introduced in the Commons on 25 May 2005. The Bill was almost identical to the failed Bill of the same name introduced in the previous Parliamentary session. **3.29**

The Home Office published a number of documents alongside the Bill: Explanatory Notes; a ten-page 'Identity Cards Briefing'; a Regulatory Impact Assessment; and a Race Equality Impact Assessment. **3.30**

The Bill had its second reading in the House of Commons on 25 June 2005. It was opposed by both the two main opposition parties as well as a significant number of Labour MPs. However it passed all of the stages in the Commons without opposition amendment, but the government lost a number of votes on key amendments in the House of Lords.[22] The government conceded on the clauses that would have allowed the scheme to be made substantively compulsory and made concessions on the costs of the scheme. In the end, the Identity Cards Act 2006 obtained Royal Assent on 30 March 2006. All passport applicants from 2008 will be placed on a national ID database. However, passport applicants can opt out of obtaining an ID card until 2010, after which it will become compulsory to obtain an ID card. Contentiously, then Home Secretary Charles Clarke indicated that people applying for passports from 2008 will have to pay for ID cards, whether or not they opt out. **3.31**

---

[19] *Hansard*, HC col 376 (29 November 2004).

[20] *The Identity Cards Bill, Bill 9 of 2005–06*, House of Commons Research Paper 05/43 (13 June 2005) 15.

[21] Labour party, *Britain forward not back: the Labour Party manifesto 2005* 52–53.

[22] See the Parliamentary Progress Table in Appendix 2.

B. THE IDENTITY CARDS ACT 2006

1. Territorial Extent

3.32 The Identity Cards Act applies to the whole of the UK. The official explanatory notes to the Identity Cards Bill explained that this territorial reach was for the ID cards scheme to 'operate on a UK-wide basis to deal with matters which are reserved to the UK Parliament, notably, immigration and nationality'.[23]

3.33 The legislation allows, but does not require, devolved administrations in Wales and Northern Ireland to make regulations making the production of an ID card a condition of providing a public service for which these administrations are responsible.

3.34 Any requirement for production of an ID card to be a condition of a public service in Scotland which is within the legislative competence of the Scottish Parliament would require authorization by an Act of the Scottish Parliament.

3.35 The new offences created by the Identity Cards Act 2006 are applicable throughout the UK.

3.36 The provisions relating to passports also operate on a UK-wide basis.

2. Effect of the Act

(a) *Registration*

3.37 Registration is dealt with in ss 1 to 5 of the Act.

3.38 Section 1 establishes the National Identity Register, the database which underpins the entire ID cards scheme. It sets out the statutory purposes of the Register, and explains what personal information may be held, the 'registrable facts'. This includes the physical characteristics of a person that are capable of being used for identification purposes, such as biometric information. Every person registered on the National Register will be assigned a unique number, the National Identity Registration Number, to be attached to the information recorded about him or her.

3.39 Section 2 sets out who may be entered on to the Register and the Secretary of State's duty to make arrangements to enable these entries to be made. The language of s 2 is permissive, referring to the individuals who are 'entitled' to be entered on the Register, and entries that 'may' be made. This is because registration will initially be voluntary or linked to the issuing and renewal of passports. A future Act is likely to require particular groups of individuals who have not been required to register as a result of applying for designated documents (such as passports) to register. Eventually virtually everyone will be required to register.

3.40 Entitled individuals include those who have attained the age of 16 and are

---

[23] Explanatory Notes to the Identity Cards Act 2006, para 9.

residing in the UK. The threshold age of 16 can be lowered by the Secretary of State by order. They also include individuals of a description prescribed in regulations made by the Secretary of State who have resided in the UK, or who are proposing to enter the UK. The Explanatory Notes to the Bill state that: 'This is to allow flexibility since because although the ID card will be for all UK residents, it may be in the future that the Government would want through regulations to allow for example, British citizens resident overseas to register before returning to live in the UK'.[24]

The Secretary of State has the power, by regulations, to exclude individuals from the entitlement to be entered on the Register. This power is likely to be used in relation to asylum seekers, the specific example given in the Explanatory Notes.[25] The Secretary of State also has the power, in some circumstances, to do the reverse: to add a person to the Register even though he or she has not applied or is not entitled to be so entered. **3.41**

Section 3 sets out the information that may be recorded in the Register. Information may be recorded only if it is included in Sch 1, is otherwise necessary for the administration of the scheme, or it is provided for in s 3(3) (information included at the request of the individual registered). Schedule 1 may be amended by secondary legislation following a resolution in both Houses of Parliament to add to the list of information that may be recorded on the Register. **3.42**

Information recorded on the Register may be kept for as long as this is consistent with the statutory purposes (s 3(1)). This will create an audit trail of changes, so previous addresses, previous immigration status and so on will be likely to be permanently retained. **3.43**

Section 3(4) was a later addition to the Identity Cards Act, providing that an individual's entry in the Register must include any information falling within para 9 of Sch 1 (the audit trail) that relates to an occasion on which information has been provided to a person without the individual's consent. **3.44**

Section 4 provides for the Secretary of State to have the power by order to designate documents for the purposes of the Act. Any orders will be subject to an affirmative resolution procedure in Parliament. These documents are referred to in the Act as 'designated documents', and persons responsible for issuing designated documents are referred to in the Act as 'designated documents authorities'. Pursuant to s 4(2), only certain documents may be designated, characterized by documents which certain persons are authorized or required to issue. Those persons are only a Minister of the Crown, a government department, a Northern Ireland department, the National Assembly for Wales and any other person who carries out functions on behalf of the Crown (s 4(3)). At the time of writing, designated documents are likely to include passports and biometric immigration documents, although driving licences and employment **3.45**

---

[24] ibid, para 23.   [25] ibid, para 24.

checks through the Criminal Records Bureau (CRB) could be included at some future time.

3.46   If a document is designated, anyone applying for one will also need to apply to be entered in the Register unless he or she is already entered (s 5(2)). Application procedures for designated documents must include the information necessary for the ID cards scheme. This means that if passports become designated documents, anyone applying for a passport (new or renewed) would also automatically be applying to be entered on the National Identity Register and to obtain a national ID card, and the UK Passport Service would be obliged to request any information necessary for the ID cards scheme from its passport applicant. Passports alone will be subject to an opt-out until January 2010, however. If CRB checks become designated documents, anyone applying for a job which involves a compulsory check will be obliged to apply to enter the Register and obtain an ID card.

3.47   Section 5(1) provides that an application for entry on the Register can be made either on its own, or by being included in an application for a designated document. An applicant may then be obliged to attend at a particular time and place, and to provide certain biometric information which will be recorded. The requirements can be changed by regulations made by the Secretary of State under the affirmative resolution procedure, and such regulations must not require a person to provide information to another person unless it is information required by the Secretary of State for the statutory purposes.

3.48   Any application for registration or confirmation of entry on the Register must be accompanied by such information as may be prescribed by the Secretary of State. The information required may vary for different categories of person. For example, the government has suggested that third country nationals may be required to provide information regarding their immigration status. Applicants may also be required to provide additional information to the Secretary of State if requested. Failure to provide such information will attract a civil penalty of up to £1,000 (s 7(5)).

3.49   The original clause 6[26] was the substantive compulsion clause, the crux of the proposed scheme, but it was lost in the battle between the Lords and Commons and is missing from the Identity Cards Act 2006. It would have provided a power to require any individual to register. This power would apply regardless of whether a person applied for a designated document. It is expected that future legislation, modelled on clause 6, will allow the Secretary of State to designate groups of people who are required to register, and, therefore, for whom entry to the National Identity Register and obtaining an ID card are compulsory.

3.50   The clause would have provided the facility to phase in compulsory registration. The full scheme would be introduced in a number of stages. Initially

---

[26] Identity Cards Bill, clause 6 (HL 28, 19 October 2005).

it would not have been compulsory to register, although in applying for a designated document from the time that that document is designated, it would be mandatory to register or confirm an entry already made in order to obtain the designated document (s 5 of the Act). Under the proposed clause (and under likely future provisions) the Secretary of State may then designate groups of people as subject to compulsory registration, regardless of whether or not they apply for designated documents. Eventually, it is envisaged that all UK residents (and any other individuals prescribed by regulations made under s 2(2)) will be subject to compulsion.

The government suggested that the proposed clause would be used to make it **3.51** compulsory for third country nationals to register before the scheme becomes compulsory for European Economic Area or UK nationals. The Explanatory Notes to the 2005–06 Bill also suggested that 'people over a certain age may initially or permanently be excluded from the requirement to register', which indicates that rollout even under the future provisions, modelled on clause 6, may not be total.

The proposal would have ensured that in making registration compulsory, the **3.52** order to do so may include an obligation on individuals to apply for registration in accordance with s 5 by a particular future date.

The maximum civil penalty for failure to register when required to do so by **3.53** such an order made under the rejected proposal, or for contravening a requirement under s 5(4) (by not providing the further information required by the Secretary of State) when obliged to register under that order, would have been a civil penalty of up to £2,500. However, if the individual continued to fail to satisfy the obligations, there would have been liability for a further civil penalty of up to £2,500 each time the Secretary of State gives notice requiring an application and there is a failure to do so before the set deadline.

The finalized s 5 no longer attracts a civil penalty, of any amount. Further, the **3.54** maximum civil penalty payable is now set at £1,000.

(b) *ID Cards*
ID cards themselves are dealt with in ss 6 to 8 of the Act. **3.55**

Section 6 defines ID cards as including both the cards and the verifying data **3.56** on the Register. It sets out the procedure for the issue of the cards. It is clear that ID cards under the Act do not need to be uniform in appearance. An ID card may form part of a designated document; for example, if a residence permit issued to a foreign national were a designated document the ID card could form part of that, and be physically attached to it. An ID card can also be a separate card issued together with a designated document, such as the British passport. An ID card can also be a separate card, issued on its own as a stand-alone card unconnected to any designated document.

Section 6(3) provides for prescribed information to be recorded on an ID **3.57** card and parts of it to be in an encrypted form. The exact specification and design of ID cards will be set out in regulations. They will need the agreement of Parliament via affirmative resolution (s 6(9)).

3.58   ID cards will have a limited validity. Validity periods will be set out in regulations, and different periods may be specified for different categories of person.

3.59   Under s 6(4) it is not generally possible to be entered in the Register without also obtaining an ID card. Except in prescribed cases, ID cards must be issued to individuals who are entitled to be, and whose personal information has been, entered on the Register. The special cases in which entry on the Register will occur without the issuing of a card are to be specified in regulations, but the standard example given by the government is that of foreign nationals residing in the UK for less than three months but whose passport has been surrendered for bail purposes.

3.60   Nothing in this part of, or elsewhere in, the Act places any constraints on the type of organizations which may be involved in the issuing process. This was noted in the official explanatory notes to the 2005–06 Bill, which suggested that, 'for example, private sector organizations may have certain parts of the process contracted out to them, such as actual production of the card'.

3.61   Section 7 provides for the renewal of cards. It is compulsory to apply for a new card before the old ID card expires (s 7(2)). Again, the Secretary of State may require an individual applying for a renewed ID card to provide certain information and to do certain things for the purpose of verifying information. An individual who fails to renew or to provide the information requested to verify an application is liable to a civil penalty not exceeding £1,000 (s 7(5)).

3.62   Section 8 sets out the functions of designated documents authorities. They are issuers of designated documents. This section does not set out common standards for all designated documents authorities in carrying out their functions under the Act, but it does establish how those common standards will be set in place: by regulations made by the Secretary of State and subject to the affirmative resolution procedure.

(c) *Maintaining the Accuracy of the Register*

3.63   Sections 9 to 11 deal with ongoing maintenance of the Register.

3.64   Section 9 creates new data-sharing and data-verification powers. It establishes powers to permit data to be shared with the Secretary of State and designated documents authorities for the purpose of verifying information already on or due to be placed on the National Identity Register where no such powers already exist. These powers are restricted to ensuring the accuracy of the Register and it does not confer the power to share data for wider purposes; neither does it allow the Secretary of State or a designated documents authority to request information that is not relevant for the purposes of validating the Register.

3.65   If it appears to the Secretary of State or a designated documents authority that a person may have information which could be used for verifying information connected to another individual's entry on the Register, a duty is placed on that person to provide the information. This obligation is mandatory (s 9(3)). The 'person' must be specified by order subject to the affirmative resolution procedure.

Section 10 sets out how changes in circumstances should be notified in order to maintain the accuracy of the Register. A registered person is under a duty to notify the Secretary of State of any change in his or her circumstances that may be prescribed, and to notify the Secretary of State of every error in the information held about him or her of which he or she is aware. Further information may also be required from the registered person, such as an iris scan or other biometric. **3.66**

These duties will apply to all registered persons, regardless of whether they are compulsorily registered as proposed under the original clause 6, they volunteered to register, or they applied for a designated document and were subject to the s 5 procedure. Failure to comply with these duties may lead to a maximum civil penalty of £1,000. **3.67**

The Secretary of State can make regulations under the affirmative resolution procedure amending the circumstances in which an individual is required to provide information to another person, but such regulations must not require a person to provide information to another person unless it is information required by the Secretary of State for the statutory purposes. **3.68**

Regulations can be made under s 11 to oblige a cardholder to report to the Secretary of State if he or she knows or has reason to suspect that his or her ID card has been lost, stolen, damaged, destroyed or tampered with. In certain circumstances, the cardholder is required to surrender his or her ID card. Failure to comply with s 11 or any pursuant order will attract a civil penalty not exceeding £1,000 (s 11(6)). **3.69**

(d) *Use of Information for Verification or Otherwise Without Consent*

Section 12 sets out the circumstances in which information recorded in a person's Register entry can be provided to others by the Secretary of State. Section 12(10) ensures that the restrictions on the provision of data do not interfere with rights to be provided with information under other Acts, for example subject access rights under the Data Protection Act 1998. **3.70**

A further safeguard was added following the 'ping-ponging' of the Act between the two Houses. If the Secretary of State wants to make regulations modifying this section, s 12(5) provides that the power to modify does not extend to omitting s 12(2) (which sets out the only information that can be provided to another person) and does not allow the Secretary of State to modify the information falling within para 9 of Sch 1 (the audit trail) according to either s 12(2) or (3) (which sets out exhaustively the information that can be provided to another person with consent). **3.71**

Section 12 enables an accreditation scheme to be established under regulations so that approved organizations would be able to make checks on the ID cards of individuals who have consented to verification checks against the Register. **3.72**

3.73   Finally, the Secretary of State can only provide information to another person where that person satisfies the conditions imposed under s 12(7)(a) and (b), namely, that the person has registered prescribed particulars about himself and where the person is approved by the Secretary of State in the prescribed manner.

(e) Required Identity Checks

3.74   Sections 13 to 16 deal with the issue of identity checks using the Register or ID cards. Section 13 provides a power to make public services conditional on identity checks, and s 15 a power to provide for checks on the Register. Section 14 sets out the procedure for regulations under s 13, including how they will apply to devolved administrations. Section 16 provides a temporary prohibition on requirements to produce ID cards.

3.75   Regulations made under s 14 may be permissive or mandatory: they may allow or require a person who provides a public service to make it a condition of providing the service that an individual produces an ID card and/or other evidence of his registrable facts. In some circumstances, the ID card on its own may suffice; in other situations, the service provider may check someone's identity against the Register, for example by using an iris scan to check the recorded biometric.

3.76   Such regulations cannot make provision of a public service which is free of charge or payments which are provided for in legislation contingent on production of an ID card or registrable facts to be verified against the Register, *unless* the individual is subject to compulsion. Once an individual is designated under these proposals, free NHS treatment or provision of social security benefits may be made contingent on production of an ID card.

3.77   Section 15 provides powers to the Secretary of State to enable checks to be made of information recorded in the Register by people providing public services, and to regulate identity checks, including an accreditation scheme for user organizations and the equipment they are using. The powers are only exercisable where the provision of information satisfies the conditions set out in s 15(4)(a) and (b), namely, that the person has registered prescribed particulars about him or herself and where the person is approved by the Secretary of State in the prescribed manner.

3.78   Regulations may specify the manner and circumstances in which applications for checks of the Register are to be made, the information that may be provided, and the means of providing that information. However, regulations cannot authorize the provision to any person of information falling within para 9 of Sch 1 (the audit trail), according to s 15(2). The regulations are subject to an affirmative resolution procedure. Before any draft regulations are laid before Parliament, the Secretary of State must take steps to ensure that members of the public in the UK are informed and consulted on any proposals (s 15(7)).

3.79   Section 16 appears to amount to a prohibition on requirements to produce ID cards. This section heavily featured in ministerial speeches on the Bill during its passage through Parliament. However, s 16(3) sets out a number of caveats, the crucial one being that the s 16 ban falls away once a group of persons is subject to compulsory registration.

After the Bill was debated in both Houses, further prohibitions on the 3.80 requirement to provide an ID card were added. In particular, s 16(1) provides that it is unlawful to make the provision of an ID card conditional on making an application under s 12(1) of the Act (the provision of information with consent), exercising a subject access request right under s 7 of the Data Protection Act 1998, or providing a person with information about what is recorded in his or her entry in the Register.

(f) Other Purposes for which Information can be Provided from the Register

Sections 17 to 21 set out further purposes for which information from the Regis- 3.81 ter can be provided. There is very little detail in this part of the Act, which simply sets out the bare framework and leaves the detail to regulations. The summary of what is now s 17, for example, in the official explanatory notes to the 2005–06 Bill, readily demonstrates the lack of detail on the face of the Act: it 'provides the power to provide specified information held on the Register to public authorities or other specified persons for specified purposes without the consent of the registered person'.

Information may be provided without consent to various specified national 3.82 security and intelligence agencies, police, Her Majesty's Revenue and Customs, or to a prescribed government department for purposes connected with the department's functions. The provision must be to a prescribed entity and for a prescribed purpose. Information may also be provided outside those entities, including to overseas bodies or persons, when it relates to the prevention and detection of crime and s 18 is made out.

Information may also be provided to a person or organization who has sup- 3.83 plied information in order to verify an entry in the Register where information provided proved to be inaccurate or incomplete.

Section 21 sets out general rules for using information without the indi- 3.84 vidual's consent. Again, regulations will provide the detail: the Secretary of State may make regulations imposing requirements relating to provision of information.

(g) Supervision of Operation of Act

Sections 22 to 24 deal with the supervision of the mechanisms established under 3.85 the Act.

Section 22 establishes a National Identity Scheme Commissioner to oversee 3.86 certain aspects of the operation of the ID cards scheme and the National Identity Register. The Commissioner is to be appointed by the Secretary of State, a matter which proved controversial during passage of the Bill through Parliament. He or she has no jurisdiction to deal with civil or criminal penalties under the Act. Section 23 requires the Commissioner to make annual reports, although these are to be made to the Secretary of State rather than to the Prime Minister, Cabinet or Parliament.

3.87   The Commissioner's remit does not cover the provision of information to the intelligence and security agencies. Instead, this is under the jurisdiction of the Intelligence Services Commissioner. Section 24 amends the Regulation of Investigatory Powers Act 2000, which sets out the functions of the Intelligence Services Commissioner and the Investigatory Powers Tribunal. It adds to their functions oversight of the provision of information held on the National Identity Register to the intelligence and security agencies under the Identity Cards Act 2006.

(h) *Offences*

3.88 New criminal offences are created by ss 25 to 30. They include possession of false identity documents (s 25), providing false information (s 28), and tampering with the Register (s 29). They also include a new 'whistleblower's offence' for civil servants or others who make unauthorized disclosures of information that they are obliged to keep confidential (s 27).

3.89   The offences created by ss 25, 28 and 29 are 'either way' offences, triable summarily or on indictment. On conviction on indictment, the ss 25 and 28 offences have a maximum sentence of two years' imprisonment and a fine; s 29, ten years' imprisonment and a fine.

3.90   The s 27 offence is triable only on indictment, with a maximum sentence of two years' imprisonment and a fine.

3.91   Section 30(2) adds the false documents offence (s 25) to s 31(3) of the Immigration and Asylum Act 1999. This means that those who destroy any false documents will commit an offence under s 2 of the Asylum and Immigration (Treatment of Claimants, etc) Act 2004.

3.92   Section 30(3) also adds the false documents offence to s 14(2) of the Asylum and Immigration (Treatment of Claimants, etc) Act 2004. This gives immigration officers power to arrest without warrant for the offence and ancillary powers to search for and seize documents.

(i) *Civil Penalties*

3.93 The procedure for the imposition of civil penalties is dealt with in ss 31 to 34.

3.94   A broad discretion is given to the Secretary of State as to the quantum of the civil penalty. He may impose such a penalty as he thinks fit in a given individual case, provided it does not exceed the specified amount.

3.95   In imposing a civil penalty, the Secretary of State must do so by notice which sets out certain matters, including the reasons for imposition, the amount payable, the date before which the penalty is due, the methods of payment and the steps the defaulter may take if he or she objects (s 31(3)). Section 31(6) operates as a form of ouster clause: in proceedings for recovery of the imposed penalty no question may be raised as to whether the defaulter was liable to the penalty, whether the imposition of the penalty was unreasonable, or the amount of the penalty.

If the individual does object this may be raised on an objection to the Secretary of State (s 32) or an appeal to the civil courts (s 33). On objection, the Secretary of State has the power to increase the penalty (s 32(3)), and so there is an inbuilt discouragement of objection in s 32. An appeal under s 33 is by way of a rehearing of the Secretary of State's decision to impose the penalty. **3.96**

Section 34 sets out provisions relating to a code of practice on penalties. This provision was not present in early versions of the Identity Cards Bill. The Secretary of State has the duty to issue a code of practice setting out the matters that will be considered when determining the amount of a civil penalty as well as determining whether a civil penalty should be imposed in the first place. The Secretary of State must have regard to the code when imposing a penalty or considering a notice of objection. A court must also have regard to the code when determining any appeal. Before issuing the code, the Secretary of State must take steps to ensure that members of the public are informed and consulted about the proposed code, and then a draft must be laid before Parliament.[27] It then comes into force as specified by order which is exercisable only after being subject to the affirmative resolution procedure. The order can be annulled by either House. **3.97**

(j) Fees and Charges
Fees and charges are dealt with in ss 35 to 37. **3.98**

Section 35 enables fees to be set, by regulation, for applications for entries to the Register, modification of entries, the issue of ID cards, provision of information from the Register, and so on. Regulations may permit payment by instalments. The Secretary of State is entitled, in prescribing fees, to take into account the wider costs associated with the ID cards scheme. The charges do not need to be uniform for all cards, and different fees may be charged to different groups of people. Treasury consent is required before regulations are made. Once the fees come into force the Secretary of State has power to vary the fees as he thinks appropriate. **3.99**

Section 36 amends the Consular Fees Act 1980, to allow for additional factors to be taken into account in setting fees for consular functions, including the issuing of passports. Passports may now be issued subject to different levels of fees for different cases. This enables the cross-subsidy of passport fees between fees charged to different applicants. Section 44(5) provides that s 36 will come into force two months after Royal Assent, on 30 May 2006. The amended fee-setting powers could be applied at any period after that time, including in advance of the introduction of ID cards. **3.100**

Section 37 was a late addition to the Identity Cards Act 2006, compelling the Secretary of State to prepare and lay before Parliament a report setting out his estimate of the costs of the ID card scheme over the next ten years. The report **3.101**

---

[27] See the draft Code of Practice in Appendix 3.

must be prepared within six months of the Act being passed, so before 30 September 2006. The report must estimate the amount of public expenditure on the scheme, including the cost of establishing and maintaining the Register, the issue, modification, renewal and so on of ID cards themselves, and the provision of information recorded on the Register by the Secretary of State to other persons.

3.102 This reporting requirement is ongoing, requiring the Secretary of State to lay such a report every six months (s 37(2)).

3.103 The potential cost of the ID card scheme has been a matter of much speculation and debate as the Act worked its way through the legislature. The government has consistently argued that to release information about the costs of the scheme would prejudice the tendering process on lucrative contracts arising out of the scheme. Section 37(4) represents a compromise on the reporting procedure, allowing that the Secretary of State need not include information about the costs of the scheme in his report that he considers to be prejudicial in securing the best value from the use of public money.

(k) Provisions Relating to Passports

3.104 Sections 38 and 39 contain provisions concerning passport applications and related legislation.

3.105 Section 38 mirrors s 9, permitting data sharing in relation to passport applications in the way s 9 permits it for ID card applications.

3.106 Section 39 simply makes a series of amendments to existing legislation relating to passports. Legislation which establishes circumstances in which a passport may be required is amended to add ID cards as an alternative; legislation under which a person is required to surrender his or her passport is amended to add a requirement to surrender an ID card able to be used as a travel document. This includes the Football Spectators Act 1989 (banning orders) and the Criminal Justice and Police Act 2001 (travel restriction orders).

3.107 The Secretary of State can modify any enactment or any provision of any piece of subordinate legislation to include a reference to an ID card by order, subject to the affirmative resolution procedure. The order can be annulled by either House.

(l) Supplemental

3.108 Sections 40 to 44 deal with certain supplemental matters, although some important detail is buried in this part of the Act. For example, potential new criminal offences are created by s 40(5), and the definition of 'false' in s 42(1) is very broad, which has knock-on effects on the criminal offences created by the Act and associated asylum, immigration and nationality legislation.

3.109 Section 40(3) provides that orders and regulations under the Act will be made through a negative resolution procedure except in cases specifically provided for, and that different application procedures for ID cards may be provided for groups specified in regulations (likely to include the very elderly or those with severe mental health problems). Section 40(5) also provides that if the age for entitlement to registration is lowered by the Secretary of State in future, any obligations arising under the Act may fall on the child's parents or other responsible adult. This means that the parent would become responsible for notifying the Secretary of State of changes in address or other details, but also that the parent would be responsible for informing the Secretary of State if the child has reason to believe that his or her ID card may have been tampered with or damaged. Failure to comply would lead to civil or criminal liability under the Act. This creates a series of proxy criminal offences for parents, to be triggered by regulations of the Secretary of State.

Section 41 deals with the Secretary of State's expenses in connection with the operation of the Act, which are to be paid from sums provided by Parliament. **3.110**

Section 42 is the general interpretation clause. Section 42(1) provides for interpretation of defined terms in the Act. Section 42(2) defines what is meant by a 'public service'. The Explanatory Notes to the Act recognize how widely this definition is drawn: 'This is broadly defined and is not restricted to what might be commonly understood as "public services", such as the NHS, and could include the granting of a firearms certificate or the requirement to notify changes of address imposed on certain sex offenders'.[28] **3.111**

The phrase 'subject to compulsory registration' was changed after clause 6 mandating compulsory registration was scrapped. It now means 'required to be entered in the Register in accordance with an obligation imposed by an Act of Parliament passed after the passing of this Act', which further suggests that compulsion is only a matter of time. **3.112**

Section 43 deals with Scotland. It provides that the use in relation to Scotland of the Register or an ID card is authorized only in matters which are reserved or which are in accordance with an Act of the Scottish Parliament. Section 43(2) ensures that regulations may not be made under s 13 which allow or require the imposition of a condition on the provision of a public service in Scotland, except where it is in relation to a reserved function. Separate legislation by the Scottish Parliament would be required if, for example, it were proposed in the future to require an ID card to be produced as a condition of accessing a devolved public service in Scotland. However, nothing in s 43 restricts any of the provisions of the Act authorizing information from the Register to be provided, and it does not restrict the Act's powers to make other provision authorizing such information to be provided to a person in Scotland. **3.113**

Section 44 deals with the short title, repeals, commencement and extent. It allows the preceding provisions of the Act to be brought into force by order made by the Secretary of State. Different parts of the Bill may come into force on different dates. Section 44(5) provides that ss 36 and 38 (amendments relating to passport fees and data-sharing powers for passport applications) shall come **3.114**

---

[28] Explanatory Notes, para 220.

into force two months after the Act is passed (on 30 May 2006). This section also clarifies that the Act includes a power to enable roll-out of the scheme to be undertaken by geographical areas; and that a trial may be undertaken in relation to particular areas or persons (s 44(4)). This includes a power to make transitional provisions for the period between the trial stage and the full commencement of the scheme. Section 44(6) provides an extension power so that clauses may be applied to the Channel Islands or to the Isle of Man via Order in Council, and s 44(8) provides that the Act extends to Northern Ireland.

(m) *Schedule 1*

3.115 Schedule 1 sets out the information that may be recorded in the Register. This includes:

- personal information—names, date and place of birth, gender, addresses;
- identifying information—photograph, signature, fingerprint, other biometric information;
- residential status—nationality, entitlement to remain, terms and conditions of that entitlement;
- personal reference numbers—for example the National Identity Registration Number and other government-issued numbers, and validity periods of related documents;
- record history—information previously recorded, audit trail of changes and date of death;
- registration and ID card history—dates of application, changes to information, confirmation; information regarding other ID cards already issued, details of counter-signatures, notification under clause 11(1) and requirements to surrender an ID card;
- validation information—information provided for any application, modification, confirmation or issue; other steps taken in connection with an application or otherwise for identifying the applicant and verifying the information; particulars of any other steps for ensuring there is an accurate entry in the Register; and particulars of notification of changes;
- security information—personal identification numbers, password or other codes, and questions and answers that could be used to identify a person seeking provisions of information or the modification of an entry; and
- records of provision of information—how and when any information from an entry was provided to any person or body.

3.116 Under s 3(6), however, the Secretary of State may, by order, modify the information set out in Sch 1.

(n) *Schedule 2*

3.117 Repeals can be found in Sch 2 to the Act.

4

THE IDENTITY CARD

A. INTRODUCTION

There is very little information on the face of the Identity Cards Act 2006 **4.01** concerning the ID card itself. Even now, the precise form of the ID card, including its technological capabilities, is not exactly clear. What is known is that the first stand-alone ID cards will not be issued until late 2008,[1] so it will be one of the last pieces of the infrastructure of the national identity scheme to go 'live'.

In the context of the national identity scheme currently being constructed **4.02** by the government, the very notion of an ID card is, in itself, confusing. Since the Home Office began the consultation process on 'entitlement cards' in 2002, the government has consistently indicated that it wishes to establish 'one secure record of identity to which a variety of identity documents would be linked'.[2] Rather than the scheme being based around a single ID card, it is centred on the Register entry, which is in turn linked to 'a family of ID cards based on new and existing documents'.[3] Further, the definition of the term 'card' in the Identity Cards Act 2006 goes far beyond ordinary usage, and includes a 'stamp' and a 'label', provided it may be used to establish or verify identity in some context.

---

[1] EURIM, *Draft Summary Report of the EURIM Identity Cards Bill Subgroup Meeting, 6 October 2005.*
[2] *Entitlement Cards and Identity Fraud: The Government's Response to the Consultation Points* 9, 23.
[3] Home Office Parliamentary Labour Party Briefing, *Identity Cards*, 26 April 2004.

4.03   Despite this, the ID card itself has been a political flashpoint since consultation began. In November 2004, protestors from lobby group No2ID greeted then Home Secretary, David Blunkett, as he arrived to give a speech on the proposals by burning a giant ID card bearing his photo.[4] Privacy International has argued that the card is the physical manifestation of 'the most powerful element of the system', the number which allows for data-sharing between government departments: 'The modern ID card is not merely a simple piece of plastic. It is the visible component of a highly complex web of interactive technology that fuses the most intimate characteristics of the individual with the machinery of the state.'[5]

4.04   Those who support the introduction of ID cards have also focused on the impact of the card itself. The Home Office has suggested that it will be a 'badge of citizenship', a physical manifestation of the individual's right to be in the UK: 'Identity cards will provide every person in this country with an easy and secure way of demonstrating their right to be here and asserting their place in the community'.[6]

4.05   Although most opposition to the Identity Cards Bill within Parliament focused on its potential impact on the right to privacy, and thus on the Register, the ID card itself raises particular issues relating to discrimination. In other countries, there have been reports of discriminatory use of police and immigration officials' powers to demand identification from ethnic minorities. The Commission for Racial Equality has argued that stop and search patterns in the UK indicate that minority ethnic individuals will be likely to be stopped and asked to verify their identity—possibly by providing a biometric rather than producing their ID cards themselves—and that such differential treatment may be replicated in service provision and recruitment procedures.[7] Such differential treatment is a double-edged sword, however: as the purposes of the Identity Cards Act 2006 include preventing illegal immigration, illegal working, and terrorism, it may be argued that these risks are not evenly distributed across society, ethnicities, nationalities and so some differential impact is inevitable.

4.06   The Identity Cards Act 2006 does include safeguards designed to prevent such discriminatory impact, including an explicit guarantee that the ID card itself does not need to be carried (s 16). The likely effectiveness of these safeguards is explored further below and in chapter 7.

---

[4] 'Blunkett concern on loyalty cards', *BBC News*, 17 November 2004, available at http://news.bbc.co.uk/1/hi/uk_politics/4018939.stm.

[5] Privacy International, *Submission to the Citizenship & Immigration Committee of the Canadian Parliament: National Identity Cards*, 4 October 2004.

[6] David Blunkett, Foreword, *Identity Cards—The Next Steps* (Cm 6020, November 2003) 3.

[7] CRE Briefing, *Identity Cards Bill: House of Lords Report Stage*, 16 January 2006.

B. ISSUING ID CARDS

1. Overview

Section 6 sets out the procedure for issuing ID cards. It is envisaged that they will **4.07** eventually be issued to every person over age 16, entitled to be enrolled on the Register, and residing in the UK for longer than a specified period (three months).

The Identity and Passport Service expects 'most people to get their ID card **4.08** when they apply for a new adult passport, either a first passport or a renewal'.[8] The passport booklet and new ID card will be issued together. Many foreign nationals from outside the European Economic Area will get an ID card with, or as part of, their Asylum Registration Card or biometric residence permit, a new document expected to be issued by the Immigration and Nationality Directorate (IND) from 2007. If the Secretary of State chooses to designate other documents—a process whereby he, with Parliamentary approval, may specify certain documents which will automatically be issued with an inbuilt or accompanying ID card—ID cards may also be issued with such documents as Criminal Records Bureau (CRB) checks and firearms certificates.

As the scheme progresses it will be possible to apply for an ID card separately, **4.09** called a stand-alone ID card. This will be an option for those individuals who have not already obtained an ID card as part of or with a designated document. It will not be possible to apply for a stand-alone ID card until late 2008.[9] Once the first cards are issued, the government anticipates 'ramping up issuing capacity over 18 months' to full capacity before 2010.[10] Full capacity is currently predicted as involving the issue of between 5 and 7 million cards per year.

Until 1 January 2010, those applying for a passport may 'opt out' of being **4.10** issued with an ID card. This provision was introduced as part of the compromise deal negotiated by the Labour government with many opposition MPs and Lords in order to ensure that the Identity Cards Bill reached the statute book. Government ministers have also guaranteed to Parliament (once in relation to the Identity Cards Bill[11] and once in relation to the Road Safety Bill[12]) that ID cards will not be issued with, or as part of, driving licences.

Shadow Home Secretary David Davis MP reportedly described the compro- **4.11** mise as a 'major climb-down by Government' which meant that 'nobody who does not want an ID card need have one before the next election—and that in itself is worth having'.[13] However, there remain circumstances in which ID cards may

---

[8] Identity and Passport Service website, http://www.identitycards.gov.uk/scheme-what-produced.asp#applying.

[9] ibid. [10] EURIM report (n 1 above) para 4.

[11] *Hansard*, HC col 1175 (13 February 2006) (Charles Clarke MP).

[12] *Hansard*, HC col 839 (8 March 2006) (Alastair Darling MP).

[13] Quoted in 'Deal paves the way for ID cards', *BBC News*, 30 March 2006, available at http://news.bbc.co.uk/1/hi/uk_politics/4856074.stm.

or must be issued to individuals who do not want them or have not applied for them.[14]

2. Definition of ID Card

4.12 An 'ID card' has a specific meaning under the Act. It is defined by s 6(1) and (2).

4.13   First, it is a card that is issued to an individual by the Secretary of State (s 6(1)(a)). The card may form part of a designated document (such as a passport or biometric residence permit) or it can be a separate card issued together with a designated document.[15] It can also be a stand-alone card issued as an ID card. 'Card' is a broad term in this context. It includes a 'document' and/or 'other article', in or on which information may be recorded (s 42(1)). 'Document', in turn, includes a 'stamp' or a 'label' (s 42(1)). This means that a chip capable of storing information or a visa stamp may be a 'card' under the Act.

4.14   Second, whatever form the document takes, it must do certain things to constitute an 'ID card' for the Act's purposes (s 6(1)(b)). Those things are recording personal information already recorded on the Register (s 6(2)(a)) and carrying data enabling the card to be used for verifying information on the Register (s 6(2)(b)).

3. Issuing

4.15 An ID card may be issued in three broad circumstances: if (i) an individual applies to be entered in the Register, (ii) an individual applies for a designated document (subject to the compromise on passports), or (iii) an individual confirms an entry which has been made for him or her on the Register by the Secretary of State, whether or not that entry has been made with his or her consent. In a case falling under (iii), the individual will be obliged to confirm that the entry that has been made or else face a civil penalty of up to £1,000.[16]

4.16   The interaction of ss 6(4), 6(6), 2(2) and 2(4) is complex and potentially confusing. This may be due to the last-minute nature of the compromise deal agreed by the government on the eve of Royal Assent. There is an apparent conflict, in particular, between the provisions in s 6(4) (an ID card *must* be issued to qualifying individuals) and s 6(6) (an ID card *must not* be issued without an application or confirmation from the individual). Both are mandatory provisions.[17]

4.17   According to s 6(4), if an individual is 'entitled' to be entered on the Register

---

[14] The way in which this may occur is explained in para 4.19 below.

[15] Note s 43(6) which provides that references to a designated document being issued together with an ID card include references to the two documents being comprised in the same card.

[16] For further information, see s 9 in chapter 6.

[17] It is suggested that the only way in which these two provisions can correctly interact with each other in practice is if regulations made by the Secretary of State under each of them mirror each other: the prescribed individuals exempted from the s 6(4) requirement must be those individuals who fall outside s 6(6).

(or is subject to compulsory registration[18]) and his or her personal information has in fact been entered on the Register, an ID card must be issued. This general rule may be subject to certain exceptions, in cases to be prescribed by the Secretary of State.

Section 6(5) provides that in certain cases, to be prescribed by the Secretary of **4.18** State, someone who is not required to be issued with an ID card may be issued with one anyway, as long as registrable facts about him have been entered in the Register. This could apply, for example, to a foreign national who has resided in the UK for less than three months but whose passport has been surrendered for bail purposes and who therefore requires another form of proof of identity.[19] As an entry in the Register may be made for an individual if the information is 'otherwise available' to the Secretary of State, whether or not the individual has applied to be, or is even entitled to be, on the Register (s 2(4)),[20] this subsection's effect is that ID cards may be issued to those who are not otherwise entitled to be within the scheme.

According to s 6(6), an ID card will only be issued either if the individual has **4.19** applied for its issue (s 6(6)(a)) or has confirmed (with or without changes) an entry of his or hers already in the Register (s 6(6)(b)). In the latter scenario an individual may not have much of a choice, as the Act includes the power for the Secretary of State to include an individual in the Register even if he or she has not applied for or does not want enrolment (s 2(4)), and once entered the individual may be subject to a duty to verify those details and notify any errors or changes. Refusal to comply could result in a civil penalty of up to £1,000.

Any application for an ID card must be made in the prescribed manner (yet **4.20** to be determined) (s 6(8)(a)), to the Secretary of State or the designated documents authority (s 6(8)(b)), and it must include certain information (yet to be determined) (s 6(8)(c)).

Regulations made under this section must comply with the Disability Dis- **4.21** crimination Act 1995. The prescribed information that must be provided before an ID card will be issued must take into account the fact that some individuals will be unable to provide information relating to certain registrable facts. For example, some disabled individuals will be unable to provide biometrics such as thumbprints or iris scans. The European Information Society Group (EURIM) (an all-party Parliamentary-Industry grouping which included the then Home Secretary, Charles Clarke) indicated during the passage of the Bill through Parliament that 'valid reasons would be accepted for the absence of a particular biometric'.[21]

Under s 6(7), an individual who does not already have an ID card must apply **4.22**

---

[18] No individuals may be subject to compulsory registration without a further Act of Parliament.
[19] Explanatory Notes to the Identity Cards Act 2006, para 51.
[20] The Secretary of State must consider that the entry is consistent with the statutory purposes. For further information, see chapter 5.
[21] EURIM (n 1 above) para 2.47.

for one (in the manner prescribed) when applying for a designated document. Until 1 January 2010, an individual applying for a new or renewed passport need not be subject to this obligation. He or she will be entered in the Register regardless of whether he or she exercises the 'opt out' option, but unless an ID card has been issued he or she will not be obliged to notify the Secretary of State of any change in his or her circumstances pursuant to s 10.[22] The numbers of individuals likely to be automatically enrolled in the national identity scheme as the result of applying for designated documents will also be affected by the government's Parliamentary promise that driving licences will not be designated: 'In the light of some of the recent publicity, I should make it clear that, along with my right hon. Friend the Secretary of State for Transport, I have looked actively at designating driving licences, but we have decided not to do so'.[23]

4.23   The impact of these two changes to the planned designated documents policy is likely to be substantial. Passports and driving licences are the most common forms of identity document within the UK, held by 80 per cent of the population. Without an automatic link between their issue or renewal and ID cards, roll-out of the scheme will not be as fast as had been earlier predicted by the Home Office.

4.24   From late 2008, when stand-alone ID cards will be ready for issue, an application for an ID card may be made separately from any application for the designated document. This will allow the authority to issue an ID card that is not part of the designated document. Until that time, any ID cards issued will be part of designated documents. In theory, during this interim period any requirement or request to produce an ID card will mean that the individual must produce the designated document itself. It must be presumed that the procedure will be designed to avoid difficulties such as, for example, if the designated document is a CRB check which the individual has failed or a biometric residence permit when the individual does not want to reveal his or her nationality.

4. Renewal of ID Cards

4.25   ID cards will have a specified period of validity. Under s 11(4)(d), an individual with an expired card may be required to surrender it to the Secretary of State. If he or she fails to do so, he or she may be liable to a civil penalty of up to £1,000.

4.26   Section 7 sets out the procedure for the renewal of ID cards for those individuals who are compelled to be entered in the Register. Until there is a fresh Act of Parliament, no individuals may be subject to compulsory registration, so this section will not be triggered until there is a further piece of legislation.

4.27   Section 7(2) provides that if an individual holds a valid ID card that is due

---

[22] For further information, see chapter 6.
[23] *Hansard*, HC col 1175 (13 February 2006) (Charles Clarke MP).

to expire within the prescribed period, or if he or she does not hold a valid ID card, he or she must apply for an ID card (within a specified time). This section ensures that compulsion stretches beyond the point at which ID cards are first required.

Section 7(3) provides that the Secretary of State may require an individual applying for an ID card under this section to do certain things in order to verify the information provided or to otherwise ensure that there is a complete and up-to-date entry about the individual on the Register. This mirrors the provisions set out in s 5(5). The things that an individual may be required to do are set out in s 7(4) and include attending specified appointments, allowing his or her fingerprints and other biometric information to be taken and recorded, allowing himself or herself to be photographed, and 'otherwise to provide such information as may be required by the Secretary of State' (s 7(4)(d)). This final category is broad, allowing the Secretary of State room to increase the requirements under s 7(4). **4.28**

Section 7(5) provides for a maximum civil penalty of £1,000 to be imposed for an individual who contravenes a requirement imposed by s 7.[24] **4.29**

C. THE CARD

1. Overview

The exact design and specification of ID cards is yet to be determined. Parliament must approve the format of any such card by the affirmative resolution procedure, whether it is a stand-alone ID card, an ID card issued alongside a designated document, or an ID card issued as part of a designated document. **4.30**

The Home Affairs Select Committee expressed concern about the absence of detail relating to the card itself in its 2004 report. They concluded that: **4.31**

The type of card to be used is a decision of the same order of importance as the architecture of the database, since it has consequences for issues such as how the card will be used and the number of readers and the infrastructure needed.[25]

They also observed that some of the government's choices relating to the card, such as the nature of the chip, follow on from the decision to use the passport as the basis for an ID card rather than any independent assessment of what will be the most appropriate for the ID card itself.[26]

Section 6(3) provides that an ID card issued to an individual must record only the prescribed information and must record prescribed parts of it in encrypted form. **4.32**

---

[24] For further detail on the operation of the civil penalties scheme, see chapter 10.
[25] Home Affairs Select Committee, Fourth Report of Session 2003–04, *Identity Cards*, 30 July 2004 (HC 130-I) para 197.
[26] *Hansard*, HL col 960 (15 November 2005).

4.33   Further, the ID card is only to be valid for the prescribed period. The Home Office's planning assumption has been that there will be a ten-year re-registration cycle, as for a passport.[27] It is likely that different prescribed periods will apply to different categories of person, such as linking a foreign national's ID card validity to his or her length of stay.[28]

4.34   Section 6(3)(d) provides that the ID card will remain the property of the issuer, ie the Secretary of State or the designated documents authority. The purpose of this clause is to ground the provisions in s 11 relating to the surrender and cancellation of ID cards.

4.35   The cards need not be uniform, either in their appearance or technologically. Regulations may distinguish between different categories of people. Only British citizens will have the technology to allow them to use their cards for international travel, for example, and nationality will be listed on the face of some cards, but not others.

2. Appearance of the Card

4.36   As the cards themselves are 'still the subject of much work',[29] the precise appearance cannot be outlined. However, it is highly likely that any such card is likely to be a credit card sized plastic card with a photograph containing a secure chip where biometric data will be stored.[30]

4.37   Only certain information will appear on the face of the card. Further information may be stored in the card, on a chip, perhaps with an accompanying encryption mechanism to hide the data unless an authentification process is completed. Finally, there will be information which is neither apparent on the card, nor stored in the chip, but will be stored in the individual's entry on the Register (which will be linked to the card).

4.38   It is unclear how many of the 'registrable facts' stored in the Register will be replicated on the face of the card. There are indications that only basic information, such as name, age or date of birth, and the National Identity Register number will be printed on the card. The government has stated that the information on the card will resemble what is on the passport.[31] The individual's address will not appear on the face of the card, nor will it be on the chip—it will only be stored on the Register itself.[32] The address may then be one of the items which may be used to verify remotely the individual's identity against his or her Register entry.

4.39   During the pre-legislative scrutiny stage and the passage of the Identity Cards Bill through Parliament, this issue was highlighted by many lobby groups. Although the government had indicated that sensitive information

---

[27] EURIM (n 1 above) para 2.47.   [28] Explanatory Notes, para 50.
[29] EURIM (n 1 above) para 2.44.
[30] See the UK government's identity card website at http://www.identitycards.gov.uk/index.asp.
[31] *Hansard*, HL col 79 (30 January 2006).   [32] ibid.

would not be included on the face of the card, critics argued that whether or not information was sensitive depended on the circumstances of the particular individual.

The cards will not be uniform in appearance. There will be a 'plain card, **4.40** which will not be valid for travel'. The government indicated in Parliament that, 'you will clearly be able to differentiate one from the other'.[33] Some UK nationals will have two ID cards, one which lists their nationality on the face of the card, which will be confiscated if the government wishes to prevent them from travelling, and one not listing their nationality, which they would retain while the other was confiscated in order to access domestic services.[34]

Information provided in Parliament was not clear on this issue, in part due to **4.41** the repeated use of the phrase 'foreign national' without clarification of which categories of non-UK nationals were included each time. In November 2005 Home Office Minister Baroness Scotland said that EU nationals resident in the UK would be eligible for a UK ID card, 'but it will not show nationality'.[35] In March 2006 she stated that she wished to make clear that 'the residence permit of a foreign national' would include his or her nationality on the face of the card.[36] On this occasion she appeared to include EU nationals within her description of foreign nationals who 'will apply for a residence permit'.[37]

3. Technical Requirements

The technical side of the cards is still being explored, particularly in relation to **4.42** chip technology. This is partly because the government or Home Office were unable to proceed fully with the procurement process until the Act had received Royal Assent.[38] It is also in part due to the sheer size and complexity of the project, which requires a great deal of development work prior to finalizing the operational details.[39]

Despite these inevitable restrictions, a large amount of preparatory work was **4.43** undertaken prior to Royal Assent on 30 March 2006. In October 2005 EURIM noted that:

Headline media coverage on the politics surrounding the ID Cards Bill contrasts with the large amount of work being undertaken in preparation for procurement. Recognizing the anxiety and impatience among some potential suppliers to the scheme for more information, it was stated that significant resources (involving some 170 people) are employed in translating the legislative framework into the requirements of the market, compared with 4 people working on the Bill.[40]

---

[33] *Hansard*, HL col 1009 (23 January 2006).
[34] *Hansard*, HC Written Answers, col 758W (27 March 2006).
[35] *Hansard*, HL col 1008 (15 November 2005).   [36] *Hansard*, HL col 579 (6 March 2006).
[37] ibid.   [38] PLP Briefing (n 3 above).
[39] Home Office, *Identity Cards Bill: Regulatory Impact Assessment*, 25 May 2005, para 6.
[40] EURIM (n 1 above) para 2.1.

4. International Civil Aviation Organization Standards

4.44 The present assumption is that cards will have a chip that has 'ICAO functionality'. It will comply with International Civil Aviation Organization standards for international travel. This will require at least two biometrics to be stored on the card itself (in the chip). Further biometrics may be stored on the Register only.

4.45 It is intended to issue cards valid for travel only to UK citizens. This may mean that ID cards issued to others may not have ICAO functionality.

5. Chip and Pin

4.46 The government has been holding discussions with the private sector concerning the possibility of the cards being EMV-compliant.[41] 'EMV' (Europay Mastercard Visa Integrated Chip Card Standard) is an acronym referring to the standardization of 'chip and pin' systems for payments. If the cards were made EMV-compliant, a simple card validation method would be available over the existing chip and PIN network, which currently comprises over 800,000 readers (mainly in banks and retailers).

6. Biometrics

4.47 A biometric is a unique personal physical characteristic. Examples of biometrics include iris patterns, vein patterns, fingerprints, facial structure, hand geometry and voices. Biometric technologies extract data from these unique physical attributes and store that data for later verification. If the individual later presents the same physical information, the system should verify that there is a match. As the core purpose of the Identity Cards Act 2006 is to provide a reliable means of verifying identity, and the government wishes to prevent multiple registration, biometrics will be central to the scheme's effectiveness.

4.48 The Act allows for the recording of any biometric data.[42] The kinds of data that may be recorded in the Register can be amended by an order of the Secretary of State (s 3(6)).

4.49 Biometric collection capabilities are appearing in travel documents around the world. The US has already implemented a fingerprint requirement on all visitors to the US, including British citizens, who have not requested a visa, under a scheme known as the 'visa waiver scheme'. The EU has mandated biometric passports, incorporating facial image and fingerprint biometrics, for its citizens.[43] Since early 2006, the Identity and Passport Service has begun rolling out a 'first generation' biometric passport, which incorporates a chip that stores passport data and a digital photograph as a 'facial recognition biometric'.

---

[41] ibid, para 2.45.   [42] See Sch 2 and s 2, in particular s 2(d).
[43] Pursuant to Council Regulation 2252/2004 [2004] OJ L385/1. See also *The Identity Cards Bill*, HC Research Paper 05/43, 30–31.

Biometrics are already used for many purposes within the UK. Fingerprints **4.50** have long been used for law enforcement purposes.[44] More recently, voice recognition biometrics have been used to support electronic monitoring schemes for those on Home Detention Curfew following early release from prison, individuals sentenced to curfew orders, and asylum seekers. The IND has introduced a 'fast-track' method to clear immigration control in certain UK airports, the Iris Recognition Immigration System, which allows individuals to enrol in the system on the spot and enter the UK through an automated barrier incorporating an iris recognition camera.

The police are currently investigating the possibility of wider use of biometric **4.51** identifiers. The Police Information Technology Organisation's Forward Plan states that 'deployment and wider deployment' of fingerprint scanning systems will be undertaken, and additional biometrics will be investigated. They are also working to 'establish the police requirement and business case for a facial images national database, drawing on the Home Office Police Science and Technology Strategy'.[45]

Despite the increasing popularity of biometric data capture, the technology is **4.52** not without its errors. An amendment tabled at the Identity Cards Bill's reading in the House of Lords, requesting a consideration of the reliability of recording biometrics, drew attention to the Cabinet Office report indicating that 'around 10 to 15 percent of genuine people fail the biometric tests set at the highest level of corroboration' and that there are problems capturing accurately the biometrics (such as facial recognition) of certain people such as those persons of ethnic minority groups, those with disabilities, people who are smiling,[46] those with brown eyes, and those who are bald.[47]

The government argues that biometric technology is constantly improving **4.53** and, in any event, facial recognition will not be the only means of verifying a person's identity but will be part of a larger strategy incorporating many other forms of biometric data. In any event, any one method used to authenticate and verify a person's identity will need to be part of a larger strategy which takes into account the potential limitations of each component part of the identifying array. It has been indicated that the scheme will allow for 'false negatives' when biometric data is checked against that held on the Register, due to changes in a person's physical appearance or iris properties.[48]

Some academics have decried the use of biometrics as a means of enhancing **4.54**

---

[44] See further P Bogan, *Identification: Investigation, Trial and Scientific Evidence* (London: Legal Action Group, 2004) 267–275.

[45] I Brown, 'Technology development and its effect on privacy and law enforcement', *UK Information Commissioner Study Project: Privacy and Law Enforcement*, combined papers 1 and 2, February 2004, 3, available at http://www.informationcommissioner.gov.uk/cms/DocumentUploads/Report%20Parts%201&2.pdf.

[46] *Hansard*, HL col 1048 (15 November 2005) Amendment 8.

[47] *Hansard*, HL col 961 (15 November 2005) Amendment 12.

[48] EURIM, *Draft Summary Report* (n 21 above) para 2.47.

security. They argue that whilst biometric data is useful as a means of authenticating a person's identity (that is, one-to-one matching of the card to the cardholder), it has serious limitations as a means of identifying a person (that is, uniquely and reliably identifying an individual cardholder with respect to many individuals whose biometrics are stored on a database).[49]

4.55   The ability of data-matching software to match a cardholder to a person on, for example, a database of known terrorists, is dubious. First, there is no guarantee that the foundation documents used to secure an ID card were not forged in the first place. Any ID card can only be as reliable in linking to a person's true identity as the source data on which it is based. Second, detection systems are not infallible; there will always be a margin of error allowing false positives (innocent people wrongly matched to suspects on a watch list) and false negatives (failing to match a person to a suspect that is rightly on a watch list).[50] There are some statistics which show that even if a facial recognition system is 99.9 per cent accurate (which is not the case at the moment) there is still a 1 in 1,000 chance of a false positive and a 1 in 1,000 chance of a false negative for every data comparison made.[51]

4.56   The national identity scheme is, in financial terms, heavily reliant on the private sector becoming involved and paying fees for that involvement. The government anticipates that many private sector bodies will apply for 'accreditation' in order to access the Register to verify the identity of their customers or potential employees, and will be willing to pay for this system. For the verification system to be commercially viable, the biometric technology must be accurate and secure.

4.57   If biometric data is to hold the promise of the future for the system, the government will need to improve the accuracy and reliability of such data, and understand its limitations so that it can be effective in authenticating and verifying a person's identity. The form that any future ID card assumes, as well as the breadth of biometric information stored therein, remains to be seen.

7. Radio Frequency Identification

4.58   The US is going further than the UK in terms of its identification technology. It has begun issuing passports embedded with radio frequency identification chips, and they will be issued in all passports from October 2006 onwards.[52] Such chips

---

[49] See R Bijon, 'The Case Against Biometric National Identification Systems (NIDS): "Trading Off" Privacy Without Getting Security' (2005) 19 Windsor Rev of Legal & Social Issues 45 at 58.

[50] ibid 60–61.

[51] ibid 62, citing B Schneider, *Beyond Fear: Thinking Sensibly about Security in an Uncertain World* (New York: Copernicus Books, 2003) 189.

[52] P Prince, 'United States sets date for e-passports', *RFID Journal*, 25 October 2005; G Gross, 'United States to Require RFID in Passports', IDG News Service, available at http://www.pcworld.com/news/article/0,aid,123246,00.asp.

will contain the name, nationality, gender, date of birth and place of birth of the passport holder, as well as a digitized photograph of the person. The State Department has issued security rules governing the technology designed to protect it from accidental disclosure of personal information, and intentional 'skimming' or unauthorized acquisition of data.

D. CARRYING ID CARDS

The Identity Cards Act 2006 explicitly rules out the possibility of regulations making the carrying of an ID card compulsory (s 16). The government has repeatedly emphasized that it is not its intention to impose a requirement to carry a card, either pre- or post-compulsion. A Home Office spokesperson indicated this at the first ID card hearing of the Home Affairs Select Committee in 2003:   **4.59**

> There is absolutely no question of people at any point being required to carry the card as a matter of compulsion. It is not going to be compulsory to carry a card and that has been ruled out very clearly . . . The desire of the Home Office is to have a compulsory scheme. Certainly as now, if the police stop you for speeding, they can ask to see your driving licence, but there is no expectation that you will always have it with you. We would expect exactly the same situation, the same culture. Ministers have been very clear, right from the outset, that they do not want a compulsory to carry scheme. For that very reason we do not want to move to a 'Big Brother State' where you are having to produce a card at all times.[53]

There are two factors which are likely to limit the effect of the statutory guarantee that ID cards will not be required to be carried at all times. First, it may nevertheless become a de facto requirement to carry the card as many public and private sector organizations begin to request it in order for the individual to access services.   **4.60**

Second, technology allows for identity verification against the Register even without the card being present. There has been a recent increase in the use of remote systems of identity verification by law enforcement agencies and others. For example, operations carried out by the British Transport Police and the IND involving 'spot checks' on suspected illegal immigrants on the London Underground have involved the use of handheld computers to check the individual's identity against Home Office records.[54] Some police forces have introduced or are examining the possibility of handheld fingerprint scanners or iris scanners in order to verify identity.   **4.61**

---

[53] HASC, Minutes of evidence (11 December 2003) Q23 (Nicola Roche).
[54] CRE Briefing (n 7 above) para 23.

E. MULTIPLE CARDS

4.62 The Identity Cards Act 2006 is intended to prevent individuals having or registering 'multiple identities'. However, it became clear during its passage through Parliament that, although 'the majority of us would have just the one identity card',[55] in some circumstances multiple cards may legitimately be issued to a single individual.

4.63 If a UK national's ID card is confiscated, along with his or her passport, as a bail condition or under a football banning order (s 39):

> To ensure that anyone subject to restrictions for an extended period of time can demonstrate their identity for domestic purposes, they will be able to obtain an identity card which will be issued to the same standards as other cards but which will not be valid for travel. This will be achieved by not specifying the nationality of the card holder on the face of the card.[56]

4.64 Transsexuals may be issued with two cards, one in each gender.[57] The government has also referred to the possibility of an Irish national from Northern Ireland being issued with two cards, with only one of them listing his or her UK citizenship.[58]

---

[55] *Hansard*, HL col 78 (30 January 2006).
[56] *Hansard*, HC Written Answers, col 758W (27 March 2006).
[57] *Hansard*, HL col 78 (30 January 2006).   [58] ibid.

5

REGISTRATION

A. INTRODUCTION

Despite its name, the Identity Cards Act 2006 is not just about ID cards. The **5.01**
Act also establishes a National Identity Register, a monolith of information
stored about individuals who are registered. During the debates about the Bill in
the House of Lords, many of those opposed to the Bill suggested that the title of
the Bill was wrong and misleading and that other names would be more
appropriate, such as the National Identity Register Bill[1] and even the National
Control of the Subject Bill.[2] The Earl of Northesk stated during the debates as
follows:

I turn to the second of my previous criticisms of the Bill—that is, the fact that the real
aim of the proposed scheme is to establish a centralized national identity database rather
than an ID card system. This issue caused concern to the constitutional committee in its
previous report on the Bill. Indeed, the noble Lord, Lord Holme, touched upon it earlier
today. As the committee commented:

---

[1] *Hansard*, HL col 968 (15 November 2005).   [2] *Hansard*, HL col 1011 (15 November 2005).

'When the scheme is fully in place, the role of identity cards themselves will be secondary to the database of information regarding the personal history on a life-long basis of every individual in the Register.'[3]

5.02 The original Identity Cards Bill purported to confer a power on the Secretary of State to make registration compulsory. The question of compulsion was the most contentious facet of the Bill and resulted in a lengthy and multi-staged debate between the House of Commons and the House of Lords.

5.03 The power of the Secretary of State to require registration was provided for in the original clause 6 of the Bill. Compulsion was to be achieved initially by requiring everyone who applied for a passport to be registered on the ID card database and to be supplied with an ID card. The Bill allowed the government to introduce compulsory registration at some time in the future for all those persons who had yet to become registered. The regulations that would make the scheme compulsory were to be created through the super-affirmative resolution procedure, whereby the government would have to publish a report outlining its reasons for compulsion to be laid before Parliament in draft form, followed by a debate and a vote.

5.04 The opposition parties in the House of Lords vigorously argued against compulsion, not swayed by the safeguards offered by the super-affirmative process for making the scheme compulsory. Eventually, a compromise was agreed, delaying compulsion until following the next general election. In the meantime, as of 2008, anyone who renews a passport will be put on the national identity database but will not be forced to obtain an ID card until 2010. Further, people are entitled to opt out of the scheme until 2011 (following the next general election). Those who opt out will not have to inform the government of changes of address and so will not be subject to the fees and charges that apply to the entire scheme.

5.05 This compromise makes the question of a compulsory ID cards scheme an election issue, given that the Conservatives have indicated a desire to scrap the ID cards scheme should they gain power at the next general election.[4] If the Labour government retains power after the next election, compulsion appears inevitable.

B. THE NATIONAL IDENTITY REGISTER

1. Overview

5.06 The Identity Cards Act 2006 establishes a National Identity Register which is a database of information retained about individuals who are registered under the ID cards scheme. The duty to establish and maintain the Register falls on the

---

[3] *Hansard*, HL col 75 (31 October 2005).

[4] David Davis, Shadow Home Secretary quoted in 'Clarke attacked on ID card costs', *BBC News*, 30 March 2006, http://news.bbc.co.uk/1/hi/uk_politics/4862556.stm.

Secretary of State (s 1(1)). The fact that the control of identities of registered individuals rests with the government of the day was described as 'deeply worrying' by those who opposed the Bill.[5]

2. Statutory Purposes

There has always been concern about the nature and scope of the information **5.07** that can be held on the Register. This concern is meant to be partly alleviated by the fact that the Act only allows for certain confined statutory purposes for which the Register is to be established and maintained. In particular, s 1(3) provides that the two explicit statutory purposes are to facilitate a convenient method for individuals to prove their identity and to facilitate a secure and reliable method for an individual's identity to be checked, wherever it is necessary to do so in the public interest.

Something is necessary in the public interest under s 1(4) if and only if it is in **5.08** the interests of national security, for the purposes of the prevention or detection of crime (which includes action to prevent terrorism, identity fraud and theft), for the purposes of the enforcement of immigration controls, for the purposes of the enforcement of prohibitions on unauthorized working or employment, or for the purpose of securing the efficient and effective provision of public services. This list, whilst exhaustive, is quite broad, contemplating a wide variety of circumstances in which identity checks will be permitted.

3. Registrable Facts

An individual's identity is specified by a set of personal information known as **5.09** 'registrable facts' that is recorded about that individual and stored on the Register. 'Registrable facts' are defined exhaustively in s 1(5) to mean an individual's identity (further defined in s 1(7)), the address of his or her principal place of residence in the UK, the address of every other place in the UK and elsewhere he or she has previously been resident, the times at which he or she was resident at different places in the UK or elsewhere, his or her current residential status (further defined in s 1(8)), residential statuses previously held by him or her, information about numbers allocated to him or her for verification purposes and about the documents to which they relate (further clarified in s 1(6)), information about occasions on which information recorded about him or her in the Register has been provided to any person and, finally, information recorded in the Register at an individual's own request.

What is meant by an individual's identity is expounded in s 1(7), defined as a **5.10** reference to an individual's full name, other names by which he or she is or has previously been known, his or her gender, his or her date and place of birth and

---

[5] *Hansard*, HL col 75 (31 October 2005).

the date of death (if applicable),[6] and any external characteristics that are capable of being used to identify him or her (which is a reference to biometric information). 'Biometric information' is defined in s 42(1) as data about a person's external characteristics, including the features of an iris or any other part of the eye.

5.11 An individual's residential status is defined in s 1(8) as his or her nationality, his or her entitlement to remain in the UK and, where that entitlement derives from a grant of leave to enter or remain in the UK, the terms and conditions of that leave.

5.12 Reference to information about numbers allocated to an individual for identification purposes and the documents to which they relate in s 1(5)(h) specifically excludes any sensitive personal data as defined by the Data Protection Act 1998 or anything the disclosure of which would tend to reveal such data. This is meant to exclude numbers such as a police national computer number which would tend to reveal such sensitive personal data.[7] This restriction only applies to numbers allocated to an individual and related documents and, as such, it is not a restriction on collecting sensitive personal data in general. Indeed, the Act itself contemplates collecting and retaining sensitive personal data such as iris patterns and fingerprints. The government has indicated that the Act does not allow the collection of DNA and that further primary legislation would be required to collect that data.[8]

C. INDIVIDUALS ENTERED IN THE REGISTER

1. Overview

5.13 Section 2 sets out who may be entered on the Register and the Secretary of State's duty to make arrangements to enable these entries to be made.

5.14 Section 2(1) provides that an entry must be made in the Register for every individual who is entitled to be in it and who applies to be entered in it. Those individuals who are entitled to be registered are set out in s 2(2): everyone over the age of 16 who resides in the UK and everyone of a 'prescribed description' who has resided in the UK or who is proposing to enter the UK. This provision provides the potential for the Act to extend its reach eventually to those British citizens who are resident overseas and who are considering returning to the UK,[9] as well as potential immigrants who have made applications for leave to enter the UK.

5.15 Section 2(6) provides that the Secretary of State may modify the age of entry

---

[6] 'An identity card for a dead man is a somewhat novel concept', *Hansard*, HL col 1136 (16 November 2005) (Lord Phillips of Sudbury).
[7] *Hansard*, HL col 1627 (23 November 2005).   [8] *Hansard*, HL col 1657 (23 November 2005).
[9] Explanatory Notes to the Identity Cards Act 2006, para 22.

on the Register from 16 years to a different age by order subject to the affirmative resolution procedure (s 2(7)). There was some debate as to whether the age should be raised to age 18 to take into account the fact that the accepted age of adulthood is 18 years or older. Baroness Walmsley and others argued that to include children within the ambit of the registration requirements under the Act could be contrary to Article 8 of the European Convention on Human Rights (the right to respect for private and family life) and Article 16 of the UN Convention on the Rights of the Child (the right to privacy).[10]

The government defended its decision to extend the legislation to those aged **5.16** 16 years and over on the basis that age 16 fits with the age of issue of an adult passport, it is the school leaving age, and also the age at which children may start to work.[11] The amendment to raise the age from 16 to 18 years was eventually withdrawn.

A person who has not applied or who is not entitled to be entered on the **5.17** Register may be entered anyway if the information likely to be recorded is otherwise available and the Secretary of State considers that the addition of his or her entry is consistent with the statutory purposes (s 2(4)). This power would allow the entry on the Register of a failed asylum seeker, for example, who had not applied for an ID card but whose biometric information was available. This would prevent him from applying for asylum under a new name as his biometric data would be recorded. This section does not constitute a power to obtain biometric data in the first place.[12]

2. Exclusions

Certain individuals may be excluded from being entered in the Register by way **5.18** of regulations made by the Secretary of State. Section 2(3) sets out that such regulations can exclude an individual if he or she does not meet the prescribed requirements in relation to the time of residence in the UK or if he or she is residing despite having no entitlement to remain (such as failed asylum seekers).[13]

3. National Identity Registration Number

Every individual who is entered in the Register will be assigned a unique number, **5.19** known as the National Identity Registration Number, which will be attached to all the information recorded about an individual (s 2(5)). The format of the National Identity Registration Number will be specified in regulations. Paragraph 4 of Sch 1 provides that other numbers may be recorded about an individual, including the number of any ID card issued, national insurance number,

---

[10] *Hansard*, HL col 65 (31 October 2005).
[11] *Hansard*, HL col 34 (31 October 2005); *Hansard*, HL col 1679 (23 November 2005).
[12] Explanatory Notes, para 26.   [13] ibid, para 24.

the number of any immigration document related to him or her, passport number (within or outside the UK), any work permit number, any driving licence number or the number of any other designated document held by him or her.

D. INFORMATION RECORDED IN THE REGISTER

1. Overview

5.20   Section 3 sets out the information that may be recorded in the Register. Information may only be recorded if it is authorized by Sch 1, provided for in s 3(3), or where it is information of a technical nature that is necessary for the administration of the scheme. Information must be recorded about the audit trail of information about an individual, which is provided for in para 9 of Sch 1, where such information relates to an occasion on which information contained in an individual's entry has been provided to a person without that individual's consent (s 3(4)).

5.21   Once an individual's information is recorded in the Register it may be kept for as long as it is consistent with the statutory purposes to be kept (s 3(1)). This gives rise to a potential to retain large amounts of information by way of a data trail of changes and requests for information.

2. Information Recorded in the Register

5.22   Information may be recorded in the Register if it is authorized by Sch 1 to the Act. The information that can be recorded in the Register as set out in Sch 1 is very broad, and includes personal information, identifying information, residential status, personal reference numbers, record history, registration and ID card history, validation information, security information, and records of the provision of information. Schedule 1 may be amended by secondary legislation following a resolution in both Houses of Parliament to add to the list of information that may be recorded on the Register (ss 3(6) and (7)).

5.23   The government contends that one safeguard in preventing Sch 1 from being greatly expanded by future resolution is the definition of 'registrable fact' as defined in s 1(5). According to the government, s 1(5) represents the 'outer limits' of anything that the government could subsequently try to bring within the ambit of information that can be recorded on the Register.[14] This raised a question about whether there was a need to allow the power to expand the categories of information that can be recorded in the Register in Sch 1 as Sch 1 already appears to cover all of the information that it could possibly carry within the boundaries of s 1(5).[15] The government responded that other

---

[14] *Hansard*, HL col 1095 (16 November 2005).
[15] *Hansard*, HL col 1137 (16 November 2005).

modes of communication which have not yet been invented might yet be added to Sch 1.[16]

The government has indicated that certain types of information, such as criminal records, medical records or political opinions, cannot be included in Sch 1 because they do not fall within the definition of registrable facts and so are not consistent with the statutory purposes. Criminal records could only be included where further primary legislation was enacted to record criminal records as registrable facts.[17]   **5.24**

There is a power in s 3(8) to annul a statutory instrument that contains an order amending the information that can be recorded in the Register as set out in Sch 1, as long as the order has not been laid in draft form before Parliament for debate.   **5.25**

Section 3(3) enables other information that is not listed in Sch 1 to be recorded if an individual has asked the Secretary of State for it to be included, where regulations include it as information that may be subject to such a request, and where the Secretary of State considers it practicable and appropriate for the information to be recorded in the Register. For example, an individual may ask for emergency contact details to be included on the Register.[18]   **5.26**

Where the Secretary of State and the individual agree on what is to be recorded in the Register and where the Secretary of State has given a direction that what is to be recorded is determined by agreement, that information is conclusively presumed for the purposes of the Act to be accurate and complete (s 3(5)). This situation could arise where an individual is in doubt as to his true registrable facts, such as his place or date of birth. Where the individual and the Secretary of State agree to record such facts, this would prevent any false document offences in s 25 from arising if the information is found to be false.[19] This subsection could also be used where a person needs to establish a new identity, such as under a witness protection programme.[20]   **5.27**

E. DESIGNATION OF DOCUMENTS

ID cards do not have to be simply stand-alone cards issued by the government. The Act confers a power in s 4 on the Secretary of State to designate documents for the purposes of the Act—documents which can then operate as ID cards and/or which link to information on the Register. Such documents are known as 'designated documents'.   **5.28**

Not all documents will qualify as documents that can be so designated. Section 4(2) and (3) provides that the only documents that can be designated are   **5.29**

---

[16] *Hansard*, HL col 1138 (16 November 2005).
[17] Explanatory Notes, para 32; *Hansard*, HL col 1627 (23 November 2005).
[18] Explanatory Notes, para 35.   [19] ibid, para 34.   [20] ibid.

documents which only certain persons can issue, namely a Minister of the Crown, a government department, a Northern Ireland department, the National Assembly for Wales or any other person who carries out functions conferred by or under any enactment that are carried out on behalf of the Crown. The persons who have the power to issue designated documents are known as 'designated documents authorities'. This presumably prevents the designation of documents issued by purely private companies, such as a video card or a coffee club card. The oft-cited example of a document that is likely to be designated is a passport.

5.30   The Secretary of State can designate documents only by order subject to an affirmative resolution procedure (s 4(4)).

5.31   Once certain documents have been designated by the Secretary of State, certain obligations will fall on individuals who apply for such documents. For example, once a document is designated, anyone applying for one will also have to apply for an ID card unless he or she already holds one (s 5(2)). This is discussed further in the section below.

F. APPLICATION FOR ENTRY IN THE REGISTER

5.32   Section 5 sets out how an application for entry in the Register should be made. An application may be made either by being included in an application for a designated document or by making an application directly to the Secretary of State.

5.33   As stated above, once the Secretary of State designates certain documents and an individual makes an application for that designated document, the application must also include an application to be entered in the Register or state that the individual is already entered in the Register and confirm the contents of the entry, or state that the individual is already entered in the Register and confirm the contents of the entry subject to any changes set out in the application (s 5(2)). References to confirming an entry relate only to the information contained in paras 1 to 5 of Sch 1 (which sets out the information that may be recorded in the Register) or information that is added voluntarily (see s 42(4)).[21] In practice, information on the designated document application form is likely to include all the information included on the Register or to verify an existing entry.[22]

5.34   The Secretary of State can prescribe certain information that must be submitted by an individual when he applies for registration or confirmation of an entry on the Register (s 5(3)). The information required may vary for different categories of people, which might make information about an individual's immigration status required of third country nationals.[23]

---

[21] ibid, para 40.   [22] ibid, para 41.   [23] ibid, para 42.

The Secretary of State may also make further requirements of applicants in order to verify the information to be entered on the Register and to ensure that the information is complete, up-to-date and accurate (s 5(4)). Section 5(5) expounds the things that an individual may be required to do, such as attending at a specified place and time, allowing his or her fingerprints and other biometric information to be recorded, allowing him or herself to be photographed, and otherwise to provide such information as required by the Secretary of State. **5.35**

Section 5(6) operates as a safeguard, providing that regulations under this section must not require an individual to provide information to another person unless it is information required by the Secretary of State for the statutory purposes. This means that the list of information that must be provided by individuals cannot be expanded without new primary legislation amending the list of registrable facts.[24] **5.36**

A further safeguard was added during the debates in the House of Lords, mandating that the power of the Secretary of State to make regulations under this section must be subject to the affirmative resolution procedure (s 5(7)). **5.37**

G. VOLUNTARY OR COMPULSORY REGISTRATION

Clause 6 of the original Identity Cards Bill was the most controversial part of the Bill as introduced by the government. Clause 6 allowed the Secretary of State to compel an individual to register. Compulsion was to be phased in by a process of mandatory registration when individuals applied for certain designated documents (such as passports). Eventually, full compulsion was envisaged, whereby an individual would have to register whether or not he or she applied for a designated document. This would have meant that the ID card scheme would have likely become compulsory for certain groups of people, such as foreign nationals who must obtain a residence permit, before becoming compulsory for others. **5.38**

Under the original Bill, the maximum civil penalty for failing to register when compelled to do so or for not providing further information when required by the Secretary of State would have been a civil penalty of up to £2,500. However, under the Identity Cards Act 2006, the maximum civil penalty is now £1,000. This penalty also captures those individuals who are required to register and who do so, but who then fail to provide further information as required by the Secretary of State (see also ss 7(5), 10(7), 11(6)). **5.39**

Compulsory registration under clause 6 was meant to be subject to the super-affirmative process. In order to make registration compulsory, the Secretary of State would have been required first to prepare and publish a report containing **5.40**

---

[24] ibid, para 45.

a proposal which set out his reasons for making the scheme compulsory (including how compulsion would operate, the categories of individuals to whom compulsory registration would apply and a timetable for implementation).[25] The Secretary of State would have had to lay the report before Parliament and both Houses would have debated on and voted on the proposal, and could have suggested modifications. Any draft order consistent with the proposal would have needed approval by both Houses. Each of the resolutions for approving the draft must have been agreed more than 60 days after the day on which it was laid before Parliament. If either House did not approve the proposal or if the government was unhappy with the proposal as amended, it would have needed to start the process again with a fresh report.

5.41   Compulsion was the sticking point in the debates between the two Houses. The government argued that the ID cards scheme was a manifesto commitment and, according to the principles of the Salisbury convention, the House of Lords should not interfere with the elected will of the people. Others argued that the Labour government's election manifesto was ambiguous. The relevant part reads as follows: 'We will introduce ID cards, including biometric data like fingerprints, backed up by a national register and rolling out *initially* on a voluntary basis as people renew their passports'.[26] (Emphasis added.)

5.42   The fact that the manifesto commitment suggested that the scheme would be initially voluntary appeared to leave room for a compulsory scheme to be introduced at a later time. A proposed compromise by the government to remove clause 6 from the Bill but retain the provisions allowing the Secretary of State to designate documents, applications of which must include the provision of information on the Register and obtaining an ID card, was described by those opposed as 'compulsion by stealth'.[27]

5.43   One further question was whether or not to retain the current scheme of allowing compulsion by way of statutory instrument (as in the original Bill, through the super-affirmative process in clause 7) or whether further primary legislation should be required before the scheme became compulsory.

5.44   In the end a compromise was agreed delaying compulsion until following the next general election. Further primary legislation will be needed in order to make the registration provisions of the Act compulsory. In the meantime, as of 2008, anyone who renews a passport will be put on the national identity database but will not be forced to obtain an ID card until 2010. Further, people are entitled to opt out of the scheme until 2011 (following the next general election). Those who opt out will not have to inform the government of changes of address and so will not be subject to the fees and charges that apply to the entire scheme.

---

[25] Explanatory Notes to the Identity Cards Bill, 25 May 2005, para 51.
[26] *Hansard*, HC col 748 (18 October 2005).   [27] *Hansard*, HL col 1008 (12 December 2005).

H. ID CARDS FOR THOSE COMPULSORILY REGISTERED

5.45 Section 7 provides for the renewal of ID cards and applies to those individuals who are subject to compulsory registration or who are already entered in the Register. If an individual holds a valid ID card that is due to expire within the prescribed period or if he or she is subject to compulsory registration and has not yet obtained a valid ID card, he or she must apply for one during the prescribed period.

5.46 The Secretary of State may again make further requirements of applicants who are applying for renewed ID cards in order to verify the information to be entered on the Register and to ensure that the information is complete, up-to-date and accurate (s 7(3)). Section 7(4) expounds the things that an individual may be required to do, such as attending at an agreed place and time, allowing his or her fingerprints and other biometric information to be recorded, allowing him or herself to be photographed, and otherwise to provide such information as required by the Secretary of State.

5.47 An individual who fails to renew or to provide the information requested to verify an application is liable to a civil penalty not exceeding £1,000 (s 7(5)).

I. FEES AND CHARGES

1. Overview

5.48 One of the concerns about the ID card regime is that it will be expensive to operate and that much of the expense will fall on the individual ID card holder. Along with the power to impose penalties, the Act makes provision for the payment of fees in a broad range of circumstances including applying for and issuing ID cards.

2. Fees in Respect of Functions Carried out under the Act

5.49 Under s 35 the Secretary of State has the power to make regulations that impose fees in such amounts as he sees fit in respect of a myriad of matters, such as:

- applications for entries to be made in the Register, applications for the modification of entries or applications for the issue of ID cards;
- the making or modification of entries in the Register;
- the issue of ID cards;
- applications for the provision of information from the Register;
- the provision of information from the Register;

- applications for confirmation of information;
- issue or refusal of such confirmations;
- applications for the approval of a person or apparatus;
- the grant of such approvals.

This list is not intended to be exhaustive but it is already quite broad.

5.50　Treasury consent is required before such regulations can be made (s 35(4)).

5.51　There was some suggestion during the Parliamentary debates that certain individuals, such as students, would be adversely affected by the fees and charges provisions in the Act, given their propensity to move house more frequently than others:

> Even though the citizen does not know what is on the register, he is under a duty on pain of a penalty of £1,000 to notify any inaccurate information that may be on the register—which he has never seen. He has to notify every change of address from the age of 16 onwards. Does anybody begin to appreciate the bureaucracy and form-filling that that means for students, who move from one address to another?[28]

5.52　The payment of fees by instalments is permitted under s 35(2). In prescribing fees, the Secretary of State is allowed to take into account the wider costs associated with the ID card scheme (s 35(3)). In other words, a charge may need to cover not just the issue of an ID card but the costs of updating the card as well. This subsection includes the power to charge different fees for different circumstances allowing for cross-subsidizing for different cards to occur.[29]

5.53　Section 35(5) allows for the fees for designated documents to cover the costs of dealing with matters under the Act when those matters are dealt with in relation to an application for and the issuing of designated documents. For example, charges for residence permits[30] or passports[31] could be made using existing powers and could include costs associated with the ID card scheme.

5.54　Fees received by the Secretary of State will be paid into the Consolidated Fund (s 35(8)), just as with civil penalties.

3. The Power to Raise Fees

5.55　Section 35(6) gives the Secretary of State the power to raise fees where appropriate. This could occur any time after the commencement of the power to charge including in advance of the introduction of ID cards.[32] This was of prime concern when the Bill was passing through Parliament as the introduction of compulsion under clause 6 led to concerns about a two-tier system of charging emerging: one that operates for certain people who are subject to the compulsory regime and one for the others. Depending on the groups of people who

---

[28] *Hansard*, HL col 51 (31 October 2005).　[29] Explanatory Notes, para 193.
[30] Explanatory Notes to the Identity Cards Bill, 25 May 2005, para 198.
[31] ibid, para 195.　[32] ibid, para 196.

would have been affected (such as foreign nationals), accusations of discrimination might have been levied.

Section 35(7) provides that the power of the Secretary of State to make regulations containing a provision authorized by s 35(1) is exercisable only if a draft of the regulation has been added before Parliament and has been approved by a resolution of each House.   **5.56**

4. Amendment of the Consular Fees Act 1980

Section 36 amends s 1(4) of the Consular Fees Act 1980 to allow flexibility in the setting of fees for the carrying out of consular functions which includes the setting of passport fees.   **5.57**

As with fees in s 35, there is a power to set different levels of fees for different cases and to make exceptions for different types of cases including the exemption of fees altogether. This would enable cross-subsidizing of passport fees to occur between fees charged to different applicants.   **5.58**

Section 44(5) indicates that this section will come into force two months after the Act comes into force, so on 30 May 2006. Thus, the fee setting powers could be applied at any period after 30 May 2006, including in advance of the introduction of ID cards themselves.   **5.59**

J. REGULATORY IMPACT ASSESSMENT

The Government's Regulatory Impact Assessment of the Identity Cards Bill makes it clear that the Act is enabling legislation, designed in part to set up a National Identity Register of basic personal information, to specify the information that may be recorded on the Register (including biometric data), and to specify safeguards to ensure that the information is only available to those with lawful authority.   **5.60**

The Assessment reveals that there is a potential for a 'forced subject access' route to information on the Register, similar to one which can arise out of the Data Protection Act. This could arise as employers will be entitled to make potential employees prove that they are who they say they are before hiring them, a requirement which might force potential employees to obtain access to information about themselves on the Register.[33]   **5.61**

---

[33] For further information on remedies, see chapter 12.

6

MAINTENANCE OF THE REGISTER

A. INTRODUCTION

The National Identity Register (the Register) is the core of the new identity 6.01
scheme introduced by the Identity Cards Act 2006. The Act is not simply about
the introduction of ID cards for individuals: it is the establishment of a whole
system of identity verification by the recording of information about individuals
on a government-controlled central database.

The Register will hold personal identity information and biometric data for 6.02
everyone who has enrolled in the scheme. It will also contain other information,
however. Whenever an individual's personal information changes, this must be
included in the Register. Every time an individual moves house, the Secretary of
State must be notified. The Register will also create a 'data trail' of information
about every individual enrolled upon it: when public or private sector organizations check a card or biometric against the Register, a record will be created of
who checked an individual's record, and when. Each time Royal Mail checks an
individual's ID card when he or she picks up a piece of mail, or when a bank
checks an individual's ID card to access his or her bank account, this transaction will be recorded in the Register. The Register will eventually contain a vast
amount of information, updated daily, in relation to over 60 million individuals.

The Identity and Passport Service suggests that the Register 'will contain 6.03
only identity-related information'.[1] This has been disputed by the Information
Commissioner. He has argued that, although robust initial measures for verifying an individual's identity may be necessary under the scheme, once this process

---

[1] Identity and Passport Service website, http://www.identitycards.gov.uk/scheme-what-
run.asp#nir.

is complete there can be little justification for the retention of all such details in a central Register. In particular, the continuing data trail will involve gathering and retaining information irrelevant to an individual's identity:

> The requirement on individuals to keep notifying changes is excessive and disproportionate. For example individuals are obliged to tell the government about all the addresses they have lived at and any new places where they reside. It is difficult to see the relevance of all such details, once identity has been verified to the 'gold standard' the government sets for itself. If a person issued with a card buys a second home this cannot affect their identity which would already have been verified and tied to them by a unique biometric. The requirement to register another address is excessive and irrelevant to establishing that person's identity.[2]

6.04 Although other aspects of the Identity Cards Bill caused the Information Commissioner concern, it was the Register and the resulting data trail which he highlighted during the Bill's passage through Parliament. He argued that the data trail was excessive, and went beyond what was required to verify identity: 'The primary aim of Government with this legislation should be to establish a scheme which allows people to reliably identify themselves rather than one which enhances its ability to identify and record what its citizens do in their lives'.[3]

6.05 There are three ways in which the Secretary of State will maintain the accuracy of the Register under the Identity Cards Act 2006: by requiring organizations or individuals to provide information to verify Register entries (s 9), or verifying information provided with applications for passports (s 38), and by requiring individuals to notify him when their information in the Register needs to be updated (s 10).

6.06 A failure to comply with a duty arising under s 9 may lead to civil proceedings instituted by the Secretary of State. A failure to comply with a requirement under s 10 renders the individual liable to a civil penalty of up to £1,000.[4]

6.07 There is a further power set out in the Act which is linked to the accuracy of the Register. Under s 11 the Secretary of State may recall, re-issue or cancel ID cards in certain circumstances, including when the information on which the card was based is considered to be inaccurate, incomplete or out-of-date.[5]

B. VERIFYING INFORMATION ON THE REGISTER

1. Overview

6.08 Section 9 creates the power to require data to be shared with the Secretary of State and designated documents authorities for the purpose of verifying

---

[2] *The Identity Cards Bill—The Information Commissioner's Concerns* (June 2005) 2.
[3] ibid, 3.   [4] For further information, see chapter 10.
[5] This provision is considered separately in chapter 10.

information that is to be placed or that is currently placed on the Register. Public and private bodies may be subject to this requirement. Home Office Minister Baroness Scotland outlined the purpose of s 9 during the House of Lords' Committee Stage of the Identity Cards Bill:

The rationale behind this clause is the rigorous biographical footprint check that will be undertaken when a person applies to be entered onto the register. That is the most important moment when we have to be absolutely sure that the person being entered is the person that they say they are. We therefore need to ensure as far as possible that no false or inaccurate details are entered into the register.[6]

The government has indicated that the procedure envisaged by s 9 follows   **6.09**
processes which the Passport Service has had in place since 2005. This followed the Cabinet Office's recommendation[7] that a wider biographical check be carried out before issuing passports, to prevent people obtaining multiple documents on the basis of false information:

When information is supplied to the Passport Service on an application form, a wider range of checks is done to verify it against other Government databases, although private sector information such as credit references are also used. Hon. Members will be able to read about that procedure when the Passport Service annual report is issued to them in the next few days; there will be a report on the success of those procedures. I think hon. Members will see that the service has already succeeded in exposing some applications that needed to be caught and would not otherwise have been caught.[8]

Section 9 limits data-sharing to the purpose of ensuring the accuracy of the   **6.10**
Register and does not, on its face, confer the power to share data for wider purposes. As such, the Secretary of State and designated documents authorities are not permitted by this section to request information that is not relevant for the purposes of validating the Register.[9] However, given the scope of the 'registrable facts' that may be recorded in the Register, this section nevertheless has the potential to encompass a wide range of information.[10]

2. Requirements

Either the Secretary of State (s 9(1)) or a designated documents authority (s 9(2))   **6.11**
may require an organization to provide information.

The Secretary of State may exercise the s 9 power if it appears to him that a   **6.12**
person or organization 'may have information in his possession' which could be used for verifying virtually any information related to the Register, namely, for verifying:

---

[6] *Hansard*, HL col 1272 (14 December 2005).   [7] Cabinet Office, *Identity Fraud* (2002).
[8] *Hansard*, HC col 272 (14 July 2005).
[9] Explanatory Notes to the Identity Cards Act 2006, para 68.
[10] For further information, see chapter 5.

(a) an individual's entry in the Register;

(b) something provided to the Secretary of State or a designated documents authority for the purpose of being recorded in an individual's entry in the Register, or

(c) something otherwise available to the Secretary of State for being recorded about an individual in the Register.

6.13 Category (c) is intended to encompass information that neither had been supplied to nor existed on the Register, but which is nonetheless relevant to an individual's entry. In Parliament the government sought to reassure the opposition that, 'the provision is not a catch-all power to go fishing, as the phrase goes, for all sorts of data sources, nor is it meant to pick up on information that is not strictly limited to the registrable facts'.[11]

6.14 The government's examples indicate that s 9(1)(c) will be of most relevance in immigration and failed asylum cases. Andy Burnham described it as a 'necessary corollary' to the power in s 2(4) to enter in the Register someone who has not applied to be so entered. Biometric and biographical details for failed asylum seekers who have been deported could be obtained from the Immigration and Nationality Directorate and recorded in the Register to prevent unauthorized re-entry.[12]

6.15 Designated documents authorities have the same power to require information as the Secretary of State, but the circumstances in which they may exercise that power are more limited. Where it appears to them that a body may have information in its possession relating to one of two matters, they may require that body to provide them with the information. The two matters are either:

(a) the information could be used for verifying something that is recorded in the Register about an individual who has applied to the authority for the issue or modification of a designated document or an ID card, or

(b) the information could be used for verifying something that has been provided to that authority for the purpose of being recorded in the entry of such an individual in the Register.

6.16 During Committee Stage in both Houses of Parliament on the Identity Cards Bill, various amendments were advanced by the Liberal Democrats and the Conservatives which would have had the same broad effect: to include a condition of 'reasonableness' in s 9(1) and (2). In other words, the Secretary of State or the designated documents authority could only issue a requirement to an organization to provide data if the requirement were reasonable in all the circumstances. The government replied that there was no need for this explicit condition: 'that people will act reasonably is an assumption on which the Bill is based. We expect the Secretary of State to exercise his powers in a reasonable manner.'

---

[11] *Hansard*, HC col 278 (14 July 2005).   [12] *Hansard*, HC cols 277–278 (14 July 2005).

This response was undoubtedly correct. In the exercise of a public function, **6.17** the Secretary of State is bound to act reasonably.

3. Duty to Provide Information

The duty created by s 9 is mandatory (s 9(3)). **6.18**

The Home Office has indicated its view that the s 9 duty overrides other **6.19** obligations under which the person may hold that information. It is not yet clear how this duty will interact with the Data Protection Act 1998, Human Rights Act 1998 or the Regulation of Investigatory Powers Act 2000.

The timeframe for compliance with the request will be set by the party **6.20** requesting the information (the Secretary of State or the designated documents authority).

4. Bodies which May be Required to Share Data

The section envisages data-sharing as between government bodies, but there is **6.21** scope for the power to capture private sector organizations and private individuals. Only bodies or persons specified in an order made by the Secretary of State may be required to provide information under s 9. Any such order will be subject to the affirmative resolution procedure (s 9(8)).

According to s 9(5), the bodies who may be specified in such an order include **6.22** ministers, government departments, Northern Ireland departments, the National Assembly for Wales, or 'any other person who carries out functions conferred by or under an enactment that fall to be carried out on behalf of the Crown' (s 9(5)(e)). Although the Scottish Executive is absent from the list, the government has indicated that it anticipates requiring information from it pursuant to s 9(5)(e).[13]

The five categories of bodies set out in s 9(5) do not constitute an exhaustive **6.23** list. Any other organizations or private individuals could be included in an order. In both the Commons and the Lords, amendments were tabled to convert the list of five examples of possible bodies which could be specified in an order into an exhaustive list.[14] The Home Office ministers responded by indicating that, although the initial focus of the s 9 power would be public sector databases, 'it is important for the power to widen that check to remain in the Bill in case it were to become apparent over time that people were slipping through the verification net'. Information held on credit reference agencies' databases and private databases had proved useful for the Passport Service, as 'some private sector organizations hold pretty wide databases with up-to-date biographic information'.[15]

---

[13] *Hansard*, HL col 1276 (14 December 2005).   [14] *Hansard*, HC col 279 (14 July 2005).
[15] *Hansard*, HC col 281 (14 July 2005).

6.24 Nevertheless, the amendments were withdrawn, and an order could specify credit reference agencies or other private bodies.

6.25 The government has indicated the primary focus of the s 9 power: 'The checks mentioned in the clause will be modest and generally limited to other Government databases, for example those of the Driver and Vehicle Licensing Agency and the Department for Work and Pensions'.[16]

6.26 This approach has been criticized as topsy-turvy by commentators:

> If we were thinking this through clearly (which of course we're not), it might occur to us that, if the National Identity Register is intended to be the 'gold standard' of identification, then what we should really be doing (and will end up doing anyway) is using other databases (including the electoral registers) to maintain the accuracy of the gold standard, rather than vice versa.[17]

6.27 Certain checks appear likely to occur routinely, rather than on the basis of individualized suspicion. Addresses are likely to be routinely cross-checked against the DVLA database, and national insurance numbers against the Department for Work and Pensions database. Home Office immigration records were also repeatedly referred to during the Parliamentary debates.

6.28 If discrepancies are discovered between the individual's Register entry or application and information in an existing database, it is unclear what next steps will be taken. If, for example, an address included in a DVLA or Experian database is out-of-date or differs from the address given as the individual's principal residence for the Register, it is assumed that no alterations will be made to the individual's entry without first verifying the accuracy of the information with him or her. This is essential for two reasons. First, if information is included in the Register on the basis of inaccurate information contained in another database, the individual may become liable to a civil penalty. Second, the Act provides the Secretary of State with the power to levy fees in order to modify information in the Register, even though the error may not be the individual's fault (s 35).

6.29 Individuals may apply for confirmation that the information they have supplied coincides with the information recorded in the Register. However, a fee may be payable in order to make such an application (s 35(1)(f)), and a further fee may be charged for the issue or refusal of confirmations (s 35(1)(g)).

6.30 The Act does give the Secretary of State the power to provide information to an organization such as the DVLA without an individual's consent in order to correct inaccurate or incomplete information (s 19).[18]

---

[16] *Hansard*, HC col 280 (14 July 2005).

[17] J Lettice, 'Government moots ID card link for new UK voter database', *The Register*, 16 December 2005.

[18] For further information, see chapter 8.

5. Enforcement

The mandatory duty created by s 9 is enforceable in civil proceedings by the **6.31** Secretary of State or the designated documents authority (s 9(6)). As was noted in Parliament, s 9(6) allows the possibility of a minister suing a minister within the national government, or a Westminster minister raising proceedings against a minister in Edinburgh, Cardiff or Belfast, however unlikely this may be in practice.

The potential remedies available include an injunction (s 9(6)(b)(i)) and **6.32** specific performance (s 9(6)(b)(ii)). Section 9(6)(b)(iii) also allows 'any other appropriate remedy or relief'. This includes judicial review and other normal public law remedies for public authorities. The Explanatory Notes expressly contemplate judicial review.[19] It also includes remedies in Scots law, such as interdict.[20]

This subsection requires regulations to trigger it, which are subject to the **6.33** affirmative resolution procedure (s 9(8)).

6. Payments

Section 9(7) provides that the Secretary of State may make payments to a person **6.34** providing information under this section, in such cases (if any) as he sees fit. It is unlikely that this subsection will be used. The reason for its inclusion in the Act has been described by the Home Office as follows: 'That was included after pre-legislative scrutiny so that if the verification proved unduly complicated or burdensome—that is a big if, because really only a simple check should be involved—people could be compensated'.

If used, this subsection is likely to cover only 'further' checks, and not initial **6.35** checks. The Home Office has accepted that:

It would be unreasonable to require extensive information or time-consuming checks without compensating the organisations involved. It is more reasonable to say that in the limited circumstances in which we require a further check, we will compensate people for the inconvenience caused.[21]

The payment would be in respect of the provision of information only, and not **6.36** its gathering or the cost of the infrastructure to maintain it. This is because there is no duty under s 9 to gather information one does not already have. The duty only applies if the information is already in the possession of the body from whom it has been requested. The payments, if any, are thus likely to be small, as they will cover only the checks themselves and the transmission of information to the body requesting it.

---

[19] Explanatory Notes, para 71.   [20] *Hansard*, HC col 289 (14 July 2005).
[21] *Hansard*, HC col 284 (14 July 2005).

C. VERIFICATION OF PASSPORT INFORMATION

6.37   Section 38 mirrors s 9 (the power to require information for validating the Register) but relates to passports. It is a provision to permit data-sharing for the purposes of verifying information provided in relation to an application for or withdrawal of a passport.

6.38   The obligation to provide the information relating to passports is mandatory and the Secretary of State may specify a period of time within which the person must comply. In the face of non-compliance, the Secretary of State may seek a remedy through the civil courts (s 38(5)). The requirement may be imposed on a Minister of the Crown, a government department, a Northern Ireland department, and the National Assembly for Wales, but could be extended by order to any other person not named in this list (s 38(3)). This section will come into force on 30 May 2006 pursuant to s 44(5).[22]

D. NOTIFICATION OF CHANGES

1. Overview

6.39   Section 10 sets out how changes in circumstances should be reported in order to maintain the accuracy of the Register. An individual to whom an ID card has been issued must notify the Secretary of State about every prescribed change of circumstances affecting his or her entry in the Register, and every error in the entry of which he or she is aware. Although the notifications are mandatory, individuals are likely to have to accompany their notifications with a fee (s 35(1)).

6.40   Crucially, the duties arising under this section do not apply to those who have an entry in the Register but to whom an ID card has not been issued. Under the terms of the compromise struck by the government with opposition parties in March 2006 in order to get the Identity Cards Bill passed, individuals who obtain new or renewed passports until 1 January 2010 will be entered on the Register but will not be issued with an ID card. Until then, these individuals are under no obligation to notify the Secretary of State of changes in their details under s 10.

2. Duty

6.41   Under s 10(1) there is a duty on every individual to whom an ID card has been issued to notify the Secretary of State about every prescribed change of circumstance affecting the information that is recorded about him or her in the Register

---

[22] For further information, see chapter 8.

and every error in that information that he or she knows about. This includes any change in circumstance about a registrable fact (set out in s 1(5)) including a person's name and address.[23]

This duty is likely to impact more on certain groups rather than others. The **6.42** duty may have a disproportionate impact on young people, including students living away from home, who are less likely than adults to have a settled address. Teenagers, those with mental health issues and others whose lifestyles may not be conducive to personal organization may be more likely to fall foul of notification requirements, and risk escalating penalties. Those on lower incomes may be more likely to rent property rather than own it, and thus more likely to move regularly. Further, 40 per cent of London's population moves at least once a year. Individuals at risk of domestic violence may be unwilling to provide their new address to a database which also retains their old address. It is also unclear how the ID card scheme will operate in the context of homeless people who do not have a fixed address, as well as those persons who must change their identity as part of a witness protection programme.

Should a data entry mistake be made and an ID card then be issued with an **6.43** apparent error (such as a misspelling of a name) the individual must then notify the Secretary of State of this error and pay to do so, or risk imposition of a civil penalty. Further, it is possible that those with unusual names may face particular difficulties. The duty arises not only when the individual's circumstances change, but also when he or she becomes aware of any error in the information recorded about him or herself in the Register.

3. Notification

The way to notify the Secretary of State of such changes or errors is set out in **6.44** s 10(2). The notification must be given in the prescribed manner and within a prescribed period, which are not yet specified in the Act but which will be set out in regulations.[24]

4. Requirements

Where an individual has given a notification, s 10(3) provides that further infor- **6.45** mation may be required by the Secretary of State for verification purposes. The verification is not limited to information arising from the change or error; the Secretary of State has the power to require the individual to do a number of things to 'otherwise [ensure] that there is a complete, up-to-date and accurate entry about the individual in the Register' (s 10(3)(b)).

This requirement to provide further information may include personal atten- **6.46** dance at a specified place and time, being fingerprinted, having other biometric

---

[23] Explanatory Notes, para 74.   [24] ibid.

information taken and recorded, being photographed, or otherwise providing information as may be required by the Secretary of State (s 9(4)).

6.47   The only information that individuals may be required to provide under s 10 is 'information required by the Secretary of State for the statutory purposes': s 10(5). The statutory purposes are set out in s 1(3) of the Act. As they include 'facilitatory' purposes, such as 'facilitating a secure and reliable method for registrable facts about such individuals to be ascertained or verified whenever that is necessary in the public interest', and 'securing the efficient and effective provision of public services',[25] this may not, in practice, limit the requirements imposed upon people. However, the information which may be requested must be included in the 'registrable facts' listed in Sch 1.

5. Civil Penalties

6.48   Failure to comply with a requirement imposed under s 10 means that the individual may be liable to a civil penalty of up to £1,000.[26] Civil penalties are imposed by the Secretary of State and may be objected to (s 32) or appealed (s 33).

6. Regulations

6.49   Regulations made under this section are governed by s 10(6). On the first occasion that the Secretary of State makes regulations under s 10, he is obliged to comply with the affirmative resolution procedure. Thereafter, he may make regulations in the usual way.

7. Fees

6.50   Section 35(1) allows fees to be imposed by the Secretary of State for the making of or modification of entries in the Register. Regulations may permit the payment of fees by instalments.

6.51   The fees chargeable may take into account general running costs of the National Identity Register and the Identity and Passport Service, so even a simple change may nevertheless incur a fee unrelated to the cost of making that change. The regulations may provide for different fees to be charged to different categories of person.

6.52   It is arguable that the imposition of fees when changes to the Register are mandated and the potential to incur fines for not reporting changes of registrable facts on the Register, is excessive. This is particularly so in the context of mandatory notifications arising from errors for which the individual was not responsible, either due to a data-entry error or the provision of inaccurate

---

[25] This forms part of the definition of 'public interest' set out in s 1(4).
[26] For further information, see chapter 10.

information from a public or private sector database pursuant to s 9. Lord Thomas of Gresford argued during the debates in Parliament 'that I cannot imagine that the people of this country will stand for form-filling every time there is a change of circumstance on pain of being described as a defaulter and pursued for large sums of money. The people of this country will rise up and reject it.'[27]

8. Auditing

During the passage of the Identity Cards Bill through Parliament, lobby groups **6.53** critical of the Bill noted that the maintenance of the accuracy of the Register is largely achieved through obligations on individuals to notify about changes in relevant information, changes which could prove costly. They noted the absence of a corresponding obligation arising under the Act to audit the information contained in the Register. An audit requirement could take the form of a duty on the Secretary of State to ensure the accuracy of the data and could perhaps be fulfilled by a system of self-verification requiring details of individuals to be sent to them twice yearly for verification.[28]

---

[27] *Hansard*, HL col 1024 (12 December 2005).
[28] *Liberty's Briefing for Second Reading in House of Lords* (February 2005) para 31.

7

IDENTITY CHECKS

A. INTRODUCTION

1. Parliamentary Background

The possibility of ID cards and the National Identity Register being used **7.01** for identity checks by public officials, the police, employers or the private sector has been both one of the most popular and one of the most criticized aspects of the Home Office's proposals since the scheme was first outlined in July 2002.

Its strongest supporters were in favour of identity checks as a way of ensur- **7.02** ing public services were only made available to those entitled to them. They argued during the passage of the successive Identity Card Bills through Parliament that the proposals did not go far enough and that in order for the system to work effectively the cards should be mandatory to obtain and to carry at all times. Otherwise, they argued, the full benefits of the scheme could not be realized: the only people who would use the cards would be those with nothing to hide, and 'health tourism', benefit fraud and identity fraud would continue unchecked.

Its strongest critics, on the other hand, argued that even giving discretionary **7.03** powers to public and private sector officials to make identity checks in certain circumstances would have discriminatory results, and prevent vulnerable, marginalized or minority groups accessing services to which they were entitled. The ID card would become, in effect, a 'licence to live'.

The policy genesis of the Identity Cards Act 2006 was the Home Office's **7.04** consultation paper, *Entitlement Cards and Identity Fraud: A Consultation*

Paper.[1] This document proposed a card scheme which, it was suggested, would lead to both short-term and long-term benefits. Short-term, they would be required by individuals wishing to access free public services, such as free National Health Service (NHS) healthcare and obtaining welfare or disability benefits. The then Home Secretary, David Blunkett, expressed a hope that the debate on ID cards would unfold in the context of these important issues of 'citizenship and entitlement to services' rather than counter-terrorism and serious crime.[2] Long-term, the consultation paper suggested, if the cards were widely held by the population, such a scheme could also 'make a contribution' to tackling identity fraud: 'Some of the measures could involve increased co-operation between the public and private sectors and increased use of information sharing about individuals'.[3]

7.05   Although, following this consultation, the Home Office proposals shifted from a voluntary 'entitlement card' scheme to an ID card scheme which would eventually become compulsory, its focus remained the original twin issues of entitlement to public services and identity fraud. The Draft Bill of 2004 and the Explanatory Notes to both the 2004–05 Bill and the 2005–06 Bill stated that the government's main reason for introducing ID cards is to 'secure the efficient and effective provision of public services' (s 1(4)(e)) by simplifying checks on eligibility for services and reducing the fraudulent use of services.[4]

7.06   The newly formed Identity and Passport Service, which came into being two days after the Identity Cards Act 2006 received Royal Assent, outlines ten 'key benefits' to the national identity scheme. All of these benefits, in order to be realized, require identity checks of some kind:

(1)   help protect cardholders against identity theft and fraud;

(2)   provide a reliable way of checking the identity of people in positions of trust;

(3)   make travelling in Europe easier;

(4)   provide a secure way of applying for financial products and making financial transactions, including those made over the internet;

(5)   offer a secure and convenient way of proving your age;

(6)   help to confirm your eligibility for public services and benefits—and reduce fraud relating to those services and benefits;

(7)   help in the prevention of organized crime and terrorism;

(8)   help combat illegal working and reduce illegal immigration to the UK;

---

[1] *Entitlement Cards and Identity Fraud: A Consultation Paper* (Cm 5557, July 2002), available at http://www.homeoffice.gov.uk/documents/entitlement_cards.pdf?view=Binary.

[2] David Blunkett, Foreword to *Entitlement Cards and Identity Fraud*, ibid.   [3] ibid.

[4] Explanatory Notes to the Identity Cards Bill, 25 May 2005, para 99, with reference to *Identity Cards—The Next Steps* (Cm 6020, November 2003), available at http://www.archive2.official-documents.co.uk/document/cm60/6020/6020.pdf.

(9) allow the police to more quickly identify suspects and people they arrest;

(10) provide a secure way of applying for financial products and making financial transactions, including those made over the internet.

It remains to be seen whether, in practice, alternative methods of establishing identity will be accepted by the service provider in these circumstances, or whether checking of ID cards or the Register become standard.   **7.07**

2. Identity Checks and the Identity Cards Act 2006

As the Identity Cards Act 2006 is 'enabling legislation',[5] there is little detail in the body of the Act itself as to how identity checks will operate in practice. The powers to make services conditional on identity checks are exercisable through regulations.[6] At the time of writing, there have not yet been any regulations made.   **7.08**

The Act allows the provision of public services to be made conditional on an individual producing an ID card or other evidence of his or her registrable facts (such as a fingerprint or PIN number) which can be checked against his or her entry on the National Identity Register. Public authorities may also have the power to require ID cards or other evidence of identity when an individual is subject to stop and search powers, arrested, makes an application for a firearms certificate or a Criminal Records Bureau check, or is subject to a legal requirement to notify the police or Probation Service of any change of address. Under the Act, the Home Secretary may allow public and private sector organizations to make checks against the Register before allowing an individual to do such things as open a bank account, obtain dental treatment, or take up employment.   **7.09**

Many of the regulation-making powers in this part of the Act involve double delegation, or delegation one step removed—and, in the case of Northern Ireland, delegation two steps removed. In Northern Ireland the First Minister may (by regulation) designate a Northern Ireland department which then has power to make regulations itself (s 14(1)(b)). A designated Northern Ireland department, the National Assembly for Wales, the Scottish Parliament or the Secretary of State has power to make regulations which may, in turn, delegate a discretionary power to public authorities to decide for themselves whether or not to make service provision reliant upon identity checks (s 13(1)). The regulations may delegate the choice as to whether identity checks will be voluntary or mandatory in given circumstances. The Explanatory Notes to the Act explain this outsourcing of discretion: 'This will give service providers flexibility in deciding   **7.10**

---

[5] See a quotation by Tony Blair in *The Guardian*, 27 June 2005, available at http://politics.guardian.co.uk/homeaffairs/story/0,11026,1515716,00.html.

[6] Regulations may be made to make public services conditional on identity checks pursuant to s 13, and to provide for checks on the Register pursuant to s 15. See paras 7.17 et seq below.

what proof of identity is the most appropriate in the particular circumstances and what level of identity check is necessary'.[7]

7.11 Without another Act of Parliament making the scheme compulsory for some or all of the population, regulations cannot require production of an ID card or other evidence of identity based on the Register for two things: a public service that has to be provided free of charge (such as emergency health-care), or a legal entitlement to receive a payment (such as disability or welfare benefit).

7.12 Identity checks are dealt with in ss 12 to 16 of the Identity Cards Act 2006. Section 12 provides that information may be provided from an individual's entry in the Register to a third party if he or she gives authority or consents. Section 13 provides that regulations may make provision allowing or requiring a person who provides a public service to make the service conditional on production of an ID card or other evidence of registrable facts. It also includes a number of safeguards on the use of this power. The procedure by which regulations may be made is governed by s 14 (and s 43 when dealing with a devolved power in Scotland). The Secretary of State has the power to enable checks to be made of information recorded in the Register by people providing public services (s 15). He may also regulate identity checks by creating an accreditation scheme for user organizations and their equipment. Section 16 introduces a narrow prohibition on organizations requiring ID cards or other evidence which may be checked against the Register in particular circumstances. Individuals may enforce this prohibition in the civil courts.

7.13 When or if the national ID scheme becomes compulsory (which requires another Act of Parliament), regulations could make the receipt of benefits or free public services conditional on identity checks. The right to go to court under s 16 would also fall away. On the current governmental timetable, it is anticipated that compulsion will be rolled out from 2010 or 2011.[8]

7.14 Compulsion will not be introduced in a 'big bang' manner, but incrementally, with certain groups being subject to compulsory registration before others.[9] This means that before compulsion applies to everyone, there will be a two-tier ID card scheme—one for those who are already subject to compulsion and one for those who are not yet subject to compulsion. The former group, which is likely to include foreign nationals, will be prevented from accessing free services, and will be subject to certain penalties inapplicable to those not yet subject to compulsion.[10] If the scheme leads to disadvantages in this way, such as by creating obligations and penalties on foreign nationals before they apply to UK citizens, the scheme could be found to be discriminatory pursuant to the Human Rights

---

[7] Explanatory Notes to the Identity Cards Act 2006, para 93.
[8] *Hansard*, HL col 1001 (29 March 2006).
[9] See 'ID Card Plans Too Risky', *BBC news*, 21 March 2005, available at http://news.bbc.co.uk/1/hi/uk_politics/4366307.stm.
[10] *Identity Cards—The Next Steps* (Cm 6020, November 2003).

Act 1998. If, as is likely, distinctions are drawn between non-UK EU nationals and UK citizens, issues will also arise under EU law.[11]

3. Jurisdiction

Regulations relating to public services which are linked to transferred or devolved functions are exercisable only by the relevant national authority (the Welsh National Assembly, the Scottish Parliament or government departments in Northern Ireland designated by the Assembly).   **7.15**

The Secretary of State has a residual power to make regulations in all other circumstances (s 14(1)(c)).   **7.16**

B. PUBLIC SERVICES

Central to this part of the Act is the definition of 'provision of a public service', as this is the trigger for the identity check powers. The definition is contained in s 42(2) and (3). The definition is extremely broad, and stretches the ordinary meaning of those words almost to breaking point. An individual who is stopped and searched by police, for example, is receiving the provision of a public service from the police. A private employer who checks a potential employee's immigration status against the Register is providing a public service to the employee.   **7.17**

The Explanatory Notes to the Act state that: **7.18**

Subsection (2) defines what is meant by the provision of a public service. This is broadly defined and is not restricted to what might be commonly understood as 'public services' such as the NHS and could include the granting of a firearms certificate or the requirement to notify changes of address imposed on certain sex offenders.[12]

The definition of 'provision of a public service' in s 42(2)(a), (b) and (d) is institutional, referring to the definition of a 'public authority', which is further defined in s 42(1) as having the same meaning as in s 6 of the Human Rights Act 1998.[13] However, the definition of 'provision of a public service' in s 42(2)(c) and (e) is problematic. In particular, the definition in s 42(2)(c) encompasses the doing by any person of anything in relation to a statutory function and therefore would include an employer, for example, who was complying with a statutory duty under the Employment Act 2002 or the Race Relations Act 2000. Section 42(2)(e) turns the definition of the '*provision* of public services' on its head, as it includes not just 'provision' but also the 'notification' or 'receipt' of information,   **7.19**

---

[11] ibid, 4.   [12] Explanatory Notes, para 220.

[13] Note that this definition is currently being challenged. See Joint Committee on Human Rights, Seventh Report of Session 2003–04, *Meaning of Public Authority Under the Human Rights Act* (HL 39/HC 382).

which would make the mere requirement on a sex offender to notify the police of his or her address a provision of a public service.

7.20 The Identity and Passport Service considers that 'all kinds of businesses and organisations, public services and government departments' will be covered by this definition. It gives a wide range of examples, including banks, the police, the Criminal Records Bureau, Royal Mail and other delivery and courier services, video/DVD rental companies, telephone companies, travel agencies, property rental companies, universities and 'retailers of all kinds, including internet-based companies'. The Service also anticipates that many private employers 'will use the scheme to check the immigration status of potential employees and to ensure those applying for positions of trust are who they say they are'.[14]

C. CONDITIONAL PUBLIC SERVICES

1. Overview

7.21 According to s 13(1), regulations may make public services conditional on producing an ID card (s 13(1)(a)), other evidence of registrable facts about a person (s 13(1)(b)), or both (s 13(1)(c)). By allowing registrable facts to be produced, someone's identity could be checked against the Register when the card is not present.

7.22 The regulations may be mandatory, requiring service providers to request certain pieces of evidence before providing the service, or they may be discretionary, allowing the service provider to decide what level of identity check is appropriate in the circumstances.

7.23 'Evidence of registrable facts' may take a number of forms. The individual may be asked to provide a piece of information, a Personal Identification Number (PIN) or a biometric, such as a fingerprint or iris scan. These may be verified against his or her entry in the Register.

7.24 Biometric fingerprint readers will allow confirmation of identity from the Register remotely, sometimes without the ID card being present. The Identity and Passport Service anticipates that banks will use biometric readers which also need the ID card itself to operate.[15] The ID card will be inserted into the reader, and the individual will then be asked to place his or her finger on the screen. The scanner will return a positive or negative response, indicating whether the card and the biometric match, and whether the card is registered as lost or stolen.

7.25 The card does not have to be present if different technology is used, however. The Immigration and Nationality Directorate (IND) and the police already use

---

[14] See the Identity and Passport Service website at http://www.identitycards.gov.uk/how-organisations.asp.

[15] ibid.

technology which allows biometrics to be checked against existing databases. The IND checks the fingerprints of asylum seekers who arrive in the UK against a database called Eurodac to see if there have been previous applications for asylum in any other EU country. In July 2005 Northamptonshire Police piloted a mobile fingerprint reader scheme.[16] Roadside checks on drivers included taking a fingerprint using a handheld biometric fingerprint reader, and this reader running a check against the national police fingerprint database. The Police Information Technology Organisation is in the process of making a business case for a national mobile fingerprint reading system.

Biometrics will not always be needed. The Identity and Passport Service **7.26** anticipates that for some transactions, a simple card reader will be used. They give the example of a courier company which asks an individual to produce his ID card to prove his identity. The card is inserted into a card reader and handed to the individual. He is asked to enter his PIN. The card reader will then indicate whether the ID card is genuine and whether it has been registered as lost or stolen.

2. Public Services that May Not be Conditional

Section 13(2) provides that there are two situations in which provision of a **7.27** public service may not be made conditional on an identity check:

Regulations under this section may not allow or require the imposition of a condition on –
(a) the entitlement of an individual to receive a payment under or in accordance with any enactment, or
(b) the provision of any public service that has to be provided free of charge,
except in cases where the individual is of a description of individuals who are subject to compulsory registration.

(a) *Statutory Entitlement to Receive a Payment*
This includes obtaining benefits, such as social security or disability benefits. It **7.28** should also include the provision of housing benefit under the Housing Acts,[17] as, although payment will then be made to the landlord by the tenant, the provision of the benefit is pursuant to a statutory entitlement and it is a payment.

(b) *Free Public Services*
This is a narrow exception, as it applies only to public services that *must* be **7.29** provided free of charge, and not the broader category of public services that are, in fact, provided free of charge. It also does not cover subsidized public services.

---

[16] 'Police patrol cars get mobile fingerprint readers', Silicon.com, 1 July 2005, available at http://management.silicon.com/government/0,39024677,39145037,00.htm.
[17] The Housing Act 1996 or the Housing Act 2004.

7.30   It certainly includes free NHS treatment,[18] but it does not cover NHS dental provision or prescriptions.

(c) *Compulsory Registration*

7.31   Different rules will eventually apply depending on whether ID cards are compulsory or not. The s 13(2) provision is time-limited, as if registration becomes compulsory for all there will be no individuals to whom this section applies. In this way, it will not always act as a safeguard against making the receipt of benefits and free public services conditional on production of an ID card. However, until such time as the national ID scheme becomes compulsory, regulations made under s 13 cannot make the receipt of benefits or free public services conditional on providing an ID card or other evidence of registration.

3. Carrying ID Cards

7.32   The Home Office has described the belief that citizens will be required to carry their card with them at all times as one of 'the more persistent myths surrounding the scheme'.[19] While it could be compulsory to produce an ID card or provide a fingerprint in order to receive certain services, s 13(3)(a) specifically excludes the possibility of an order making the carrying of cards compulsory at all times. It also prevents regulations being made which would have the effect of requiring an individual to carry a card at all times (such as a regulation providing that the card must be produced on demand if requested by the police). The government wants to make clear that 'compulsory' means compulsory to register with the ID card scheme, not compulsory to carry an ID card.[20]

7.33   Further, s 13(3)(b) provides that nothing in s 13 authorizes the making of regulations that would have the effect of requiring an individual to produce such a card, unless it is for the provision of a public service as defined by the Act.[21]

7.34   It is suggested that these twin safeguards, although important, may be of limited use in practice if extensive use is made of the regulation-making power under s 13(1). The protection against being required to carry one's ID card at all times is of limited value if regulations permit one's fingerprints to be checked against the Register at all times if so requested by the police. The protection against requests to produce one's card only applies in circumstances which do not involve the provision of a public service—and, given the broad definition of that phrase, the protected area will inevitably shrink gradually as regulations are made.

---

[18] Explanatory Notes, para 94.

[19] Home Office, *Identity Cards Bill: Race Equality Impact Assessment*, 25 May 2005, para 4.1.

[20] Identity Cards Bill Team, *Identity Cards Bill: Briefing for MPs* (8 June 2005) 11.

[21] For further information, see s 16(3), the prohibition on carrying ID cards, which is set out further in para 7.66 below.

4. Regulations

Sections 14 and 43 set out the procedure for making regulations under s 13. **7.35**
Information and consultation with persons likely to be affected by the regulations
is mandated by s 14.

(a) *Bodies which may make Regulations Under s 13*

Under ss 14(1) and 43(2) the power to make regulations under s 13 is exercisable **7.36**
by the devolved administrations if the public service in question is within their
legislative competence, and in all other cases the power is exercisable by the
Secretary of State. The Secretary of State's power is therefore residual: what is
left once the devolved functions have been taken away.

The devolved administrations' powers are determined by their institutional **7.37**
competence, and not their geography. The Secretary of State has the power to
make regulations relating to Wales, Northern Ireland or Scotland in relation to
public service provision in areas in which Westminster has retained competence,
such as immigration and defence.

(b) *Wales*

The power to make regulations under s 13 relating to the provision of Welsh **7.38**
public services is exercisable by the National Assembly for Wales (s 14(1)(a)).

'Provision of Welsh public services' is defined in s 14(2)(a) as the provision of **7.39**
public services in Wales, so far as their provision is a matter in relation to which
the National Assembly has functions.

The National Assembly was created by the Government of Wales Act 1998. **7.40**
The functions of the Assembly are set out in two Transfer of Functions Orders[22]
and various pieces of primary legislation which have conferred additional functions on the Assembly since devolution.[23] Essentially, the former responsibilities
of the Secretary of State for Wales have been transferred to the Welsh National
Assembly. It now has power to develop and implement policy within a range of
areas, such as education and training, housing, health and health services, and
transport. Regulations providing that the provision of services in such areas may
or must be conditional on identity checks may only be made by the National
Assembly for Wales, and not by Westminster.

(c) *Scotland*

Section 43(2) provides that the regulation-making powers under ss 13 and 14 do **7.41**
not extend to public services provided in Scotland that are within the legislative
competence of the Scottish Parliament.

Under the Scotland Act 1998 the Scottish Parliament has 'devolved' powers. **7.42**

---

[22] National Assembly for Wales (Transfer of Functions) Order 1999 (SI 1999/672) and National
Assembly for Wales (Transfer of Functions) Order 2005 (SI 2005/1958).
[23] At time of writing there is currently a Government of Wales Bill before Parliament.

The definition is negative and residual: the Parliament has powers in those areas which are not 'reserved' to Westminster.[24] Essentially, the powers of the Scottish Parliament are determined by what it does not have legislative competence in rather than in what it can do.

7.43   The devolved powers are extensive, including matters such as education and training, health, housing, transport, and prisons. If the Scottish Parliament wishes to make the production of an ID card a condition of providing public services in these devolved areas, it would first have to pass its own Act.[25]

(d) *Northern Ireland*

7.44   In Northern Ireland the power to make regulations relating to the provision of Northern Ireland public services is exercisable by a Northern Ireland department designated for the purpose (s 14(1)(b)).

7.45   'Provision of Northern Ireland public services' is defined as the provision of public services in Northern Ireland, so far as their provision is a transferred matter (s 14(2)(b)). Section 4(1) of the Northern Ireland Act 1998 defines the transferred matters. Again, the definition is negative and residual: transferred matters are those matters which are not 'excepted'[26] or 'reserved'.[27]

7.46   Before regulations may be made under s 13, a Northern Ireland government department must be designated. The designation must be by order made by the Office of the First Minister and the Deputy First Minister (s 14(1)(b)). At the time of writing the Northern Ireland Assembly is suspended.[28] The Office of the First Minister and Deputy First Minister remains a fully functioning department of the Northern Ireland administration, but the Secretary of State for Northern Ireland has assumed responsibility for its functions.[29] Until suspension of the Assembly ends, the regulation-making power is therefore exercisable from Westminster in relation to Northern Irish public services.

(e) *Procedure*

7.47   Section 14(3) requires that draft regulations to be made under s 13 by the Secretary of State must be laid before and approved by resolution in both Houses of Parliament. Draft regulations to be made in Northern Ireland must be laid before and approved by the Northern Ireland Assembly.

7.48   Under s 14(4) information and consultation on the proposals is mandated in England, Wales and Northern Ireland. Before draft regulations are laid before Parliament or the Northern Ireland Assembly, or regulations are made by the National Assembly for Wales, the person proposing to make the regulations must take such steps as that person thinks fit for securing that members of the public likely to be affected by the regulations are informed about the matters mentioned in s 14(5), and for consulting them about the proposal.

---

[24] The reserved powers are set out in Scotland Act 1998, Schs 4 and 5.
[25] Explanatory Notes, para 222.   [26] Northern Ireland Act 1998, Sch 2.
[27] ibid, Sch 3.   [28] Northern Ireland Act 2000, s 1.   [29] Pursuant to ibid, Sch, para 4(1)(a).

Section 14(5) sets out two matters which must be included in the informa- **7.49** tion provided to the public: (a) the reasons for making the regulations, and (b) why reliance is not being placed on powers outside the Identity Cards Act 2006.

Although a wide discretion appears to be left to the person proposing to make **7.50** the regulations in terms of how the information and consultation processes work, as he or she has a statutory duty only to take such steps as he or she 'thinks fit', it is suggested that the government's Code of Practice on Consultation should be followed whenever it is proposed to make regulations under s 13.[30] As any regulations made pursuant to s 13 will have a potentially high impact on society as a whole, and essential public services may become unavailable to those who cannot comply with identity check requirements, it is suggested that the person making the regulations will need to consult widely in order to discharge his or her statutory duty under s 14(4).

In addition to Regulatory Impact Assessments, proposed regulations under **7.51** s 13 are also likely to require Race Equality Impact Assessments. The Race Equality Impact Assessment published with the Identity Cards Bill in June 2005 recognized that:

There were concerns that requiring the production of a card to access services increases the risk of potential discrimination. People from black and minority ethnic groups might be asked to provide the card as proof of identity more frequently than white people which in some cases might lead to people being denied access to services to which they are entitled if they cannot produce their card. There were concerns that the cards will be used detrimentally due to institutional racism existing in public and private service authorities, particularly where there was a reliance on discretion.

It also indicated that further Race Equality Impact Assessments would need to be made and published throughout the design and roll-out of the scheme.[31]

Section 14(6) provides that, in addition to the duty to inform and consult the **7.52** potentially affected public as the person introducing the regulations sees fit, there is a specific duty of consultation with interested parties before any regulations are made under s 13 if there is an equivalent requirement in other legislation governing that service to consult those interested parties.

D. IDENTITY CHECKS

1. Overview

Section 15 is a data-sharing provision. It provides a power to the Secretary **7.53** of State to enable checks to be made of information recorded in the Register by people providing public services. Specifically, regulations may authorize a

---

[30] Cabinet Office, January 2004. This would involve a minimum 12-week process.
[31] *Race Equality Impact Assessment* (n 19 above) para 24.

person providing a public service to be provided with information recorded in the Register that he needs in order to ascertain or verify facts about an individual who has applied for a public service. The Secretary of State is given the power to regulate the identity checks, in part by including an accreditation scheme for user organizations and their equipment.

7.54　The exercise of powers under s 15 is subject to s 12: the information may only be provided from the Register to the service provider if the individual has consented or given his or her authority (s 12(1)).[32] It is, as yet, unclear whether this safeguard will be effective in practice. If the service provider does not permit the individual to prove his or her identity using alternative means, he or she may be forced either to give consent, or forego the service. Given the very broad range of services which fall within the Act's definition of 'public service', foregoing the service may not be a realistic option for many people: it may involve not being able to travel, rent a property, go to the dentist, or access one's bank account.

2. Provision of Information

7.55　Section 15(1) allows the Secretary of State to make regulations that authorize a person providing a public service (broadly defined) to be provided with information recorded in the Register that he or she needs in order to ascertain or verify facts about an individual who has applied for a public service.

7.56　Regulations made under this section may not authorize the provision to any person of information falling within para 9 of Sch 1.

3. Conditions

7.57　Before a person is entitled to obtain the information, the Secretary of State may, by order, make a number of conditions. Regulations may provide for the manner in which applications for information should be made, the information that may be provided, and the way in which it should be provided. Regulations may also make the provision of that information conditional on the applicant or service provider having registered with the Secretary of State, and the equipment being approved.

7.58　Section 15(3) and (4) provide the basis for the creation of an 'identity verification scheme' for accredited organizations. Organizations and individuals who provide a 'public service' (in the broad sense, from the public and private sector) will be able to apply for accreditation for themselves and the apparatus that they use to receive and store information from the Register. Once accredited, they will be able to check an individual's identity against the Register, provided the individual consents.

---

[32] For further information, see chapter 8.

The identity verification service will work at different levels, according to what **7.59** information is needed. The Identity and Passport Service provides contrasting examples:

For a basic transaction such as proving your age it could confirm simply that your card is valid. If you are a foreign national applying for a job it could be used to confirm that the status of your visa allows you to work. If you are applying to work in a position of trust (as a nanny for example) it could be used to confirm that you do not have a criminal record.[33]

It is not yet clear whether the levels will be set by regulations or by the service **7.60** providers themselves.

4. Regulations

Pursuant to s 15(4) the regulations referred to in this section are subject to **7.61** affirmative resolution procedure.

Before any draft resolutions are laid before Parliament, the Secretary of State **7.62** must take steps pursuant to s 15(5) to ensure that members of the public in the UK are informed about the reasons for the proposal to make regulations and consulted about them. It is again suggested that the Code of Practice on Consultation should be followed prior to the making of any regulations, given their wide-ranging potential impact.

5. Process

The verification method will depend on the circumstances and the level of secur- **7.63** ity needed. The organization will not be able to access the full Register entry for the individual it is checking: it will either receive confirmation that the individual's biometric matches the Register entry, or that the card has not been lost or stolen. In employment cases, it will be possible to obtain a verification of whether the individual has the right to work or is subject to any employment restrictions.

6. Scotland

Under s 15(8) 'enactment' includes an enactment of the Scottish Parliament. **7.64** This means that, although the Scottish Parliament may determine when identity checks are justified in order to access Scottish public services, the rules governing those identity checks will be uniform throughout the UK.[34]

---

[33] Examples are provided at http://www.identitycards.gov.uk/how-idcard-daily.asp.
[34] Explanatory Notes, para 109.

E. PROHIBITION ON REQUIREMENTS TO PRODUCE ID CARDS

7.65 Section 16 is a proposed safeguard and provides a general prohibition on the requirement to produce ID cards. In theory, organizations cannot simply decide that they will not provide public services to an individual unless they produce an ID card,[35] and the police do not have the power to demand production of an ID card.[36]

7.66 However, it is suggested that the exceptions set out in s 16(3) (which include the obligation to produce the card in the provision of public services) are too broad to provide any comfort, particularly given the breadth of the definition of the 'provision of public services' in s 13.

7.67 Section 16(4) provides that an individual can enforce the general rule against producing ID cards in the courts. An individual may obtain an injunction or interdict or may apply for any other appropriate remedy or relief.

---

[35] ibid, para 110.   [36] Home Office Parliamentary Labour Party Briefing, June 2005, 9.

8

ACCESS TO THE REGISTER AND DISCLOSURE

A. INTRODUCTION

One of the large concerns surrounding the ID cards scheme is the extent to **8.01** which persons, organizations, companies or government departments will have access to the wealth of information about individuals on the Register. The Act provides a myriad of circumstances in which information about an individual contained in the Register may be accessed and/or disclosed, either with or without the consent of that individual.

The issue of disclosure dominated large parts of the debates in Parliament, **8.02** with opponents arguing that 'we must be jealous of the privacy of the citizen and jealous of allowing disclosure of information in any citizen's entry in the national identity register to any outside person or body, particularly where that is done without the consent of the individual concerned'.[1]

Certain specified information can be provided to the private sector (such as **8.03**

---

[1] *Hansard*, HL col 1305 (14 December 2005).

banks) without an individual's consent, according to s 12. In effect, s 12 creates an identity verification power, operating with the consent of the individual on the Register, complete with the means for the Secretary of State to establish an accreditation scheme for user organizations and their equipment. The kind of information that may be disclosed under s 12 is restricted, although the list may be modified by the Secretary of State by regulation.

8.04   Other information about an individual's entry on the Register can be disclosed to certain bodies without the consent of the individual. Section 17 allows the Secretary of State to disclose information about an individual on the Register to specified public authorities for purposes connected with their functions, namely, the national security and intelligence services, the police, Revenue and Customs, a government or Northern Ireland department, or a designated documents authority. Section 18 allows the Secretary of State to disclose information about an individual on the Register for the purposes of preventing and detecting crime. This section authorizes a potentially more far-reaching disclosure, including disclosure to overseas bodies or persons. Section 19 allows the Secretary of State to disclose such information in order to correct inaccurate or incomplete information. Section 20 operates as a catch-all provision, allowing the Secretary of State to disclose information to a public authority in circumstances where there is no authorization under ss 17 to 19 as long as the information is specified by order and the order is necessary in the public interest.

8.05   There are strict restrictions governing the disclosure of information falling within para 9 of Sch 1, which is information about the 'audit trail' or 'data trail', ie every occasion on which information contained in an individual's entry has been provided, particulars of every person to whom such information has been provided, and other particulars of the provision of the information. Information about the audit trail can be disclosed by the Secretary of State to national security and intelligence agencies for purposes connected to the carrying out of their functions under s 17(2), and to a designated documents authority for purposes connected with the exercise or performance of the authority under s 17(6). Information about the audit trail can be revealed to other public authorities (namely, the police, Revenue and Customs and a government or Northern Ireland department), but only where the information is provided for purposes connected with the prevention or detection of serious crime (s 18(4)).

8.06   Section 21 sets out the rules that must be followed when disclosing information about an individual on the Register without that individual's consent, which includes a caveat that identifying information (as set out in para 2 of Sch 1) can only be disclosed by the Secretary of State where he is satisfied that it would not be reasonably practicable for the person seeking the information to have obtained the information through other means. This section also allows the Secretary of State to make regulations imposing many requirements before information can be provided under ss 17 to 20. These provisions are explored in more detail in the following paragraphs.

B. USE OF INFORMATION WITH CONSENT

1. Overview

The Act provides for an identity verification service that allows individuals **8.07** to consent to their information on the Register being provided to certain organizations (likely to be within the private sector) for the purposes of verifying identity (s 12). This provision also provides for an accreditation requirement for user organizations and their equipment. The Explanatory Notes under this section make it clear that the Home Office envisages this kind of check being necessary to verify the identity of an individual whose biometric data could not be recorded at the time of enrolment (eg because of a medical condition).[2]

2. The Power to Provide Information from the Register with Consent

The Secretary of State has the power to provide a person with information from **8.08** the Register if an application is made by or with the authority of that individual or if that individual otherwise consents (s 12(1)). 'Provision of information' in the Act includes confirming that certain information is or is not recorded in a person's entry in the Register (s 42(7)).

The way in which the provision of information will work under this section will **8.09** be set out by regulation and so much remains to be determined. Section 12(6) provides that the Secretary of State may by regulations make provision as to how an 'authority' is to be given, the persons by whom and the circumstances in which an application for those purposes is to be made, and how such an application is to be made.

Only certain listed information may be provided under this section. The list **8.10** is intended to be exhaustive[3] but it is nevertheless quite broad, including the following:

- information about the individual falling within paras 1, 3 or 4 of Sch 1 (name, date and place of birth, gender and addresses, residential status, identifying numbers and validity of identifying documents);
- the information contained in any photograph of the individual in the Register;
- the information about the individual's signature that is so recorded;
- information about whether an ID card issued to the individual is in force and, if not, why not;
- information which, by virtue of s 3(3) (voluntary information recorded in the Register), is recorded in the Register at the individual's request;
- security questions (para 8 of Sch 1);

---

[2] Explanatory Notes to the Identity Cards Act 2006, para 85.   [3] ibid.

- the grant/refusal of confirmation that information falling within s 12(3) matches that which is held on the Register; and
- the grant/refusal of confirmation that the individual's entry does not contain information of a particular description within that subsection.

8.11 As the list is intended to be exhaustive, information falling in other parts of Sch 1, such as the records of provision and validity of information, may not be provided to organizations verifying identity under this section.[4]

8.12 It is not only static information that can be provided under this section, but also the confirmation of certain information as it exists on the Register (s 12(2)(g) and (h)). The information falling under s 12(3) is information comprised in a fingerprint, other biometric information, the number to be used for the purposes of applications for information about the individual in question, the password or other code to be so used, and the answers to the questions to be so used. This list is intended to be exhaustive; however, the kind of information that can be provided under this section is subject to change in the future.

8.13 Section 12(4) allows the Secretary of State to modify s 12(2) and (3) (by order subject to the affirmative resolution procedure) and to impose restrictions on the information that may be provided to a person under this section (by regulation). This subsection can be used to ensure that certain categories of people cannot have certain information about themselves provided to other organizations. For example, there is a need to protect certain sensitive information from being revealed as in the case of the previous names of transsexual people. Further, this power may also be used more broadly to restrict the information that is provided to specific types of organizations where all the information falling under s 12(2) is not necessary for their verification purposes.[5] Section 12(10) provides that any restrictions imposed by the Secretary of State on persons seeking to gain access to an individual's Register entry for the purpose of verification or otherwise do not affect the right for an individual to be provided with information about the contents of his or her own entry in the Register (s 12(10)). Such access rights could be made by way of s 7 of the Data Protection Act 1998 (via a subject access request).[6]

8.14 A late addition to this section following the debates in Parliament ensured that while the Secretary of State can modify s 12(2) and (3), he cannot omit s 12(2) in its entirety. Further, the Secretary of State is not permitted to add information falling within para 9 of Sch 1 (the audit trail) to either of the subsections.

3. Accreditation Scheme

8.15 The Act contemplates an accreditation scheme to be established so that only those organizations that have been approved will be able to make checks on the ID cards of individuals who have consented to verification checks against the Register (s 12(7)). In particular, the Act confers a power on the Secretary of

---

[4] ibid.   [5] ibid, para 87.   [6] ibid, para 88.

State to make regulations which set out conditions that must be met before information will be provided with consent under s 12.

Certain conditions are mandatory, in that they must be in place before the **8.16** Secretary of State can provide information about an individual to another person with consent. These conditions were agreed during the debates in Parliament and are set out in s 12(7)(a) and (b). Now, the person to whom the information is provided must have registered prescribed particulars about him or herself with the Secretary of State, and the person and the applicant must be approved by the Secretary of State in the prescribed way.

The Secretary of State may also make regulations about the apparatus to be **8.17** used for the purposes of the application and for the receipt and storage of the information (s 12(7)(c)); however, there is no obligation on the Secretary of State to do so. Section 40(7) sets out in more detail what regulations for the approval of a person or of apparatus might include.

C. THE PROVISION OF INFORMATION WITHOUT CONSENT

1. Overview

Some information on the Register can be shared with certain public authorities **8.18** or other specified persons without the consent of the registered person. This section generally encompasses information to be shared without consent with national security and intelligence agencies, the police, Revenue and Customs, government departments and designated documents authorities. However, other disclosures may be made if they are considered by the Secretary of State to be in the public interest. There are strict requirements for the use of information that is provided without consent as set out in s 21.

2. The Power to Share Information without Consent

The Act allows certain public bodies to share information about an individual **8.19** without that individual's consent. The power to share information in this section is broad; however, some constraints exist in the form of limitations on the bodies that are entitled to share the information and the circumstances for which the information can be shared. In particular, s 17(1) allows the Secretary of State to provide information about a person without consent if there is authorization to do so in this section and if there is compliance with any requirements imposed by or under s 21 (which sets out the rules for using information without consent).

Only certain authorities can access the information that is released without **8.20** the consent of the individual. These authorities are specified national security and intelligence agencies, the police, Revenue and Customs, a government or Northern Ireland department and designated documents authorities.

8.21   In general, information that falls within para 9 of Sch 1 (the 'audit trail') cannot be shared with public bodies. The only exceptions are in the context of specified national security and intelligence agencies and designated documents authorities which may share such information in certain circumstances.[7]

8.22   There is a further public interest constraint on the orders that the Secretary of State may make under this section authorizing the disclosure of information from the Register without consent.[8]

(a) *Specified National Security and Intelligence Agencies*

8.23   Section 17(2) provides that the provision of information is authorized by this section (ie may be provided without consent) where it is to specified national security and intelligence agencies for purposes connected with any of their functions. The phrase 'any functions' indicates a broad power for data-sharing with security and intelligence agencies.

8.24   During the debates in Parliament, a further measure to tighten this section was suggested, proposing that information can only be disclosed under this provision for purposes that are 'necessary' for the carrying out of the body's functions.[9] The amendment was rejected by the government as superfluous, reasoning that information connected with the entity's functions will largely be the same as information necessary for its functions.

8.25   The specified agencies in this section are the Security Service, Secret Intelligence Service, GCHQ and the Serious Organised Crime Agency.[10] For example, the Security Service would be able to obtain information about a person on the Register for purposes connected with the protection of national security, the support of law enforcement agencies in the prevention and detection of serious crime, and to safeguard the economic well-being of the UK, which are their statutory functions as set out in the Security Services Act 1989.[11]

8.26   Agencies specified in s 17(2) have the power to share information about an individual on the Register relating to para 9 of Sch 1 (the 'audit trail') in the interests of carrying out their functions.

(b) *The Police*

8.27   Section 17(3) provides a power to provide information to the police in the interests of national security, for the prevention or detection of crime, or for other purposes specified by order made by the Secretary of State.[12] Unlike the national

---

[7] This is discussed further in para 8.39 below.   [8] This is discussed further in para 8.36 below.

[9] *Hansard*, HL col 1305 (14 December 2005).

[10] Note that s 17(9) clarifies that 'GCHQ' has the same meaning as in the Intelligence Services Act 1994.

[11] Explanatory Notes, para 117.

[12] This provision could raise an issue under Article 8 of the European Convention on Human Rights, as incorporated into the Human Rights Act 1998, if the legitimate purposes contemplated by this section are beyond the scope of the legitimate aims allowing a restriction on the privacy right in Article 8(2). For further information, see chapter 12.

security and intelligence agencies or designated documents authorities, this section does not authorize the police to provide information that is found in para 9 of Sch 1 (the 'audit trail'). However, as will be discussed below, such information can be disclosed by the police if it is for the purpose of preventing and detecting 'serious' crime (s 18(4)).

With the exception of information about the audit trail, the Secretary of State **8.28** has a broad power to widen the aims for which information may be provided to the police, given that s 17(3)(c) allows the Secretary of State to make an order allowing information on the Register to be provided for 'other purposes'. Any order made by the Secretary of State under s 17 is subject to the affirmative resolution procedure (s 17(8)). It is important to note that the 'other purposes' cited by the Secretary of State for expanding this data-sharing provision could go beyond national security and crime detection and prevention, potentially allowing the police access to the information for unlimited purposes.[13] However, any such regulations expanding the scope of the data-sharing power are subject to the affirmative resolution procedure of Parliament providing a check against unnecessary broadening of the powers.

Section 17(9) defines what is meant by 'chief officer of police' in this section, **8.29** namely, the chief officer of police of a police force maintained for a police area in England and Wales and Scotland, as well as Chief Constables in Northern Ireland, the Ministry of Defence, the Civil Nuclear Constabulary, British Transport Police, the Isle of Man Constabulary and the chief officers of the States of Jersey Police Force and the salaried police force of the Island of Guernsey.

(c) *Revenue and Customs*

Under s 17(4) the provision of information without consent can be made to **8.30** Revenue and Customs for national security, the prevention and detection of crime, national insurance contributions and other purposes connected with the functions of Revenue and Customs or other purposes as specified by order made by the Secretary of State. Again, unlike with the national security and intelligence services or designated documents authorities, information about the audit trail cannot be disclosed under this section by the Revenue and Customs. However, as will be discussed below, such information can be disclosed by Revenue and Customs if it is for the purpose of preventing and detecting 'serious' crime (s 18(4)).

There was some concern during the Parliamentary debates about allowing **8.31** the tax authorities to have access to such a wealth of information about an

---

[13] *Liberty's Briefing for Second Reading in House of Lords* (February 2005) para 37. Again, this provision could raise an issue under Article 8 of the European Convention on Human Rights, as incorporated into the Human Rights Act 1998, if the legitimate purposes contemplated by this section are beyond the scope of the legitimate aims allowing a restriction on the privacy right in Article 8(2). For further information, see chapter 12.

individual without that individual's consent.[14] The government refused to amend this provision, arguing that the tax authorities have law enforcement responsibilities that are often undertaken jointly with the police, creating a need for such information sharing powers.[15] However, this is arguably further reason to restrict the access of tax authorities to information on the Register that is solely related to law enforcement purposes.

(d) *Government Department or Northern Ireland Department*

8.32 A similar power for the Secretary of State to provide information without consent to a government department or to a Northern Ireland department is set out in s 17(5). The Explanatory Notes clarify that this allows for the provision of information without consent to other parts of government including government departments of Northern Ireland, such as to the Department for Work and Pensions for investigation of social security fraud or to the Department for Social Development in Northern Ireland in connection with social security benefits or national insurance numbers.[16] Again, unlike with the national security and intelligence services or designated documents authorities, information about the audit trail is exempted from this data-sharing provision. However, as will be discussed below, such information can be disclosed by a government or Northern Ireland department if it is for the purpose of preventing and detecting 'serious' crime (s 18(4)).

(e) *Designated Documents Authority*

8.33 The Act allows the Secretary of State to designate certain documents which can then operate as ID cards and/or which link to information on the Register (s 4). The persons who have the power to issue designated documents are known as 'designated documents authorities'. Section 17(6) covers the provision of information to a designated documents authority without consent.

8.34   Disclosure of information to a designated documents authority without consent is authorized where the information is provided for purposes connected with the exercise or performance by the authority of any of its powers or duties by virtue of this Act or any of its other powers or duties in relation to the issue or modification of designation documents.

8.35   As with national security and intelligence agencies, there is no prohibition on providing information about an individual on the Register relating to para 9 of Sch 1 (the 'audit trail').

3. Public Interest Limit

8.36 A public interest limit on the Secretary of State's powers to make orders or regulations under this section is set out in s 17(7). For the purposes of the Act,

---

[14] *Hansard*, HL col 1308 (14 December 2005).   [15] *Hansard*, HL col 1311 (14 December 2005).
[16] Explanatory Notes, para 120.

something is necessary in the 'public interest' if it is in the interests of national security, for the purposes of the prevention or detection of crime,[17] for the purposes of the enforcement of immigration controls, for the purposes of the enforcement of prohibitions on unauthorized working or employment, or for the purpose of securing the efficient and effective provision of public services (s 1(4)).[18]

Section 17(10) ensures that this section does not restrict any powers existing elsewhere to disclose information. In other words, all of the constraints on the disclosure of information in s 17 are self-contained.

8.37

4. Paragraph 9 of Schedule 1—Information about the 'Audit Trail'

Paragraph 9 of Sch 1 allows for a record to be kept of an 'audit trail' or 'data trail', in other words, data to be kept about every occasion on which information contained in an individual's entry has been provided, particulars of every person to whom such information has been provided, and other particulars of the provision of the information. The information is different from the static information such as a person's name or address that is recorded in the Register, and it is generally exempt from being provided to the police under s 17(3), to Revenue and Customs under s 17(4), and to a government department including prescribed departments in Northern Ireland under s 17(5).

8.38

There are exceptions to this general restriction on disclosure about information relating to an individual's data trail. Under s 18(4) the provision of information set out in para 9 of Sch 1 to the police, Revenue and Customs, to a government department or to a department in Northern Ireland is permissible as long as it is for purposes connected with the prevention or detection of 'serious' crime.[19]

8.39

The retention of such information is made possible under s 3(1) which allows information, once entered in the Register, to continue to be recorded in the Register for so long as it is consistent with the statutory purposes.[20] A further subsection was added following the debates in Parliament, s 3(4), which provides that an individual's entry in the Register must include information about the audit trail that relates to an occasion on which information contained in an individual's entry has been provided to a person without that individual's consent.

8.40

The Information Commissioner has expressed concerns about the 'surveillance society' created by the Act and, in particular, the creation of such a 'data trail' as provided by para 9 of Sch 1, showing who checks a card and when. Such

8.41

---

[17] 'Detection' is further defined in s 42(1) and (9) and 'crime' is further defined in s 42(1), both relating to the Regulation of Investigatory Powers Act 2000.

[18] The public interest test in the Identity Cards Act 2006 appears to be broader than the public interests set out in Article 8(2) of the European Convention on Human Rights which justify restrictions on the right to privacy. For further information, see chapter 12.

[19] 'Serious crime' is defined in s 42(1) in relation to the Regulation of Investigatory Powers Act 2000.

[20] Explanatory Notes, para 30.

information could create a picture of an individual's card use and, thereby, create a detailed picture of how a person leads his or her life. Other systems of checks are feasible such as a local card reader and biometric reader verifying identity, removing the need for central records to be kept, and minimizing the risks and costs associated with developing a complex IT infrastructure.[21]

D. FURTHER PURPOSES CONNECTED WITH THE PREVENTION AND DETECTION OF CRIME

1. Overview

8.42 Section 18 sets out other circumstances in which information from the Register may be provided without the consent of the registered person. This section generally encompasses information to be shared without consent for purposes specified in certain parts of the Anti-Terrorism, Crime and Security Act 2001. As with s 17, there are strict requirements for the use of information that is provided without consent as set out in s 21.

2. Sharing Information without Consent for the Prevention and Detection of Crime

8.43 Section 18 mirrors s 17 (data-sharing among public authorities without consent), and provides that the Secretary of State can provide a person with information recorded on the Register without the individual's consent if it is authorized by this section and there is compliance with s 21 (which sets out rules for using information without an individual's consent).

8.44 Section 18(2) provides that information can be provided without consent for any of the purposes specified in s 17(2)(a) to (d) of the Anti-terrorism, Crime and Security Act 2001 (criminal proceedings and investigations). However, it is subject to s 21 (which sets out rules for using information without an individual's consent). Information falling within para 9 of Sch 1 (information about the 'audit trail') is generally exempt. However, information falling within para 9 of Sch 1 can be revealed if it is provided to a public authority that is set out in s 17 and where it is for purposes connected with the prevention or detection of serious crime.[22]

3. Exceptions

8.45 Section 18(3) allows the Secretary of State to prohibit the provision of information without consent for use in overseas proceedings as specified in s 18 of

---

[21] *The Identity Card Bill—The Information Commissioner's Concerns* (June 2005).

[22] 'Serious crime' is defined in s 42(1) in relation to the Regulation of Investigatory Powers Act 2000.

the Anti-terrorism, Crime and Security Act 2001. The Explanatory Notes indicate that the Secretary of State might prohibit the provision of information without consent for use in overseas proceedings if he considers that it would be more appropriate for the proceedings to be conducted in a court in the UK.[23]

4. Paragraph 9 of Schedule 1—Information about the 'Audit Trail'

As expounded above in para 8.38, para 9 of Sch 1 allows for a record to be kept of a 'data trail', in other words, data to be kept about every occasion on which information contained in an individual's entry has been provided, particulars of every person to whom such information has been provided, and other particulars of the provision of the information. Under s 18(4), the provision of information falling within para 9 of Sch 1 is authorized by this section if it is provided to a person set out in s 17(3) to (5) (the police, Revenue and Customs, a government department or a prescribed Northern Ireland department) and if it is provided for purposes connected with the prevention or detection of 'serious' crime.[24]   **8.46**

The fact that such information can only be released to prescribed persons for purposes connected with the prevention or detection of serious crime is a higher threshold[25] than the static information that can be released about a person, such as his or her name and address, as set out in s 17.   **8.47**

There was much debate in Parliament about extending the requirement that information only be disclosed in relation to 'serious' crime across the rest of the legislation. The government refused to extend the serious crime requirement, reasoning that people in society are concerned about all crimes, including shoplifting and street robbery, which do not come within the definition of 'serious' crime under the Act.[26]   **8.48**

E. CORRECTING INACCURATE OR MISLEADING INFORMATION

1. Overview

Section 19 provides a power to the Secretary of State to provide information from the Register to a person or organization, without the consent of the person on the Register, where information was supplied to help verify an entry but where the information provided proved to be inaccurate or incomplete.   **8.49**

---

[23] Explanatory Notes, para 129.
[24] 'Serious crime' is defined in s 42(1) with reference to the Regulation of Investigatory Powers Act 2000.
[25] Explanatory Notes, para 130.   [26] *Hansard*, HL col 1311 (14 December 2005).

2. Correcting Inaccurate or Misleading Information

8.50 Section 19(1) applies where information about an individual has been provided to the Secretary of State or to a designated documents authority for verification purposes and it appears to the Secretary of State that the information was inaccurate or incomplete.

8.51 In such a case, under s 19(2) the Secretary of State may, without the individual's consent, provide the person who provided the inaccurate or incomplete information with information about the respects in which it was inaccurate or incomplete and what is in fact recorded in that individual's entry in respect of this information. The provision of information is subject to the rules set out in s 21 (rules for using information without an individual's consent).

8.52 Section 19(4) clarifies what is meant by 'providing information about an individual for verification purposes'. It is a reference to providing information about that individual which is required (under s 9 or otherwise[27]) or intended to be used by the Secretary of State or a designated documents authority for verifying certain information. Such information to be verified is something in the Register, something provided to the Secretary of State or a designated documents authority for the purpose of being recorded in an entry, or something otherwise available to the Secretary of State for being so recorded.

F. POWER TO AUTHORIZE OTHER USES OF INFORMATION WITHOUT CONSENT

8.53 Section 20 appears to be a catch-all section, allowing the Secretary of State to make an order to provide information recorded in the Register, without an individual's consent, to a public authority in cases that are not covered within the ambit of ss 17 to 19. According to s 20(2), an order can only be made by the Secretary of State if the provision of information to a public authority is necessary in the public interest.

8.54 It is unclear precisely what is contemplated by this further power as it must be set out by order made by the Secretary of State. Certain restrictions apply to the power, namely, that the information must be specified by order, it can only be provided to a prescribed public authority for a prescribed purpose and there must be compliance with s 21, the rules governing the provision of information without consent. Information in para 9 of Sch 1 (the 'audit trail') cannot be provided according to s 20(1)(a).

8.55 There is some concern that the power to disclose information without consent is extended theoretically without limit by s 20. Sections 17 to 19 are

---

[27] s 9 deals with the power to require information for validating the Register. For further information, see chapter 6.

122

already extremely broad in scope and so it is difficult to imagine what further powers of disclosure are envisaged. It is possible that disclosure powers which go beyond those already contained in the Act will breach data protection requirements or contravene proportionality and legitimate purpose requirements contained in Article 8 of the European Convention on Human Rights, as incorporated into the Human Rights Act 1998. Article 8 protects the right to respect for private and family life, home and correspondence. This right is not absolute but can be restricted in certain limited purposes, namely, where the restriction is necessary in a democratic society, for a legitimate aim as set out in Article 8(2), and any restriction must not be excessive for the purpose it serves.[28]

A further constraint on the Secretary of State's power is found in s 20(3), by **8.56** which the order is subject to an affirmative resolution procedure requiring the Secretary of State to lay a draft order before Parliament and seek approval by resolution of each House.

G. RULES FOR USING INFORMATION WITHOUT CONSENT

1. Overview

Section 21 sets out the rules that must be followed when using information from **8.57** the Register that was obtained without an individual's consent as permitted by ss 17 to 20.

2. The Information Cannot be Available through Other Means

In particular, s 21(1) provides that, under ss 17 to 20, the Secretary of State may **8.58** provide a person with certain information[29] only if he is satisfied that it would not have been reasonably practicable for the person to whom the information is provided to have obtained the information by other means. So, for example, if fingerprint information is recorded on the Register, the police would first have to search their own fingerprint records before requesting information to be provided from the Register.[30]

The information that can be provided by the Secretary of State under this **8.59** section is found in para 2 of Sch 1, which sets out the information that may be recorded in an individual's entry in the Register: photograph of head and shoulders, signature, fingerprints and other biometric information about him or her.

---

[28] *Liberty's Briefing for Second Reading in House of Lords* (February 2005) para 38.
[29] Information within para 2 of Sch 1.   [30] Explanatory Notes, para 136.

3. Regulations

8.60 Sections 21(2) to (4) allow the Secretary of State to make regulations imposing requirements such as specifying the persons who may make any request for information and how it is to be made and authorized before any information is provided under ss 17 to 20.[31]

8.61 Section 21(5) allows the Secretary of State to make regulations setting out the rank, office or position of people who would be authorized to receive information on behalf of those persons listed in ss 17 to 20. For example, a police officer of a specified rank may be authorized to receive information on behalf of the chief officer of police.[32]

8.62 Section 21(7) provides that the regulations under this section will be subject to the affirmative resolution procedure.

H. PASSPORT APPLICATIONS

8.63 There is a specialized power in s 38 conferred on the Secretary of State, allowing him to require information to be shared for the purposes of verifying information provided in relation to an application or withdrawal of a passport. This section mirrors s 9, which provides a power to the Secretary of State to require information in order to verify the Register.[33]

8.64 Section 38(1) provides that the Secretary of State may require that a person provide him with information where it appears that the person may have information in his or her possession that could be used for verifying information in relation to the application or withdrawal of a passport. The obligation to provide the information is mandatory and the Secretary of State may specify a period of time within which the person must comply. This duty is enforceable in the civil courts (s 38(5)). The Secretary of State is permitted to pay for the information sought (s 38(6)).

8.65 The requirement may be imposed on a Minister of the Crown, a government department, a Northern Ireland department, or the National Assembly for Wales, but could be extended by order to any other person not named in this list (s 38(3)), including any person who carries out functions on behalf of the Crown. This could extend the disclosure requirements to private companies that are performing public functions. Any order to this effect is subject to the affirmative resolution procedure (s 38(7)).

8.66 Section 44(5) provides that s 38 comes into force two months from the date that the Act is passed, which means that s 38 will come into force on 30 May 2006. This has implications for the fees and charges that could attend an individual who has an obligation to provide information under the Act, as discussed below.

---

[31] ibid, para 137.   [32] ibid, para 138.   [33] For further information, see chapter 6.

I. FEES AND CHARGES

Section 35(1)(d) and (e) allows the Secretary of State to make regulations **8.67**
that impose fees to be paid in respect of applications for the provision of information contained in entries in the Register and for the actual provision of the
information. As the provisions in the Act mandating the disclosure of information relating to passport applications come into force on 30 May 2006, the
potential to charge fees simply awaits the Secretary of State's regulations which
are subject to the affirmative resolution procedure (s 35(7)).

9

CRIMINAL OFFENCES

A. INTRODUCTION

1. Overview

The Identity Cards Act 2006 creates six new criminal offences, set out in ss 25 to **9.01** 30. Three are indictable only offences, and three are triable either way. The offences will capture behaviour by those involved in identity fraud and hackers, but may also cover applicants, civil servants administering the scheme, and private contractors involved in producing hardware or software associated with the scheme.

The offences created by s 25 are particularly broad, and cover behaviour **9.02** entirely unconnected to the National Identity Register or ID cards themselves. Those involved in identity fraud at any level or on any scale, such as producing student IDs with fake dates of birth for under-18s, may be liable to up to ten years' imprisonment. One offence has the effect of providing that an individual who uses different names in different contexts may be prosecuted if he or she possesses a document, such as a student card or work photo ID, which lists a version of his or her name which does not appear on the Register. He or she will need to prove that he or she has a 'reasonable excuse' for using two different names in order to avoid being convicted. In effect, this abolishes the right at common law to use a pseudonym or alias without good reason and introduces the concept of 'one person, one identity' to UK law for the first time.

All of the offences may, and three of them must, be tried in front of a jury. It **9.03** remains to be seen whether defendants charged with the 'either-way' offences—particularly the strict liability offence of being in possession of a document belonging to another—will decide that being tried in the Crown Court is tactically wise, as juries may be reluctant to treat their behaviour as criminal.

9.04   The Explanatory Notes published in May 2005 with the Identity Cards Bill set out the mischiefs which these new offences seek to tackle. However, they were, in the main, already covered within existing law: the Forgery and Counterfeiting Act 1981, the Official Secrets Act 1989, the Immigration Acts, and the offences of obtaining property, services or pecuniary advantage by deception. The new offences fill gaps in the existing law and widen criminal liability considerably. The distinctions between existing offences and the new offences created under the Act are explored below.

9.05   There is, potentially, a seventh criminal offence which may be created by order of the Secretary of State, subject to the affirmative resolution procedure in Parliament. If the Secretary of State by order lowers the age at which individuals may or must be registered to below 16 years of age, he may then designate certain persons to act on that child's behalf for all purposes of the Act. This will result in 'proxy offences' for parents or guardians of children under 16.

2. Jurisdiction

9.06   The Explanatory Notes state that the reason for the jurisdictional reach is that, 'as these offences relate to documents or databases that operate on a UK basis, they will be applicable throughout the UK'.[1] However, as outlined below, half of the new offences are not limited to national documents or databases, given the extremely wide definition of 'identity document'. Nevertheless, all of the new offences will apply throughout the UK.

9.07   There is a single regional distinction in relation to the ingredients of the offences: in Scotland, the definition of a 'false' document derives from the Identity Cards Act 2006 itself, whereas for the rest of the UK the definition derives from the Forgery and Counterfeiting Act 1981. There are differences in the sentencing provisions for summary trials between Northern Ireland and the rest of the UK.

9.08   In certain circumstances, activity which takes place outside the UK may give rise to criminal liability under the Identity Cards Act 2006.

3. Parliamentary Context

9.09   The provisions creating the new criminal offences remained almost unchanged during the passage of the Identity Cards Bill through Parliament during the 2005–06 session. With the exception of some very minor technical amendments,

---

[1] Explanatory Notes to the Identity Cards Act 2006, para 12.

they remain as set out in the original Bill introduced in the House of Commons by the Secretary of State on 25 May 2005.

There was surprisingly little debate in the House of Commons about the effect **9.10** of the criminal offences. What debate there was centred on whether the penalties were severe enough.[2] In the House of Lords, early debates did examine the proportionality and necessity of the offences.

The same cannot be said for the Bill's predecessors, the Draft Bill published **9.11** by the Home Office in 2004 or the earlier 2004–05 Identity Cards Bill which failed to make it onto the statute book before the general election of May 2005. The criminal offences which the Draft Bill and the 2004–05 Bill proposed were far broader than those set out in the 2005–06 Bill and which now appear in the Act. These proposed offences provoked widespread public and Parliamentary debate.

The Draft Bill included a criminal offence of failing to notify the Secretary of **9.12** State that an individual knows or suspects that his or her ID card has been lost, stolen or damaged, even if the holder did not know or suspect that there was any problem with the card. A mens rea requirement was introduced in the 2004–05 Bill, but failure to notify the Secretary of State remained a criminal offence. In the 2005–06 Bill this criminal offence was downgraded to an action or omission attracting a civil penalty.[3]

The criminal offences provisions proved particularly controversial following **9.13** publication of the Draft Bill and the 2004–05 Bill. When the Bill returned to Parliament following the general election, these provisions had been substantially changed. Following this governmental compromise, debate on the criminal offences abated and these provisions passed through Parliament almost entirely unscathed.

4. Enactment

When the Identity Cards Bill was introduced to Parliament the Home Office **9.14** briefed Labour MPs on the plans for implementation of the scheme. They indicated that the criminal offences would come into force when the ID card scheme goes live in 2008.[4] Later, Andy Burnham MP, the Home Office Minister, indicated to Parliament that the criminal offences 'might be enacted in advance of any national identity register or ID card scheme. We will have to consider that more closely once the Bill has been passed.'[5] It is suggested that, on consideration, the government is likely to implement at least some of the offences sooner than 2008 for four reasons.

---

[2] Amendments 93 and 94 would have increased the maximum sentences for offences under s 25 from ten to twelve years (s 25(1) and (3)) and from two to four years (s 25(5)).

[3] For further information on civil penalties, see chapter 10.

[4] Identity Cards Bill Team, *Identity Cards Bill: Briefing for MPs* (8 June 2005) 17.

[5] *Hansard*, HC col 395 (19 July 2005).

9.15   First, none of the offences is reliant on the issuing of ID cards or even the establishment of the Register to be applicable. Actions such as producing false driving licences or immigration documents or revealing confidential information about the tendering process or the set-up of the Passport and Identity Service fall within the remit of the criminal offences.

9.16   Second, the Register will become fully operational before the first cards are issued, which will be linked to the issuing of biometric passports. Biometric passports are being introduced over a six to nine month period in 2006,[6] and they are expected to be routinely issued by 26 October 2006, the date by which the US requires countries with which it has a visa waiver to issue biometric passports.[7] The Register is likely to go live in late 2006, prior to the issuing of the first stand-alone ID cards.

9.17   Third, the Immigration and Nationality Directorate of the Home Office is aiming to introduce biometric residence permits for 'all third country nationals' by 2007.[8] This is pursuant to EU Regulations.[9] Again, these permits are intended to be linked to the Register and it is likely that the Register will go live prior to their issue.

9.18   Finally, the offence of unauthorized disclose of information (s 27) may be of particular use to the Home Office and the Identity and Passport Service in protecting individual privacy and commercial confidentiality during the initial stages of the scheme, before it is fully operational. This offence would also bolster existing provisions preventing civil servants or private contractors from leaking commercially or politically sensitive information, or revealing private information relating to individuals.

9.19   Enactment of the criminal offences may take place incrementally, with certain criminal offences applying to certain groups of people before others.

B. FALSIFICATION OFFENCES

1. Overview

9.20   Section 25 creates two new criminal offences relating to falsification of identity documents. Both offences are triable only on indictment. According to the Explanatory Notes, 'to be guilty of the offence the person must have the intention that the document be used for identity fraud',[10] but the offences as drafted are far wider than this. The extremely broad definition of 'identity document' raises particular problems, explored below.

---

[6] UK Passport Service website, http://www.passport.gov.uk/general_biometrics.asp.
[7] The US Senate announced a one-year extension to its deadline for this requirement, to 26 October 2006, on 15 June 2005.
[8] Home Office, *Identity Cards Bill: Regulatory Impact Assessment*, 25 May 2005, para 16.
[9] See ibid for further detail.   [10] Explanatory Notes, para 149.

(a) *Possession of a False Identity Document with Intent*

Section 25(1) creates an offence of possession of a false identity document with intent to commit identity fraud. It provides that: **9.21**

It is an offence for a person, with the requisite intention, to have in his possession or under his control –
(a) an identity document that is false and that he knows or believes to be false;
(b) an identity document that was improperly obtained and that he knows or believes to have been improperly obtained; or
(c) an identity document that relates to someone else.

The 'requisite intention' for the offence is set out in s 25(2). It is either: **9.22**

(a) having the intention of using the document for establishing registrable facts about himself or herself, or

(b) having the intention of allowing or inducing another to use it for establishing, ascertaining or verifying registrable facts about himself or herself or about any other person (with the sensible exception, in the case of a document within s 25(1)(c), of the individual to whom the document relates).

(b) *Possession of an Item Designed or Adapted to Make False Identity Documents with Intent*

Section 25(3) creates a second falsification offence, of possessing an item (apparatus, article or material) designed or adapted to make false identity documents. The defendant need not have designed or adapted the item him or herself to fall within s 25(3); it is sufficient if it is within his or her custody or control. **9.23**

Again, this offence is contingent on the 'requisite intention' being established. It is defined as in s 25(4) as both: **9.24**

(a) the intention that he or she or another will make a false identity document, and

(b) the intention that the document will be used by somebody for establishing, ascertaining or verifying registrable facts about a person.

These are cumulative requirements. Proof of only (a) or (b) will not suffice.

2. Possession or Control

'Possession' and 'control' are not defined further in the Act. In relation to the two falsification offences, the lack of definition is unlikely to cause difficulties.[11] Section 25(1) echoes the general rule that a person has in his or her possession **9.25**

---

[11] However, it is problematic in relation to the less serious offence under s 25(5), on which see para 9.55 below.

anything which is in his or her physical custody or under his or her control: *DPP v Brooks*;[12] *R v Boyesen*.[13]

9.26   It is certain that the courts will interpret 'under his control' as meaning that an individual may be in control of an item even if it is in the custody of another, such as in a 'left luggage' facility. Other statutes make this explicit: the Misuse of Drugs Act 1971, s 37(3), for example, offers no comprehensive definition of possession but does provide that for the purposes of the Act 'the things which a person has in his possession shall be taken to include anything subject to his control which is in the custody of another'.

3. False

9.27   'False' in s 25(1)(a) has slightly different meanings depending upon location. In Scotland, the definition derives from the Identity Cards Act 2006 itself. In England, Wales and Northern Ireland the definition given in Pt 1 of the Forgery and Counterfeiting Act 1981 is adopted instead. This distinction is due to the fact that the 1981 Act is not in force in Scotland.[14]

(a) *Scotland*

9.28   'False' is defined in s 42(1), but only in relation to information and not in relation to documents specifically. It states that false 'includes containing any inaccuracy or omission that results in a tendency to mislead' and it is to be construed in accordance with the 'conclusive presumption' in s 3(5) that information added to the Register with the applicant's agreement is accurate and complete.

9.29   It is suggested that this definition is of little use in relation to criminal offences involving false documents. A document may contain accurate and complete information, yet still be a false document; for example, it may be a copy of a document which contains correct information but which is being used in an unauthorized way.

9.30   The Scottish courts are unlikely to be troubled by this statutory silence as to what constitutes a false document. The common law approach to falsity, and jurisprudence arising under Pt VI of the Criminal Law (Consolidation) (Scotland) Act 1995, are likely to be used to determine its meaning in context.

(b) *England, Wales and Northern Ireland*

9.31   In England, Wales and Northern Ireland the definition of 'false' in the Forgery and Counterfeiting Act 1981 is adopted by s 25(8)(a) of the Identity Cards Act 2006. Section 9(1) of the 1981 Act provides that:

An instrument is false for the purposes of this Part of this Act –

---

[12] [1974] AC 862, PC.   [13] [1982] AC 768, HL.
[14] Forgery and Counterfeiting Act 1981, s 31(a).

(a) if it purports to have been made in the form in which it is made by a person who did not in fact make it in that form; or

(b) if it purports to have been made in the form in which it is made on the authority of a person who did not in fact authorise its making in that form; or

(c) if it purports to have been made in the terms in which it is made by a person who did not in fact make it in those terms; or

(d) if it purports to have been made in the terms in which it is made on the authority of a person who did not in fact authorise its making in those terms; or

(e) if it purports to have been altered in any respect by a person who did not in fact alter it in that respect; or

(f) if it purports to have been altered in any respect on the authority of a person who did not in fact authorise the alteration in that respect; or

(g) if it purports to have been made or altered on a date on which, or at a place at which, or otherwise in circumstances in which, it was not in fact made or altered; or

(h) if it purports to have been made or altered by an existing person but he did not in fact exist.

This definition of 'falsity' is exhaustive. The governing notion is that the document must not only tell a lie, it must also tell a lie about itself. A lie does not become a forgery because it is reduced to writing; it is the document which must be false and not merely the information in it.[15]   **9.32**

4. Improperly Obtained

The phrase used in s 25(1)(b) of the Identity Cards Act 2006, 'improperly obtained', is broader than that used in comparable offences: obtaining property, services or pecuniary advantage 'by deception'. 'Improper' is a lower threshold than 'deceptive'.   **9.33**

'Improperly obtained' is further defined in s 25(8)(b). An identity document is improperly obtained if false information was provided in connection with an application for its issue or modification to the person entitled to issue or modify it.   **9.34**

'False information' is to be construed in accordance with ss 42(1) and 3(5). Information is false if it contains any inaccuracy or omission that results in a tendency to mislead. There is a 'conclusive presumption' that information entered in the Register following an agreement between the Secretary of State and the individual is 'accurate and complete' information.   **9.35**

5. Registrable Fact

'Registrable fact' in s 25(2) has the meaning set out in s 1(5) and (6) of the Act (s 42(1)). It thus means that the ten categories of facts set out in s 1(5), including   **9.36**

---

[15] For a summary of the relevant case law in this area see David Ormerod, *Smith and Hogan: Criminal Law* (11th edn, Oxford: OUP, 2005) 869; *Archbold 2006* (London: Sweet and Maxwell, 2006) paras 22–18 to 22–21.

the individual's identity, his or her current residential status and numbers allocated to him or her such as his or her National Insurance number, fall within this definition.

6. Identity Document

9.37 Central to the s 25(1) offence is the definition of 'identity document'. This is set out in s 26(1):[16]

In section 25 'identity document' means any document that is, or purports to be –
(a) an ID card;
(b) a designated document;
(c) an immigration document;
(d) a United Kingdom passport (within the meaning of the Immigration Act 1971 (c. 77));
(e) a passport issued by or on behalf of the authorities of a country or territory outside the United Kingdom or by or on behalf of an international organisation;
(f) a document that can be used (in some or all circumstances) instead of a passport;
(g) a UK driving licence; or
(h) a driving licence issued by or on behalf of the authorities of a country or territory outside the United Kingdom.

9.38 This is an extremely broad definition, particularly given category (f). An outline of each category of identity document, (a) to (h), is provided below. Further, pursuant to s 26(4), the Secretary of State may by order modify the list of documents in s 26(1) which constitute identity documents for the purposes of the criminal offences set out in s 25. This power is subject to the affirmative resolution procedure.[17] The Secretary of State has not yet exercised this power to expand the definition in s 26(1).

(a) *An ID Card*

9.39 'ID card' does not exclusively mean an ID card issued by the Identity and Passport Service under the Act.[18] 'Card' is a deceptive term, as it may include any 'document' on or in which information may be recorded, and 'document' in turn may include a stamp or a label (s 42(1)).[19] An ID card, according to the Act, includes any 'document' that is being used for the purpose of establishing identity.

9.40 For the purposes of the criminal offences, a chip containing information relating to the Register, a visa establishing an individual's legal status, or a stamp in a passport could all be considered to be ID cards.

---

[16] Pursuant to s 25(10), 'identity document' in s 25 has the meaning given to it by s 26.

[17] Under s 26(5) the Home Secretary must lay a draft of any proposed order under s 26(4) before Parliament, and it must be approved by a resolution of each House.

[18] 'ID card' is to be construed in accordance with s 6(1) of the Act. For further information, see chapter 4.

[19] It must also be borne in mind that the definitions of 'card' and 'document' provided in the Act are non-exhaustive and illustrative only.

Once the Register goes live, Asylum Registration Cards and biometric residence permits for foreign nationals will also be considered ID cards for the purposes of these criminal offences. Their constituent elements will also be capable of being separately considered to be ID cards. **9.41**

(b) *A Designated Document*
Under s 4 of the Act the Home Secretary may, by order, designate a description **9.42** of documents for the purposes of this Act. No documents have yet been designated, but designation is likely to include documents such as passports, driving licences, biometric residence permits and certificates issued by the Criminal Records Bureau.

(c) *An Immigration Document*
'Immigration document' is defined in s 26(2). It covers three types of documents: **9.43**

(a) a document used for confirming the right of a person to enter or reside in the UK under the EU Community Treaties,

(b) a document which is given in exercise of 'immigration functions' under the Immigration Acts and records information about leave granted to a person to enter or remain in the UK, or

(c) a registration card within the meaning of Immigration Act 1971, s 26A.

These documents will also be covered by category (a) once the Register goes **9.44** live and these documents or information which they contain are linked to it.

(d) *A UK Passport*
A 'UK passport' for the purposes of the criminal offences in the Identity Cards **9.45** Act 2006 has the meaning set out in Immigration Act 1971, s 33:

'United Kingdom passport' means a current passport issued by the Government of the United Kingdom, or by the Lieutenant-Governor of any of the Islands or by the Government of any territory which is for the time being a British overseas territory within the meaning of the British Nationality Act 1981.

(e) *A Foreign Passport*
Section 26(1)(e) is self-explanatory. It includes any passport issued by a foreign **9.46** country or international organization.

Unlike the definition of UK passport, there is no requirement that the pass- **9.47** port be currently valid for travel, and so it probably includes an expired foreign passport. Nor is there a requirement that it suffice for entry clearance purposes to the UK, which means that (e) probably includes passports issued by the Imamate of Oman State, the Turkish Republic of Northern Cyprus, Yemen (Royalist Authorities), Taiwan and the Palestinian Authority.

It is not clear whether any current documents fall within the definition of **9.48** passports issued by or on behalf of an international organization. The African

Development Bank, International Red Cross, the Organisation of American States and the Organisation of African Unity issue travel documents to their officials, but they are not passports as such. Similarly, international organizations such as the UN and the EU issue travel documents, but again, they are not passports. These documents would instead fall within category (f), considered below.

(f) *Alternatives to a Passport*

9.49 Category (f) states that 'identity document' includes 'a document that can be used (in some or all circumstances) instead of a passport'. This provision is likely to cause difficulties of interpretation given its apparent breadth. If travelling from the UK to the Republic of Ireland, for example, a student card or a workplace photo ID may be used in place of a passport.

9.50 Although the words 'for travel purposes' do not appear in (f), this category appears to have been intended to cover only travel documents which may be used instead of a passport for entry to the UK, such as emergency travel documents, collective passports, visitors' cards of certain European nationals, travel documents for refugees or stateless persons, travel documents issued by international organizations or governments not recognized by Her Majesty's government, and Declarations of Identity. Debates in the House of Commons on the Bill confirm that s 26(1) was intended to be a narrow, discrete list and that (f) was assumed to relate to travel documents only. The then Shadow Attorney General, Edward Garnier MP,[20] who tabled a series of probing amendments relating to clauses 27 and 28 (now ss 25 and 26 of the Act) for the Conservative Party, assumed that category (f) covered only documents 'such as a travel document issued to an asylum applicant'.[21]

9.51 Tony McNulty MP, the Home Office Minister, stated that the list of identity documents covered only those which could be used to establish identity, rather than address or date of birth. He noted that:

We need to start from the premise that the offences in the clause were designed for documents that are useful for proving identity, and as such are extremely valuable as a day-to-day means of proving identity, such as the driving licence or passport. By any token, a bank statement is not proof of identity, although it may be proof of address, temporary or otherwise. The same is true of many of the other suggestions. Our partners may disagree, but a marriage certificate is not an identity document in any way, shape or form.[22]

If birth certificates were to be included in the list, he continued, this would 'cloud the issue'.[23] He explained that the list of documents was 'deliberately discrete'[24] and 'rightly narrow'.[25]

---

[20] At the time of writing Mr Garnier MP is Shadow Home Affairs Minister.
[21] *Hansard*, HC Standing Committee D, col 403 (19 July 2005).   [22] ibid, col 405.
[23] ibid.   [24] ibid.   [25] ibid, col 406.

It is suggested that category (f) is simply the product of unclear drafting. The **9.52** courts should interpret it narrowly given the following factors. First, (f) does not appear at the end of the list of identity documents, which could indicate its role as a general, catch-all category. Instead, it appears following two categories of travel documents and before the list moves to driving licences. Second, a minister representing the government and the Home Office, responsible for promoting the Bill, made a clear statement in Parliament indicating the legislative intention of what is now s 26(1). This statement is relevant for understanding the purpose and effect of this subsection.[26]

(g) *A UK Driving Licence*

'UK driving licence' is defined in s 26(3) as meaning either a licence granted **9.53** under Pt 3 of the Road Traffic Act 1988 (England, Wales and Scotland) or Pt 2 of the Road Traffic (Northern Ireland) Order 1981. It does not include the counterpart, ie the paper part of a photographic card driving licence.[27]

(h) *A Foreign Driving Licence*

A driving licence issued by or on behalf of the authorities of a country or **9.54** territory outside the UK is also an identity document for the purposes of s 25. This definition excludes international driving documents which are not issued by a country or territory, such as International Driving Permits issued by road safety or insurance companies.

7. Mens Rea

Although the requisite intention for these offences is set out in s 25(2) and (4), **9.55** the issue of mens rea also arises within s 25(1) and (3). In addition to proving the requisite intention, the prosecution must also prove that the defendant was in possession or control of the document or item in question, which includes a mental element. For s 25(1)(a) and (b) the prosecution must also prove that the defendant 'knows or believes' the identity document to be either false or improperly obtained. For s 25(3)(a) and (b) the prosecution must prove that the apparatus, item or material has been specially designed or adapted to be used for making fake identity documents 'to his knowledge'.

The requisite intention is stated by the Explanatory Notes to be 'the inten- **9.56** tion that the document be used for identity fraud'. The intention is made out

---

[26] *Pepper (Inspector of Taxes) v Hart* [1993] AC 593, HL; Francis Bennion, *Statutory Interpretation* (4th edn, London: Butterworths, 2002) 526.

[27] *Hansard*, HC col 1733 (10 February 2005). The counterpart was originally included in the definition but it was removed in order to 'simplify' the definition. This decision was made by the government in light of the Road Safety Bill. It will enable the Driver and Vehicle Licensing Agency to create an electronic driving record that will be available to the police and it includes a provision to remove references to the counterpart in existing legislation. At time of writing the Bill is still before Parliament. If enacted, it is anticipated that it would come into force in 2007 or 2008.

when the defendant intends to use the document to establish registrable facts about him or herself, or to induce another to establish, ascertain or verify registrable facts about himself or any other person. An active intention such as this, however, is not required, as intending to allow another to use the document suffices.

8. Specially Designed or Adapted

9.57   In relation to the s 25(3) offences, there is a potential escape route for a defendant who is in possession of an item which may be used to make false identity documents, but has not been 'specially designed or adapted' for that purpose. For example, a defendant in possession of a laminating machine, to which he has made no alterations, cannot be convicted under s 25(3) even if he intends to use the machine in order to make fake identity documents. He cannot be said to be in possession of 'apparatus which . . . has been specially designed or adapted for the making of false identity documents'. The apparatus was designed to laminate, and is capable of being used for legitimate purposes; it has not been adapted for the specific purpose of making false documents. Such a defendant would need to be charged with an alternative offence, such as forgery.[28]

9. Sentence

9.58   These offences are triable on indictment only. Upon conviction, the defendant is liable to a term of imprisonment of up to ten years and/or a fine.

10. Relationship to Other Offences

9.59   The offences created by s 25(1) and (3) partially overlap with the forgery offences in Pt I of the Forgery and Counterfeiting Act 1981. The use or making of a false passport, for example, would be captured by both Acts. In Parliament, the Conservatives queried whether the new offence was necessary:

> Will this Bill and the offences under clause 27 replace those relating to use of a forged passport under the 1981 Act, or will an almost identical offence be added? Will we be duplicating or providing a wholly separate law?

9.60   There are four distinctions between the Pt I offences under the 1981 Act and the new falsification offences created by the Identity Cards Act 2006.

9.61   First, the new offences are, in one sense, narrower, as they target forgery of identity documents only, whereas the 1981 Act covers the broader category of 'instruments', such as stamps, insurance discs, and tapes.

---

[28] Forgery and Counterfeiting Act 1981, s 1.

Second, the new offences are, in a different way, broader than the old offences. **9.62**
The 1981 Act covers only false documents and not documents which have been
improperly obtained or relate to someone else. Andy Burnham MP highlighted
this difference during the Identity Card Bill's passage through Parliament,
giving the example of an individual who has made a fraudulent application to
obtain a passport, which may be a genuine document despite being acquired
using false information.[29]

Third, the new offences are likely to be easier to establish than those under **9.63**
the 1981 Act. In order to make out the offences of forgery,[30] copying[31] or using[32]
a false instrument under Pt I of the 1981 Act, the prosecution has to prove a
double intention: (i) the intention that the false instrument shall be used to
induce someone to accept it as genuine, and (ii) the intention to induce somebody, by reason of so accepting it, to do or not do some act to his or her own or
any other person's prejudice.[33] In contrast, there is no prejudice requirement in
s 25(2) or (4).

Fourth, the new offences are more serious than those under Pt I of the 1981 **9.64**
Act. Although the maximum sentence under s 25(1) and the equivalent offences
under the 1981 Act are similar (ten years' imprisonment in both cases, with the
possibility of a fine under the 2006 Act), the 1981 Act offences are either way
offences whereas the s 25(1) offence is triable on indictment only.

It is suggested that in cases involving false passports or false immigration **9.65**
documents, the Crown Prosecution Service may soon consider using the new
offences under the Identity Cards Act 2006 rather than the offences set out
in the Forgery and Counterfeiting Act 1981. Many situations currently dealt
with in the magistrates' courts under the 1981 Act, such as possession of a
single false passport by an individual attempting to enter the UK, may instead
be dealt with in the Crown Court under s 25(1) of the Identity Cards Act
2006. The offences will be easier to establish and the minimum sentences more
severe.

C. POSSESSION OF FALSE IDENTITY DOCUMENTS

1. Overview

Section 25 of the Identity Cards Act 2006 also creates a third, less serious **9.66**
offence of simply possessing a false identity document without reasonable excuse,
even if the person does not intend to use the document for identity fraud. In
particular, it is an offence for a person to have in his or her possession or under
his or her control an identity document that is false, was improperly obtained,

---

[29] *Hansard*, HC Standing Committee D, col 401 (19 July 2005).
[30] Forgery and Counterfeiting Act 1981, s.1.   [31] ibid, s 2.   [32] ibid, s 3.
[33] *R v Campbell* (1985) 80 Cr App R 47, CA.

that relates to someone else or any apparatus that, to his or her knowledge, has been designed to make false identity documents.

2. Strict Liability

9.67 This offence applies irrespective of any intent to use the documents or the equipment and is therefore considered by the government to be a strict liability offence (although there is some doubt as to whether the wording of s 25 in fact creates a strict liability offence). There is no requirement of intention, recklessness or even negligence as to any of the elements of the actus reus.

9.68 The defence of 'reasonable excuse' inbuilt within the subsection itself does not fully ameliorate the consequences of this. The reasonable excuse defence creates a reverse onus: the individual is presumed guilty unless the excuse is established. A man carrying his wife's driving licence, for example, is prima facie guilty of an offence under this subsection, as he is in possession of an identity document that relates to someone else (s 25(1)(c)), and the onus is upon him to establish his excuse for that possession and its reasonableness. A woman carrying an old driving licence of her own bearing her maiden name, when her entry on the Register bears her married name, would also be in possession of a false document given the 'conclusive presumption' of the accuracy and completeness of the information on the Register. Again, she would be prima facie guilty of an offence and liable to establish her defence.

3. Reasonable Excuse

9.69 The onus of establishing this defence will lie on the defendant. It is unclear whether he or she will have to prove it on the balance of probabilities, or whether, once raised, the prosecution must disprove it.

9.70 Other areas of criminal law have strict liability offences subject to a defence of 'lawful authority or reasonable excuse'. The precedents are not encouraging for defendants charged under s 25(5) of the Identity Cards Act 2006, as the defence tends to be narrowly interpreted.

9.71 Section 1(1) of the Prevention of Crime Act 1953, for example, provides that:

Any person who without lawful authority or reasonable excuse, the proof whereof shall lie on him, has with him in any public place any offensive weapon shall be guilty of an offence.

Whether there is a reasonable excuse has been interpreted as a purely objective test: would a reasonable man think it excusable to carry a weapon?[34]

9.72 According to David Ormerod's analysis of s 1(1) of the 1953 Act:

Generally the courts have construed the provision strictly and exercised close control over magistrates and juries. It is not enough that D's intentions were entirely lawful.

---

[34] *Bryan v Mott* (1975) 62 Cr App R 71, Div Ct.

It is unclear whether simply being unaware that an identity document is **9.73** false will ever amount to a 'reasonable excuse', and thus provide a defence. If the reasonable man would have had actual or constructive knowledge of its provenance, the defence may not apply. However, in Parliament the government suggested that ignorance of the true nature of the document in one's possession would constitute a reasonable excuse for the purposes of s 25(5):

If a person did not know that they had a false or improperly obtained document, that fact would in itself amount to a reasonable excuse in the eyes of the law. It was said in the debate that intent is everything, but if an individual did not know that the documents were false or improperly obtained, he could use the 'reasonable excuse' provision in the clause as part of his case.[35]

In relation to other similar strict liability offences, there have been inconsistent **9.74** decisions as to whether forgetfulness is capable of amounting to a reasonable excuse. In the majority of cases, forgetfulness, with or without other factors, has been left to the jury.[36] As an identity document may be 'false' if it has an out-of-date address or name on it, it is suggested that forgetting to update it, and thus being unknowingly in possession of a document which is 'false', could give rise to the defence of reasonable excuse.

4. Possession

Regardless of whether the courts consider forgetfulness or ignorance to be **9.75** capable of grounding the defence of 'reasonable excuse', these states of mind may nevertheless raise questions under s 25(5) as to whether an individual is in 'possession' or 'control' of a false document.

The concept of possession has proved an elusive and controversial concept **9.76** in other areas of the criminal law. This is because, in the criminal law, possession cases usually involve a mental element of some kind. Mere physical custody of an object does not equate to its possession. The law separates the physical element of possession (the *corpus*) from the mental element (the *animus possidendi*), ie the intention to possess. However, the courts have tended to require only a minimal level of knowledge: famously, an individual who has custody of what he believes to be aspirin tablets may be said to be in possession of heroin tablets if that is what they, in fact, transpire to be.[37] If an individual is mistaken as to the very nature of the item, however, he may not be in possession.

The Court of Appeal has accepted that even in cases involving possession **9.77**

---

[35] *Hansard*, HC Standing Committee D, col 396 (19 July 2005).

[36] See *R v Bird* [2004] EWCA Crim 964 (D charged with possession of an offensive weapon in a public place; his explanation was that he had a knife in his work trousers and put them on, forgetting it was there; the defence of reasonable excuse should have been left to the jury); *R v Jolie* [2003] EWCA Crim 1543, [2004] 1 Cr App R 3.

[37] See *Warner v Metropolitan Police Commissioner* [1969] 2 AC 256, *per* Lord Pearce.

offences of strict liability, forgetfulness or ignorance may negate possession.[38] However, the case law is inconsistent. It is suggested that arguments relating to the individual's lack of knowledge may be on firmer ground in relation to the 'reasonable excuse' defence, but defendants in the Crown Court may nevertheless also raise these issues in relation to possession in case the defence is not left to the jury.

5. Sentence

9.78 The new offence created by s 25(5) is triable either way. A person found guilty of an offence under this subsection shall be liable to a maximum prison term of two years and/or a fine on indictment. On summary conviction in England and Wales the defendant will be liable to a maximum prison term of 12 months and/ or a fine not exceeding the statutory maximum.

9.79 On summary conviction in Scotland or Northern Ireland the defendant will be liable to imprisonment for a term not exceeding six months and/or to a fine not exceeding the statutory maximum.

9.80 Under s 30(4) of the Identity Cards Act 2006 the offence under s 25(5) is arrestable in Northern Ireland.

6. Impact

9.81 This new offence will be potentially applicable in any case involving theft of a handbag, wallet or purse which contains a driving licence or other identity document, regardless of whether the defendant who stole it intended to use or rely upon that document. Simple possession will suffice for the crime to be made out, and any defendant in this position will not be able to claim he has a 'reasonable excuse' for such possession. The Crown Prosecution Service may be unlikely to prosecute such an individual under the Identity Cards Act 2006 in addition to charging him with robbery or theft, but the fact remains that he would certainly be guilty of the offence under s 25(5).

9.82 This new offence also changes the presumption at common law that an individual may hold himself out to be anyone he chooses, provided he is not defrauding or prejudicing anyone by so doing. It undermines the right to be anybody. An individual using a pseudonym or alias for stage reasons may be able to establish reasonable excuse, but an individual doing so for purely personal or eccentric reasons may not be so able.

7. Strict Liability and the European Convention on Human Rights

9.83 The presumption of innocence in Article 6(2) ECHR states that everyone charged with a criminal offence shall be presumed innocent until proved guilty

---

[38] *R v Jolie* [2003] EWCA Crim 1543, [2004] 1 Cr App R 3; *R v Glidewell* (1999) 163 JP 557.

according to law. In addition to being specifically mentioned in Article 6(2), an individual's right to be presumed innocent and to require the prosecution to bear the onus of proving the allegations against him or her 'forms part of the general notion of a fair hearing under Article 6(1)'.[39] The presumption of innocence is the foundation of the fundamental common law rule that the onus lies on the prosecution to prove the defendant's guilt beyond reasonable doubt. On their face, reverse onuses—such as the 'reasonable excuse' defence under s 25(5)—are inconsistent with the presumption.

However, the European Court of Human Rights has held that the presump- **9.84** tion of innocence enshrined in Article 6 is not absolute.[40] In cases involving reverse onuses, the Court will examine whether the way the statute was applied offended the basic principles of a fair procedure inherent in Article 6(1). Similarly, the House of Lords has refused to find reverse onuses incompatible with the Human Rights Act 1998 (HRA) per se, instead finding that each case must be decided according to its own particular circumstances.[41] According to both the Strasbourg and the domestic case law, it appears that a reverse burden may be justified, provided three conditions are fulfilled:

(i) it is imposed in pursuit of a legitimate aim,
(ii) it is proportionate to the achievement of that aim, and
(iii) applying it in this particular case does not cause a risk of injustice.[42]

It is suggested that the s 25(5) offence is almost certainly compatible with **9.85** Article 6, in itself. This is so regardless of which interpretation of the offence is adopted. If a strict liability offence, the 'reasonable excuse' defence saves it, particularly as reasonableness is inherently context-specific and so takes account of proportionality. If the Home Office's interpretation is incorrect and it is not, in fact, a strict liability offence (as the absence of a reasonable excuse is an element of the offence which must be proved by the prosecution beyond reasonable doubt), no Article 6 issue is raised. However, in individual cases, depending on the particular circumstances, this offence may raise questions under Article 6. Proportionality may be a particular problem in relation to the possibility of criminal liability for being in possession of a document belonging to another.

---

[39] *Saunders v UK* (1997) 23 EHRR 313 at [68]; *Phillips v UK* [2001] Crim LR 817 at [40], ECtHR.

[40] *Salabiaku v France* (1988) 13 EHRR 379.

[41] *R v Lambert* [2001] UKHL 37, [2002] 2 AC 545 at [34], [152]; *Sheldrake v DPP* [2004] UKHL 43, [2005] 1 AC 264 at [21].

[42] Although this third criterion has been cited in the House of Lords in cases involving the Drug Trafficking Act 1994 confiscation provisions which explicitly include the 'risk of injustice' test, it is suggested that it should operate as a 'long stop' in all cases involving reverse burdens.

D. UNAUTHORIZED DISCLOSURE OF INFORMATION

1. Overview

9.86 Section 27 governs the unauthorized disclosure of information on the Register by people who are privy to such information by virtue of being employed in connection with the ID card scheme. It creates a new criminal offence of disclosure without lawful authority of information which the defendant or another person is 'required to keep confidential'.

2. Confidentiality

9.87 Section 27(2) sets out the circumstances in which a person is required to keep information confidential:

(a) if it is information that is or has become available to him or her by reason of his or her holding an office or employment the duties of which relate, in whole or in part, to

(b) the establishment or maintenance of the Register;

(c) the issue, manufacture, modification, cancellation or surrender of ID cards; or

(d) the carrying out of the Commissioner's functions.

9.88 The requirement of confidentiality attaches to the person's status rather than the type of quality of information. The information does not need to fall within s 27(2)(a), (b) or (c). These three categories simply describe the duties which trigger a confidentiality requirement on the part of the employee or office holder in relation to any information which becomes available to him or her by reason of his or her employment. For example, under s 27 an individual who works for the Identity and Passport Service is required to keep confidential information relating to the number of tea-bags in the office kitchen.

9.89 Section 27 will apply primarily to civil servants, not only in the Passport and Identity Service or the Home Office, but also those employed in other departments with posts which, in whole or in part, link to the National Identity Scheme. Given the intended reach of the scheme, most government departments will have employees who fall within this section.

9.90 Employees or office holders of any private contractors working on aspects of the scheme will also fall within the rubric of s 27.

9.91 The s 27 offence does not cover bodies who access information on the Register under ss 17 to 21. Although these organizations may have obligations to keep the information that they obtain confidential due to requirements arising under the Data Protection Act 1998 or the HRA, that confidentiality does not arise on the basis of s 27(2) and so the offence does not bite. Unauthorized disclosure of information by such an organization or individual may nevertheless be an offence under the Data Protection Act, or it may amount to misconduct in public office.[43]

3. Lawful Authority

'Lawful authority' is defined in s 27(3). There are four ways to establish lawful authority and this is an exhaustive list: **9.92**

(a) disclosure is authorized by or under the Identity Cards Act 2006 (such as disclosure to the Commissioner) or another enactment;

(b) disclosure is in pursuance of an order or direction of a court or a tribunal;

(c) disclosure is in pursuance of a Community obligation; or

(d) disclosure is for the purposes of the performance of the duties of an office or employment set out in s 27(2) (related to the Register, ID cards or the Commissioner).

It is suggested that s 27(3)(a) includes the HRA, and thus the right to freedom of expression under Article 10 ECHR. **9.93**

Under the Freedom of Information Act 2000 (FOI), public authorities are subject to a number of duties relating to the publication and provision of information. An individual releasing information on behalf of the public authority pursuant to FOI duties would fall within s 27(3)(d) and thus have 'lawful authority' for the release. **9.94**

4. Reasonable Belief

A person who, at the time of the alleged offence, believes 'on reasonable grounds' that he or she had lawful authority to provide the information or make the disclosure has a defence under s 27(4).[44] **9.95**

In Parliament the Home Office Minister indicated that this defence would be available to a defendant who could 'show on the balance of probabilities that, notwithstanding the lack of objective authority, he held a reasonable subjective belief that the modification was authorised'.[45] **9.96**

---

[43] There are four elements to the offence of misconduct in public office: (a) a public officer acting as such; (b) wilfully neglects to perform his duty and/or wilfully misconducts himself; (c) to such a degree as to amount to an abuse of the public's trust in the office holder; (d) without reasonable excuse or justification. See *Archbold 2006*, para 25–381.

[44] 'Self-help defences' such as these are currently narrowly interpreted by the courts: see *R v Jones* [2006] UKHL 16, *The Times*, 30 March 2006.

[45] *Hansard*, HC col 1733 (10 February 2005).

5. Sentence

9.97 This is an indictable only offence. The maximum penalty is a prison term of two years or a fine or both (s 27(5)).

9.98 This offence is arrestable in Northern Ireland pursuant to s 30(4).

6. Impact

9.99 There are two key faults in s 27. It is suggested that the courts, in order to deal with these faults, will be obliged under s 3 HRA to interpret the phrase 'without lawful authority' in s 27(1) and 'another enactment' in s 27(3) in such a way as to take into account Article 10 ECHR, the right to freedom of expression.

9.100 First, the requirement of confidentiality is based on an individual's post rather than the type of information involved. Section 27 appears to place a blanket ban on an individual whose post touches, even in the most minor way, the infrastructure of the national identity scheme, from providing or disclosing *any* information relating to his or her employment unless he or she is specifically authorized to do so. On its face, this appears to violate the requirement in Article 10(2) that any restriction on freedom of expression must be 'necessary in a democratic society'. It is accepted that s 27 is 'in accordance with law', as this is a statutory offence, and it pursues the legitimate aims of protecting the privacy of those individuals enrolled in the national identity scheme and the commercial confidentiality of suppliers and government departments.

9.101 The European Court of Human Rights has repeatedly held that exceptions to the rights recognized under the Convention must be strictly interpreted,[46] and, accordingly, that the adjective 'necessary' is a narrow term that 'implies the existence of a "pressing social need" '[47] and requires proportionality between the legitimate aim pursued and the means adopted. It is difficult to see how an offence of this breadth, with no causal link between the aim (protection of the Register and related information) and the means adopted (criminalizing individuals based on their employment status and not the information they disclose), could satisfy this requirement.

9.102 Second, although the intention behind s 27 is a laudable one, it has the effect of making 'whistleblowing' a criminal offence and will prevent full public debate about the operation of the largest database ever constructed by a UK government. An individual who discovers inaccuracies within the Register, or malfeasance in the running of the national identity scheme, for example, would be committing a criminal offence were he or she to inform journalists or opposition politicians of this.

9.103 During passage of the Bill through Parliament it was recognized that

---

[46] *Sunday Times v United Kingdom* (1979) 2 EHRR 245 at [65]; *Handyside v UK* (1976) 1 EHRR 737 at [48].
[47] ibid.

whistleblowing by those who had learned damaging information relating to the scheme in the course of their employment would be outlawed by s 27. Patrick Mercer MP suggested that:

The conundrum in the clause is whether we are talking only about someone who is guilty of giving information unlawfully or whether there is a place for someone who believes that he is working for an organisation that has become corrupt or has individuals within it who are corrupt and needs to blow the whistle.[48]

The amendment tabled to deal with this difficulty would have resulted in the s 27 offence applying only to those employees who 'knowingly or recklessly' disclosed the information. The government was critical of this, as the offence should indicate to employees 'the seriousness and importance of the information that they are dealing with' and remind them that: **9.104**

Information is to be treated with care and sensitivity and should not be disclosed casually to another person. When they are involved in making a disclosure, they should have this clause in mind. That would be a helpful pressure to ensure that information was not casually or accidentally disclosed to places where it should not go.[49]

The government was undoubtedly correct to highlight the difficulties the tabled amendment would cause. The national identity system will contain detailed and intimate information relating to individuals. They should be assured that processes and safeguards are in place to ensure that their details will not be misused or disclosed, whether accidentally or not. However, the unfortunate result of the wording of the proposed amendment was that the debate on the issue of whistleblowing did not develop, and the Home Office provided no response to Mr Mercer's 'conundrum'. **9.105**

Again, although the apparent absence in s 27 of a public interest defence for an employee who reveals confidential information does not raise issues concerning the 'in accordance with law' or 'legitimate aim' tests under Article 10(2), without such a defence the offence would be overbroad, disproportionate and amount to a violation of that employee's right to freedom of expression. **9.106**

In assessing proportionality the courts must pay regard to the importance of the right in question. Freedom of expression is recognized by the European Court of Human Rights and the domestic courts as 'one of the essential foundations of a democratic society'[50] and 'the lifeblood of democracy'.[51] This is not only because of the rights of the speaker, or the individual providing the information, but also the right of the audience to receive it.[52] In a case involving **9.107**

---

[48] *Hansard*, HC Standing Committee D, col 407 (19 July 2005).   [49] ibid, col 410.

[50] *Lingens v Austria* (1986) 8 EHRR 407 at [41]–[42].

[51] *London Regional Transport v Mayor of London* [2001] EWCA Civ 1491, [2003] EMLR 88 at [55], *per* Sedley LJ.

[52] *Sunday Times v UK* (1979) 2 EHRR 245 at [65]–[66]. The Court emphasized that the freedoms to 'receive' and 'impart' information were two independent rights; the receipt right is not merely a corollary of the right to impart.

possible corruption, inefficiency or misfeasance in the operation of a system which includes information relating to the public, this audience right would be of particular importance.

9.108 It is suggested that s 27 must be interpreted so as to be Article 10 compliant. The confidentiality requirement should attach to the relevant information rather than any and all information which an individual learns as a result of his or her post. There must be an implied public interest defence to a prosecution under s 27.

E. PROVIDING FALSE INFORMATION

1. Overview

9.109 Section 28 creates a new criminal offence of providing false information in connection with the Register or an ID card. In particular, it is an offence to provide false information to any person:

(a) for the purpose of securing the making or modification of an entry in the Register;
(b) in confirming (with or without changes) the contents of an entry in the Register; or
(c) for the purpose of obtaining for himself or another the issue or modification of an ID card.

9.110 There is a mens rea requirement, set out in s 28(2): at the time of the provision of the information, the person must either know or believe it to be false, or be reckless as to whether or not it is false.

9.111 This is a lower threshold than the intent threshold set out in the more serious offences in s 25(1) and (3), as recklessness will suffice.

2. Falsity

9.112 'False information' is defined in s 42(1). It includes containing any inaccuracy or omission that results in a tendency to mislead.

9.113 As 'false' includes the omission of information, and the mens rea threshold may be met by recklessness alone, those who are careless when providing information relating to the Register or the issue or modification of their ID cards may be subject to criminal liability, even if they have no intention to mislead or defraud, and their omission was accidental.

3. ID Card

9.114 Again, it must be noted that 'ID card' is broadly defined in the Act, and may include a biometric passport or a stamp in a passport.

4. Modification

9.115 'Modification' includes omission, addition or alteration (s 42(1)).

5. Sentence

This offence is triable either way. On conviction on indictment a person is liable 9.116
to imprisonment for up to two years and/or a fine. On summary conviction the
maximum penalty is 12 months' imprisonment and a fine not exceeding the
statutory maximum in England and Wales, and six months' imprisonment and a
fine not exceeding the statutory maximum in Northern Ireland or Scotland.

This offence is arrestable in Northern Ireland pursuant to s 30(4). 9.117

F. TAMPERING WITH THE REGISTER

1. Overview

Section 29 creates an offence of tampering with the Register if a person intends 9.118
to or is reckless as to whether the conduct will cause a modification in the
Register.

There is a mismatch between s 29(1) and (2), the actus reus and the mens 9.119
rea, which results in the offence being broadly drawn. A defendant will have a
defence if his or her behaviour was innocent under s 29(6), but, as with s 25(5),
the existence of a potential defence does not detract from the difficulties with the
boundaries of the offence itself.

2. Actus Reus

According to s 29(1): 9.120

A person is guilty of an offence under this section if –
(a) he engages in any conduct that causes an unauthorised modification of information
recorded in the Register; and
(b) at the time when he engages in the conduct, he has the requisite intent.

This casts the net of liability widely as 'conduct' includes acts and omissions 9.121
and 'modification' includes even a temporary modification (s 29(9)). The net is
also cast widely in geographical terms, as this is an offence of universal jurisdiction. The behaviour captured by s 29 may take place in the UK or elsewhere, and
it is immaterial whether the defendant is a British citizen or not (s 29(4)).

'Modification of information' is defined in s 29(3). It not only covers the 9.122
obvious scenario, where the person's conduct 'contributes to a modification of
such information', but also where the conduct makes it or contributes to making
it more difficult or impossible for the Home Secretary to retrieve the information
from a computer on which it is stored 'in a legible form'.

'Unauthorised' is defined in s 29(5). The definition is two-fold: (a) the person 9.123
is not entitled to determine if the modification may be made, and (b) he or she
does not have consent to the modification from a person who is so entitled.

3. Mens Rea

9.124 Section 29(2) sets out the requisite intent for an offence under this section:

> For the purposes of this section a person has the requisite intent if he –
> (a) intends to cause a modification of information recorded in the Register; or
> (b) is reckless as to whether or not his conduct will cause such a modification.

9.125 Section 29(2)(a) does not state that the person must intend to cause an unauthorized modification; it simply states that he or she must intend to cause a modification. An individual who, as part of his or her job, intends to cause an authorized modification to the Register, and accidentally in so doing causes an unauthorized modification (such as accidentally deleting information when he or she intended to add information which he or she was entitled to add), will thus prima facie be guilty of an offence pursuant to s 29.

4. Defence

9.126 Section 29(6) sets out the defence to an offence under this section. It is a defence if the person believed, at the time of the conduct, that he or she was entitled to make the modification or if he or she had obtained consent to make the modification, provided that belief was based on reasonable grounds.

9.127 This defence does not cover the accidental modification scenario outlined above, as the individual did not believe he or she was entitled to make that modification and simply erred in carrying out an intended other modification. Such a defendant would need to rely on the general defence of accident.

5. Sentence

9.128 The new offence created by s 29 is triable either way. The maximum penalty upon conviction on indictment is a prison term of ten years and/or a fine. On summary conviction, the maximum in England and Wales is 12 months' imprisonment and a fine, and in Scotland and Northern Ireland, six months and a fine.

9.129 This is the same penalty that applies if a person is convicted of using or facilitating the creation of false identity documents for the purposes of identity fraud under s 25(1) and (3). However, it is interesting to note that such a high penalty can theoretically attach to a person who may simply be reckless as to whether his or her conduct will cause a modification in the Register. The reckless standard does not appear in the falsification offences in s 25 which attract the same high penalty, but only where a person is in possession of false documents with the intention of perpetrating identity fraud.

G. IMMIGRATION AND ASYLUM OFFENCES

1. Immigration Documents

'Identity documents' are defined in s 26 to include 'immigration documents', and so many falsification offences currently dealt with under the Immigration Acts or the Forgery and Counterfeiting Act 1981 may now instead fall to be dealt with under the Identity Cards Act 2006. **9.130**

Section 30(2) adds the falsification and possession offences under s 25(1) and (5) to s 1(3) of the Immigration and Asylum Act 1999. This is relevant because, in general, those who enter the UK without a valid passport or identity document or deliberately destroy such a document commit an offence under s 2 of the Asylum and Immigration (Treatment of Claimants etc) Act 2004. Section 30(2) gives a specific—albeit narrow—defence to refugees with false documents.[53] The equivalent provision is also made for Scotland by virtue of s 30(2)(b). **9.131**

2. Arrest Powers

Section 30(3) adds all of the s 25 offences to s 14(2) of the Asylum and Immigration (Treatment of Claimants etc) Act 2004. This gives immigration officials power to arrest without warrant for the offence and ancillary powers to search for and seize documents. **9.132**

3. Employers

The Home Office indicated in its Regulatory Impact Assessment published with the Identity Cards Bill in May 2005 that the national identity scheme would 'help legitimate employers who would have a simple way to check status'.[54] If and when the scheme becomes compulsory, the government envisages that employers may need to use its 'accreditation' system to verify potential employees' identities against the Register. **9.133**

However, even prior to compulsory registration, the Home Office has stated that, 'the Government expects that legitimate employers would want to encourage their employees to provide verifiable proof of identity when taking up a job'. It has made clear that 'only an online check would give the employer the assurance that a record of the check would be held on the Register and would therefore provide a defence against prosecution'.[55] **9.134**

The eventual impact of this is likely to be that employers in industries which attract high numbers of illegal workers (such as construction and agriculture) will need to pay for card readers and access to the government's **9.135**

---

[53] Explanatory Notes, para 170.   [54] *Regulatory Impact Assessment* (n 8 above) para 37.
[55] ibid, para 39.

online verification service in order to cover themselves in the event of a prosecution.

9.136 Employers are currently subject to the new civil penalties regime introduced by the Immigration, Asylum and Nationality Act 2006, which may lead to a fine of £2,000 per illegal employee. In order to avoid liability under this system, employers may choose to become accredited under the Identity Cards Act 2006.

10

CIVIL PENALTIES

A. INTRODUCTION

The Identity Cards Act 2006 puts in place a civil penalty scheme for individuals **10.01** who fail to comply with certain requirements imposed upon them by the National Identity Scheme. This civil penalty scheme will be operated by the Home Secretary.

Further, there are three situations in which failure to perform a statutory duty **10.02** under the Act adequately or at all may give rise to civil proceedings for an injunction, damages or other relief.[1] These civil proceedings may be instituted by the Secretary of State or private individuals, depending on which duty has not been complied with.

Finally, it should be borne in mind that the new civil penalty scheme for **10.03** employers created by the Immigration, Asylum and Nationality Act 2006 also raises issues concerning the Register and the ID card scheme more generally. Employers who illegally employ foreign nationals may have a defence if they can show that they took certain steps via the new Identity and Passport Service, created as a result of the Identity Cards Act 2006.[2]

---

[1] ss 9(6), 16(4) and 38(5).
[2] For further information on identity checks in particular, see chapter 7.

1. Overview

10.04 Civil penalties may be imposed pursuant to ss 7, 10 and 11, and the civil penalty scheme is set out in ss 31 to 34 of the Act.

10.05 Section 31 sets out the way in which the civil penalties will operate under the ID cards scheme. There are various ways to attract a civil penalty under the Identity Cards Act 2006, such as failing to register when required, failing to notify of changes in information on the Register, or failing to surrender an ID card when required.

2. Parliamentary Context

10.06 This part of the Identity Cards Act 2006 was expanded in the 2005–06 Bill, as it was amended to take in behaviour which had previously been classified as criminal in the Draft Bill and the unsuccessful Bill of the previous Parliamentary session. For instance, in the Draft Bill a criminal offence was created if an ID card had been lost, stolen or damaged and the holder failed to notify the Secretary of State, regardless of whether the holder knew or suspected there was a problem with the card. Following objections a mens rea requirement was included in the Bill of 2004–05, and the offence would only be made out if the holder knew or suspected that there may have been a problem with the card. In the final Act a failure to notify the Secretary of State in these circumstances is no longer a criminal offence. It has been downgraded to conduct attracting a civil penalty only, under s 11.

10.07 Although the civil penalties provisions had expanded to include conduct previously intended to be caught by the criminal offences in the 2005–06 version of the Identity Cards Bill, during its passage through Parliament the civil penalties scheme shrank significantly. This was due to clause 6, the clause permitting compulsory registration of categories of person by order, being removed. This clause had included liability to a civil penalty of up to £2,500 for a failure to comply with a requirement arising from compulsory registration.

10.08 The maximum civil penalty available to the Secretary of State under the Identity Cards Act 2006 is now £1,000. The aggravated penalties linked to compulsory registration have been removed.

10.09 In a briefing to MPs in June 2005 the Home Office argued that the civil penalties were more proportionate and flexible than the criminal sanctions.[3] This is undoubtedly correct. Arguably, the shift from criminal to civil liability in the 2005–06 Bill was also a politically shrewd move, preventing ID cards from becoming Labour's poll tax. In May 2004 a poll for YouGov indicated that 16 per cent of the population (2.8 million people) would get involved in 'civil disobedience' were the cards to be introduced, and 6 per cent (around a million)

---

[3] Identity Cards Bill Team, *Identity Cards Bill: Briefing for MPs* (8 June 2005) 16.

would be prepared to go to prison rather than register for a card.[4] The civil penalty scheme for those who refuse to provide information which is required prevents the spectacle of 'ID card martyrs' being jailed.

3. Jurisdiction

The civil penalty scheme applies nationally, in England and Wales, Scotland and Northern Ireland. **10.10**

By Order in Council the Queen may provide for extension of the scheme to the Channel Islands or the Isle of Man.[5] **10.11**

B. LIABILITY TO CIVIL PENALTIES

1. Overview

There are 18 situations in which an individual may be liable to a civil penalty. In all cases the amount may be up to £1,000: **10.12**

Those subject to compulsory registration and entered in the Register

(i) He or she is subject to compulsory registration and entered in the Register, but does not hold a valid ID card and fails to apply for one.[6]

(ii) He or she holds a valid ID card that is due to expire but does not apply for a new one.[7]

(iii) He or she applies for a new or renewed card on time but then fails to comply with the Secretary of State's request to verify the information in a specified manner (eg by attending an appointment, or allowing his or her biometric information to be taken).[8]

Anyone to whom an ID card has been issued

(iv) His or her circumstances change (eg new address) and he or she fails to notify the Secretary of State of this change 'in the prescribed manner'.[9]

(v) His or her circumstances change, he or she notifies the Secretary of State, but then fails to comply with the Secretary of State's request to verify the information in a specified manner (eg by attending an appointment, or allowing his or her biometric information to be taken).[10]

(vi) He or she is aware of an error in the information recorded about him or her in the Register and fails to notify the Secretary of State of this error in the prescribed manner.[11]

(vii) He or she is aware of an error, notifies the Secretary of State, but then fails to comply with the Secretary of State's request to verify the information in a specified

---

[4] 'ID card backlash: is the poll tax effect kicking in?', *The Register*, 19 May 2004. Opposition politicians also dubbed the scheme Labour's poll tax: M Portillo, 'ID cards are to Blair what the poll tax was to Thatcher', *Sunday Times*, 3 July 2005.

[5] s 44(6).   [6] s 7(2)(a) taken with s 7(5).   [7] s 7(2)(b) taken with s 7(5).
[8] s 7(3) taken with s 7(4) and (5).   [9] s 10(1)(a) taken with s 10(7).
[10] s 10(3) taken with s 10(4) and (7).   [11] s 10(1)(b) taken with s 10(7).

manner (eg by attending an appointment, or allowing his or her biometric information to be taken).[12]

(viii) He or she knows or has reason to suspect that his or her ID card has been lost, but fails to notify the Secretary of State and 'such other persons as may be prescribed'.[13]

(ix) He or she knows or has reason to suspect that his or her ID card has been stolen, but fails to notify the Secretary of State and such other persons as may be prescribed.[14]

(x) He or she knows or has reason to suspect that his or her ID card has been damaged, but fails to notify the Secretary of State and such other persons as may be prescribed.[15] This includes any damage to the chip or anything in or on the card becoming unreadable or unusable in some way.[16]

(xi) He or she knows or has reason to suspect that his or her ID card has been tampered with, but fails to notify the Secretary of State and such other persons as may be prescribed.[17] This includes the information in or on the card having been modified or copied for an unlawful purpose.[18]

(xii) He or she knows or has reason to suspect that his or her ID card has been destroyed, but fails to notify the Secretary of State and such other persons as may be prescribed.[19]

Any person

(xiii) He or she is knowingly in possession of an ID card without the lawful authority of the individual to whom it was issued.[20]

(xiv) He or she is knowingly in possession of an ID card without the permission of the Secretary of State.[21]

(xv) It appears to the Secretary of State that a person is in possession of an ID card issued to another, and he or she is required but fails to surrender it within a specified period.[22]

(xvi) It appears to the Secretary of State that a person is in possession of an ID card that has expired, been cancelled or is otherwise invalid, and he or she is required but fails to surrender it within a specified period.[23]

(xvii) It appears to the Secretary of State that a person is in possession of an ID card that is valid but is within a category of cards which the Secretary of State has decided should be reissued. The person is required but fails to surrender it within a specified period.[24]

(xviii) It appears to the Secretary of State that a person is in possession of an ID card 'in consequence of a contravention of a relevant requirement', and he or she is required but fails to surrender it within a specified period.[25]

10.13 The prescribed periods are to be set out in statutory instruments. The Secretary of State must also issue a code of practice under s 34 of the Identity Cards Act 2006, and this will give further detail on the procedure to be followed prior to the issuing of a penalty notice. There have not yet been any relevant

---

[12] s 10(3) taken with s 10(4) and (7).   [13] s 11(1)(a) taken with s 11(6)(a).
[14] s 11(1)(b) taken with s 11(6)(a).   [15] s 11(1)(c) taken with s 11(6)(a).   [16] s 11(7).
[17] s 11(1)(d) taken with s 11(6)(a).   [18] s 11(8).   [19] s 11(1)(e) taken with s 11(6)(a).
[20] s 11(3)(a) taken with s 11(6)(b).   [21] s 11(3)(b) taken with s 11(6)(b).
[22] s 11(4)(a) taken with s 11(6)(b).   [23] s 11(4)(b) taken with s 11(6)(b).
[24] s 11(4)(c) taken with s 11(6)(b).   [25] s 11(4)(d) taken with s 11(6)(b).

statutory instruments and no code of practice has been issued. However, an 'indicative draft' code of practice has been issued by the Home Office,[26] and it provides clues as to how the scheme is likely to operate in practice.

2. Compulsory Registration

No individuals are, as yet, subject to compulsory registration. Compulsory **10.14** registration of any group of persons may only take place following another Act of Parliament (which need not necessarily be another Identity Cards Act). Section 42(1) states that:

'Subject to compulsory registration' means required to be entered in the Register in accordance with an obligation imposed by an Act of Parliament passed after the passing of this Act.

Once a category of persons, such as foreign nationals or those under a specified **10.15** age, are subject to compulsory registration, and an individual within that category is entered on the Register, he or she becomes subject to s 7 of the Identity Cards Act 2006.

An individual's refusal to comply with compulsory registration will not neces- **10.16** sarily avoid an entry being made for him or her on the Register. Pursuant to s 2(4), an entry for an individual may be made regardless of whether the individual has applied to be entered on the Register. If information 'capable of being recorded' in an entry for him or her is otherwise available, such as in an existing database, an entry may be made.

3. Individuals to whom ID Cards have been Issued

Individuals to whom ID cards have been issued become subject to the duties and **10.17** requirements set out in s 10.

It is important to remember that ID cards may be issued to individuals who **10.18** have not requested or applied for them. According to s 6(4):

except in prescribed cases, an ID card must be issued to an individual if he –
(a) is entitled to be entered in the Register or is subject to compulsory registration; and
(b) is an individual about whom the prescribed registrable facts are recorded in the Register.

Under s 2(4) registrable facts about an individual may be recorded in **10.19** the Register without his or her consent or an application by him or her if the information is 'otherwise available to be recorded', such as information relating to another database.

ID cards may also be issued with, or as part of, designed documents. In **10.20** the case of a passport, an individual has the right to refuse to be issued with an

---

[26] The draft Code of Practice is found in Appendix 3.

ID card when he or she makes a passport application before 1 January 2010 (s 6(7)).

10.21   For the purposes of the civil penalties in s 10, 'ID card' does not simply mean a stand-alone ID card as such. It also includes documents such as biometric passports or residence permits which are considered to have inbuilt ID cards (ss 6(1) and 42(1)).

C. IMPOSITION OF CIVIL PENALTIES

1. Overview

10.22   In general, s 31 empowers the Secretary of State to issue a notice to a defaulter of the imposition of a penalty and the amount of the penalty. The defaulter will have a set period (of at least 14 days: s 31(4)) after receiving the notice to pay the penalty in the manner prescribed, or to object to the penalty.

10.23   The procedure for objecting to a penalty can be found in s 32. A penalty can also be appealed to the civil courts under s 33. If a defaulter refuses to pay the penalty, the Secretary of State can use the civil courts to retrieve the outstanding amount.

2. Procedure for Imposition

10.24   Section 31 applies if the Home Secretary is satisfied that a person is liable to a civil penalty under the Act, ie one of the 18 scenarios outlined above at para 10.12 pursuant to ss 7, 10 or 11 are applicable.

10.25   If so, the Secretary of State can impose a penalty on the defaulter not exceeding the specified amount, as the Secretary of State sees fit. He must do this by giving notice to the defaulter in the prescribed manner (s 31(2)). The required contents of the notice have not yet been prescribed by statutory instrument, and the specified amounts of the various penalties have yet to be set.

(a) *Warning Letters*

10.26   Although there is no statutory requirement to send a warning letter prior to issuing a penalty notice, the draft Code of Practice on Civil Penalties indicated that this pre-notice step would be taken in the majority of cases. The draft code stated that:

3.1 Before imposing a civil penalty for non compliance with a requirement, it will normally be appropriate to send a warning letter setting out the reasons why the Secretary of State has reason to believe liability to a civil penalty has arisen and urging compliance.

3.2 If there is no response to the warning letter and continued non-compliance, consideration should be given to issuing a penalty notice. Before issuing the notice, the Secretary of State will take account of all relevant facts known to him including any response to the warning letter.[27]

---

[27]   ibid.

This provision appears to have been inserted into the draft code only after the **10.27** Liberal Democrats tabled an amendment in the House of Lords proposing a requirement that the Secretary of State issue a written warning to a suspected defaulter prior to issuing a penalty notice.

The proposed amendment stated that: **10.28**

No such notice may be given unless the Secretary of State has sent to the defaulter written warning of his intention to penalise the defaulter together with brief details of the alleged default inviting the defaulter where appropriate to give written reasons within 28 days as to either why there has been no default or mitigating circumstances of any default.[28]

In moving the amendment, Lord Phillips suggested that this would allow the **10.29** defaulter to 'say whether the Secretary of State has the wrong person or that he had a heart attack on the day he was supposed to attend an interview at Peterborough, or whatever else'. He suggested that, without this amendment, the civil penalty provisions would be fundamentally unfair: 'it is plainly not fair to get a penalty before you have said your piece'.

Lord Phillips recognized that his proposed amendment had been taken on **10.30** board, as the warning letters requirement had appeared in the draft code. Nonetheless, he argued that his amendment was necessary: 'We are now arguing about whether this vital provision should be on the face of the Bill or be left lurking in a code—a code, incidentally, which can be changed by negative resolution'.

The Liberal Democrat amendment was then, with leave, withdrawn.[29] This **10.31** issue did not subsequently arise in either the House of Commons or the House of Lords prior to Royal Assent.

(b) *Penalty Notice*

In the usual circumstances, if the Code of Practice follows the working draft, a **10.32** penalty notice will only be issued once a warning letter has first been issued and no or no satisfactory response has been received.

The penalty notice must comply with the requirements of s 31(3) and **10.33** any relevant statutory instrument. Section 31(3) sets out six pieces of information which it is mandatory for the Secretary of State to include in the penalty notice:

(a) his reasons for deciding the defaulter is liable;
(b) the amount of the penalty;
(c) a final date for payment (which must be at least 14 days from the giving of the notice);
(d) how payment may be made;

---

[28] *Hansard*, HL cols 1536–1537 (19 December 2005).
[29] *Hansard*, HL cols 1536–1542 (19 December 2005).

(e) the steps the defaulter can take if he or she objects to the penalty;

(f) the Secretary of State's enforcement powers.

10.34 The draft Code of Practice gives very little further information on the penalty notice, and simply reproduces s 33(3)'s requirements.[30]

10.35 It remains to be seen whether penalty notices issued by the Home Office will include details relating to a possible appeal to the courts. Section 33(3)(e) requires the notice to set out 'the steps the defaulter may take if he objects to the penalty'. A defaulter in this position may either object or appeal to the county court or the sheriff (Scotland), or do both. It is unclear whether the wider or narrower view of the term 'objects' will be adopted by the Home Office. The draft Code of Practice issued in January 2006 specified that information should be given relating to both possible avenues, 'objection' to the Secretary of State and an appeal to the courts.[31]

3. Paying the Civil Penalty

10.36 Defaulters will be given at least 14 days after the giving of the notice to pay the penalty. As there has not yet been an order setting out the manner in which the penalty notice must be given, it is unclear whether the 14-day minimum will run from the date of issue or the date of receipt.

10.37 The penalty imposed must be paid in the manner described by the notice (s 31(5)(a)).

10.38 During passage of the Bill through Parliament the Commons Standing Committee D debated a Conservative-proposed amendment which stated that penalty payments could be made in instalments. The minister agreed with the motivation behind the proposed amendment, but suggested that this was a matter for future statutory instruments and the Code of Practice.[32]

4. Amount

10.39 The draft Code of Practice suggests a 'general guideline' in civil penalty cases: 'Where it appears an individual is liable to a penalty and that it is reasonable in the circumstances to impose one, the Secretary of State would regard a figure of one quarter of the maximum penalty as appropriate'.[33]

10.40 As the draft code is indicative only, however, and has not been placed before or debated in Parliament, this information should be treated with caution.

10.41 Although this general guideline is set out in relation to consideration of objections, it is likely that the quarter figure (£250) will be adopted as the usual starting point for penalty notices which are issued.

---

[30] Draft Code of Practice (n 26 above).   [31] ibid.

[32] *Hansard*, HC Standing Committee D, col 429 (21 July 2005).   [33] See para 6.15.

5. Enforcement of Penalties

If the penalty is not paid, or is not paid in the manner prescribed, by the specified date, the amount is recoverable by the Secretary of State via the civil courts (s 31(5)). **10.42**

If the individual objects to the penalty and has notified the Secretary of State of this, recovery proceedings may not be instituted until the objector has been informed of the outcome of his or her objection (s 32(4)). However, no such explicit exclusion is included in the Act in the case of an appeal to the civil courts. Despite this omission in s 33, the draft Code of Practice envisages enforcement proceedings only being instituted 'where a person has exhausted his objection and appeal rights and has nevertheless failed to pay the penalty'.[34] It is suggested that this is a sensible approach and should be followed by the Home Office. **10.43**

If enforcement proceedings are instituted while an appeal to the county court or the sheriff is pending, the appellant should seek interlocutory relief, such as a stay. **10.44**

There is a statutory bar placed on the defaulter raising the grounds of objection and appeal in the enforcement proceedings (s 31(6)). In other words, in proceedings for recovery of a penalty a person is not allowed to raise questions as to whether the defaulter was liable, whether the imposition of the penalty was unreasonable, or the amount of the penalty. The Explanatory Notes state that these matters should be raised instead on objection to the Secretary of State (s 32) or on appeal to the civil courts (s 33).[35] **10.45**

Once judgment has been obtained it may be enforced in the usual manner, such as through attachment of earnings orders and warrants of execution (England and Wales, Northern Ireland) or earnings arrestment or attachment (Scotland). **10.46**

The sums received by the Secretary of State pursuant to s 31 must be paid into the Consolidated Fund.[36] In certain circumstances, the Treasury is able to repay sums paid into the Consolidated Fund in error. **10.47**

There is no power of imprisonment for failure to pay the civil penalty. **10.48**

D. OBJECTIONS TO CIVIL PENALTIES

1. Overview

Under s 32, a person has the right to object to a penalty notice issued by the Secretary of State. **10.49**

---

[34] See para 7.1.   [35] Explanatory Notes to the Identity Cards Act 2006, para 176.

[36] The Consolidated Fund was created by the Exchequer and Audit Departments Act 1866 (as amended by the National Loans Act 1968). It provides that most gross tax revenue (less repayments)

10.50   Importantly, a person need not object before he or she can appeal a penalty to the courts under s 33. There is arguably a disincentive to object directly to the Secretary of State under this section as the Secretary of State has the power, among other things, to raise the amount of a civil fine, a power that is not available to the court on appeal. However, there is a countervailing disincentive to bypass the objection procedure and simply appeal to the courts, as an individual who loses in the courts will be liable to pay costs. The amount of the costs is likely to exceed any potential increase in the quantum of the penalty which the Secretary of State may impose.

10.51   An objection may not be made upon receipt of a warning letter, as s 32 only applies once the person has been given a penalty notice (s 31(1)). Nevertheless, it is suggested that in order to preserve one's position for subsequent proceedings, and to attempt to persuade the Secretary of State not to issue a penalty notice, an individual who receives a warning letter and who believes he or she should not be liable to a civil penalty, should put his or her concerns in writing at that point.

2. Notice of Objection

10.52   A person who receives a penalty notice may give notice to the Secretary of State that he or she objects. The notice must be on one or more of the following grounds:

(a) that he or she is not liable,
(b) that the circumstances make the imposition of the penalty unreasonable, or
(c) that the amount of the penalty is too high (s 32(1)).

10.53   The notice must include both the person's grounds for objecting (ie (a), (b) or (c) above) and the reasons for those grounds (s 32(2)(a)). The notice of objection must be given in a manner and within a timeframe to be prescribed by order (s 32(2)(b)). In contrast to other provisions of the Act, a statutory instrument made under s 32 may be made in the usual manner and is not subject to the affirmative resolution procedure.

10.54   It appears from the draft Code of Practice that the prescribed manner in which the notice must be made will be relatively flexible. The draft Code states that the objection 'should be given in writing (either by post or electronically)' but 'no other formality is required'.[37]

10.55   If possible, relevant evidence should also be provided with the notice of objection. Evidence may relate to any of the three grounds of objection: liability; unreasonableness; or the amount of the penalty.

---

and all other public monies payable to the Exchequer shall be paid into the 'Account of Her Majesty's Exchequer' and form one general fund. This account is kept by the Treasury at the Bank of England. The Consolidated Fund is at any point in time the amount standing to the credit of this 'Exchequer Account'.

[37] Draft Code of Practice (n 26 above) para 4.2.

If the objector claims he or she is not liable to a penalty under s 32(1)(a), **10.56** clear evidence must be provided. The objector may not be liable because he or she failed to notify the Secretary of State of a change of address, for example, but if he or she can prove that he or she did not in fact move house, or did notify the Secretary of State, evidence of this will result in the penalty being cancelled.

If the objector claims that the circumstances make the imposition of a **10.57** penalty unreasonable pursuant to s 32(1)(b), evidence of those circumstances will strengthen the objection. If the objector claims that payment of the penalty will result in financial hardship, evidence of the objector's low wages, benefits, or dependants should be provided. The draft Code of Practice makes clear that such evidence may be taken into account and may serve to reduce the penalty payable, regardless of whether there are any other mitigating factors. If the objector is claiming that his or her non-attendance at an appointment, for example, was caused by a medical reason, a family bereavement or the fact that he or she was abroad at the time, evidence (such as a medical certificate, death notice, airline ticket or statement from his or her employer) should be provided if possible. The draft Code of Practice accepts that such circumstances may constitute a good reason for non-compliance and may make the imposition of a penalty unreasonable.

There is another potential defence for a defaulter in the draft Code of **10.58** Practice. Even in the case of deliberate default, evidence of subsequent compliance with the relevant requirement—even after receiving a penalty notice—should lead to cancellation of the penalty. This is because the purpose of the penalty scheme is stated to be 'to encourage compliance rather than to punish'.[38] This was confirmed by Baroness Scotland, the Home Office Minister, during the passage of the Bill through Parliament:

The whole point of the civil penalties is not to provide punishment but a means of enforcement to get people to provide their biometric data. I must make it clear that if, at any stage in the process, the person says 'I'll come quietly and have my biometrics taken,' the penalty can be waived.[39]

If the objector claims that the amount of the penalty is too high under **10.59** s 32(1)(c), financial evidence will usually be needed. However, the claim may simply be that this was a minor infringement or a one-off failure, and so the amount payable is disproportionate. Objecting on this basis only is extremely unlikely to result in a cancellation of the penalty, and so those objecting may be advised to object on the basis of both (b) (unreasonableness) and (c) (amount too high).

If it is difficult to obtain relevant evidence within the timeframe pro- **10.60** vided, the objector should nevertheless refer to the financial, medical or other

---

[38] ibid, para 6.9. [39] *Hansard*, HL col 1538 (19 December 2005).

circumstances. The scheme is relatively flexible and further evidence may be requested. Alternatively, the fact that the objector made the mitigating or other circumstances known at an early stage may prove useful in any subsequent court proceedings.

3. Consideration by the Secretary of State

10.61 The Secretary of State must consider 'a notice of objection given in accordance with this section' (s 32(3)). There is no statutory duty to consider an objection which has not been made in the prescribed form. If the draft Code of Practice is followed, this will simply mean that an objection made over the telephone or in person, and not reduced to writing, will not be considered.

10.62 Having considered the notice of objection, the Secretary of State may then cancel the penalty (s 32(3)(a)), reduce it (s 32(3)(b)), increase it (s 32(3)(c)) or confirm it (s 32(3)(d)).

10.63 According to the draft Code of Practice, the Secretary of State in considering the objection will usually adopt as a starting point £250, a quarter of the maximum penalty. No distinction is made between penalties arising under ss 7, 10 or 11 at this point. However, the draft code continues:

> That figure may be further reduced if appropriate, e.g. there are mitigating circumstances or if there has since been a degree of compliance; or in the light of the defaulter's financial circumstances. If the contravention is particularly serious or there is a history of previous contraventions, the penalty will be increased accordingly.[40]

10.64 The financial circumstances of the objector will be relevant. The draft Code makes clear that reductions may be made to the amount payable where there is evidence to suggest that the level of the penalty would cause 'undue financial hardship' to the defaulter. However, 'only in the most extreme circumstances should that result in cancellation of the penalty. Rather the penalty should be reduced to an amount which is affordable.'[41]

10.65 Non-exhaustive examples of the circumstances in which cancellation or reduction are likely to be appropriate are set out in para 6 of the draft Code of Practice. Cancellation may be appropriate when there is 'genuine doubt' as to whether the objector was aware of the requirement with which he or she failed to comply.[42] First failures will not usually attract a penalty. Minor failures, such as failure to notify loss or damage to a card, should not usually be considered serious enough to attract a penalty.

10.66 Repeat refuseniks, however, may be liable to having their penalty increased if they object. The draft Code of Practice makes clear that 'successive failures should normally attract successively higher penalties, subject to the appropriate maximum'.[43]

---

[40] Draft Code of Practice, para 6.15. [41] ibid, para 6.13. [42] ibid, para 6.5.
[43] ibid, para 6.8.

If the penalty is reduced, increased or confirmed, the objector must be **10.67** notified in the prescribed manner, by a prescribed date. If the objector agrees, the length of time may be extended (s 32(5)). The draft Code of Practice suggests that the 'prescribed manner' for notifying the objector of the outcome will be straightforward, and will simply require the Secretary of State to inform the objector in writing.[44] If the penalty has been reduced, the Secretary of State must, obviously, inform the objector of the new, decreased amount to be paid (s 32(6)).

If the Secretary of State decides to increase the penalty, he must give the **10.68** objector a new penalty notice under s 31 (s 32(6)). It is suggested that the clock will begin running again at this point for the purpose of the time limits to be prescribed by statutory instrument. At this point, it is highly unlikely that an objector would again exercise his or her right to object to the Home Office, and he or she would instead be advised to appeal to the civil courts pursuant to s 34.

E. APPEALS

1. Overview

Section 33 sets out another procedure for an individual who has been issued **10.69** with a penalty notice and who objects to that penalty: an appeal to the civil courts. In England and Wales and Northern Ireland an appeal lies to the county court (s 33(7)(a)); in Scotland, an appeal lies to the sheriff (s 33(7)(b)).

2. The Appeal

The grounds of appeal are identical to those which may form the basis of an **10.70** objection to the Secretary of State: (a) the person is not liable to the penalty; (b) the circumstances make the imposition of the penalty unreasonable; or (c) the amount of the penalty is too high.

There is a time limit to any appeal, as specified by the rules of court (s 33(2)). **10.71** At the time of writing no applicable time limits have been set.

The appeal is a re-hearing of the Secretary of State's decision to impose the **10.72** penalty (s 33(4)). Pursuant to s 33(5) the court may take into account all matters that it considers relevant, including matters of which the Secretary of State was unaware and matters which the county court or the sheriff would ordinarily be prevented from considering due to the rules of court.

The court must have regard to the Code of Practice in determining its appeal. **10.73** Section 6 of the draft Code sets out guidance.

---

[44] ibid, para 4.3.

3. Outcome

10.74 After hearing the appeal, there will be three possible decisions which the court can make:

(1) the court may allow the appeal and cancel the penalty (s 33(3)(a));
(2) the court may allow the appeal and reduce the penalty (s 33(3)(b));
(3) the court may dismiss the appeal (s 33(3)(c)).

10.75 There is no provision allowing the court to increase the penalty as the Secretary of State may do after an objection under s 32. The Conservatives queried this absence in Parliament.

10.76 The Home Office did not accept that it would be justified in giving the court a power to increase the penalty:

> On balance, we do not think that the amendment is desirable. It certainly would not follow the pattern of similar civil penalty schemes, such as the carriers' liability scheme in the Immigration and Asylum Act 1999, under which the court is not empowered to increase the penalties.
>
> The opportunity to appeal to the court is provided as a means of ensuring that, even though civil penalties are unilaterally imposed by the Secretary of State, the Article 6 right—that is, the right to a fair trial for those on whom penalties are imposed—is respected. The purpose of the appeal is not for the court to mete out further punishment to the appellant, but to ensure that those rights under Article 6 are respected. The Secretary of State decides what the appropriate penalty is and, at the objection stage, whether to increase it.[45]

10.77 The Conservative amendment was then, with leave, withdrawn.

F. CODE OF PRACTICE

1. Issuing the Code of Practice

10.78 Under s 34 of the Identity Cards Act 2006 the Secretary of State must issue a code of practice setting out the matters to be considered when determining whether to impose a civil penalty and, if so, the appropriate quantum.

10.79 Before issuing the code, the Secretary of State must lay a draft of it before Parliament. It must be approved by a resolution of each House (the 'affirmative resolution' procedure) (s 34(9)). The code does not come into force until the time specified by order made by the Secretary of State.

10.80 The Secretary of State may revise the code from time to time in whole or in part and issue the revised code (s 34(7)). Again, a draft must be laid before Parliament and is subject to the affirmative resolution procedure.

---

[45] *Hansard*, HC Standing Committee D, col 431 (21 July 2005).

2. Status of the Code

10.81 The Secretary of State must 'have regard to' the code when either imposing a civil penalty, or considering a notice of objection (s 34(2)).

10.82 In the House of Lords, the Liberal Democrats were dissatisfied with the relegation of what they considered to be fundamental procedural safeguards, such as the issuing of a warning letter prior to the issuing of a penalty notice, to the code.[46]

10.83 Baroness Scotland justified the code:

We all expect professionals to comply with it, and if they do not do so there will be consequences. The noble Lord knows perfectly well that codes are not soft; they are quite hard-edged. They set out the standards that we expect from other people, and they set out the routine, the parameters and the consequences. That is why we think it is very important that there is a code.[47]

10.84 The Home Office has accepted that the initial warning letter is likely to be generated based on a standard template, but as soon as an individual response to a warning letter or an objection notification is received the code will then be the appropriate framework for determination. The audience for the code is two-fold: it indicates to those enforcing the provisions of the Identity Cards Act 2006 the efficient, effective and fair approach to their duties; and it also enables the public to know exactly what is expected of them, what the consequences are, and what enforcement will be like.

10.85 The court must also have regard to the code when determining an appeal (s 34(3)). It is suggested that the code will be relevant in determining factors such as reasonableness and quantum, but not liability itself. Liability is a question of law, the construction of an Act of Parliament. That cannot be determined by a code of practice which is subject to change at any time, albeit subject to the affirmative resolution procedure. This distinction has been recently affirmed by the High Court in relation to the Special Educational Needs Code of Practice: *K v (1) Special Educational Needs Disability Tribunal and (2) Governing Body of Slough Grammar School*.[48]

G. CIVIL PROCEEDINGS

10.86 Civil proceedings may also arise under the Identity Cards Act 2006 in three other situations:

(i) Pursuant to s 9(6): if the Secretary of State makes an order specifying a person as having a duty to provide certain information to him, and that

---

[46] *Hansard*, HL cols 1539–1540 (19 December 2005).
[47] *Hansard*, HL col 1541 (19 December 2005).   [48] [2006] EWHC 622 (Admin) at [22].

person fails to comply, the Secretary of State may institute proceedings to enforce that duty.

(ii) Pursuant to s 16(4): an individual may institute civil proceedings against a person who unlawfully requires him or her to produce an ID card or imposes a requirement for failure to produce an ID card.

(iii) Pursuant to s 38(5): if the Secretary of State makes an order specifying a person as having a duty to provide certain information to him relating to passport applications, and that person fails to comply, the Secretary of State may institute proceedings to enforce that duty.

11

OVERSIGHT OF THE NATIONAL IDENTITY SCHEME

A. INTRODUCTION

The National Identity Register, ID cards and their supporting infrastructure **11.01** established by the Identity Cards Act 2006 are subject to oversight in a number of ways and from a number of sources. There are certain Act-specific types of oversight, but some provisions may also be subject to other general types of supervision, such as oversight under the Data Protection Act 1988 by the Information Commissioner. In addition to the systems overseeing the system in general, individuals who have grievances relating to their own particular experiences with the scheme have a number of possible remedies, which are dealt with in chapter 12.

Supervision of the scheme is multi-handed. The newly-created National Iden- **11.02** tity Scheme Commissioner has a number of specific oversight functions under the Act, but he or she is excluded from considering many aspects of the scheme's operation, including the civil penalty appeals process and criminal offences. The jurisdiction of the Intelligence Services Commissioner and Tribunal is expanded, so that they have responsibility for oversight of the provision of information from the Register to intelligence and security agencies. There is no general supervision of the civil penalty process, although in individual cases fresh appeals may be made to the county court (England and Wales and Northern Ireland) or the sheriff (Scotland).[1] The imposition of criminal penalties is to be carried out by the criminal courts.

---

[1] See further chapters 10 and 12.

11.03   It is unclear whether and to what extent the Information Commissioner will be able to guard against misuse of the Register. It seems likely that, given the Identity Cards Act's specification of content, retention, disclosure and purpose, and the new National Identity Scheme Commissioner's office, the Information Commissioner may only have a role in practice in relation to unlawful processing or inadequate security of the database.[2] The Information Commissioner himself has expressed concern at the 'gaps in the oversight arrangements, including lack of comprehensive powers for the Information Commissioner to check on data protection compliance'.[3]

11.04   There are four main bodies with supervision powers over the national identity scheme: Parliament, the new National Identity Scheme Commissioner, the Intelligence Services Commissioner, and the Office of Surveillance Commissioners. The role of each is considered below.

B. PARLIAMENT

1. Overview

11.05   The Identity Cards Act 2006 has been repeatedly described by government as 'enabling' legislation: it simply sets out the framework, and the detail will be added through regulations at a later stage. This feature of the legislation understandably caused Parliament concern, as MPs and Peers did not want important decisions which would have significant financial, security and civil liberties implications to be made by the Executive without adequate oversight.

11.06   There are over 60 occasions envisaged within the Act on which the Secretary of State may exercise his regulation-making power. He is also responsible for establishing and maintaining the Register, the core of the scheme, and he is responsible for overseeing the civil penalties system and dealing with objections received from individuals.

11.07   Despite the breadth of the powers afforded to the Secretary of State under the Act, there are two ways in which Parliament certainly has continuing oversight of the developing national identity scheme: it may reject statutory instruments making regulations or orders pursuant to the Act, and the Secretary of State must report to Parliament on the operation costs of the scheme at least every six months. Given the enabling nature of the Act itself, it is suggested that there are two matters which may be of particular relevance to Parliament in exercising their oversight powers: impact assessments and 'function creep'.

11.08   In addition, the Parliamentary Commissioner for Administration may have a role in responding to individual complaints relating to the scheme's operation.[4]

---

[2] 'Confidence and Data Protection: news and views' (2004) 4 *Privacy and Data Protection* 14.
[3] *The Identity Cards Bill—The Information Commissioner's Concerns* (June 2005).
[4] See chapter 12 for a further discussion on remedies.

2. Statutory Instruments

Statutes which confer powers to make regulations or orders by statutory instrument generally specify which of three general types of Parliamentary procedure must be followed: **11.09**

(i) Affirmative resolution procedure: the statutory instrument is laid before Parliament in draft and can only be made when approved by affirmative resolution in each House. This means that it is always subject to debate in each House.

(ii) Negative resolution procedure: the statutory instrument containing the regulations or order is laid before Parliament and must be revoked if either House passes a resolution against it within 40 Parliamentary days. A statutory instrument subject to the negative procedure is normally laid at least 21 days before it is to come into effect to ensure scrutiny of the instrument before its provisions come into force.

(iii) Approval after being made: the statutory instrument is laid before Parliament after being made. It ceases to have effect after 28 Parliamentary days unless it is approved by resolution of each House during the 28-day period. Should the regulations cease to have effect at the end of the 28 days, anything done under the regulations during the period remains effective and new regulations may be made.

The Identity Cards Act 2006 uses all three forms of statutory instrument. The Bill as originally introduced in Parliament also relied on an enhanced form of (i) above, a 'super-affirmative' procedure. This was the procedure proposed for clause 6, when the Secretary of State would make certain groups of persons subject to compulsory registration. As this clause was removed during the passage of the Bill through Parliament, the 'super-affirmative' procedure has disappeared from the final version of the Act. **11.10**

The default position is set out at s 40(3): unless otherwise stated, a statutory instrument is subject to the negative resolution procedure. **11.11**

Many of the sections in the Act which proved controversial in Parliament are subject to an affirmative resolution procedure before the Secretary of State can trigger their use. No fewer than 18 sections of the Act include the affirmative resolution safeguard.[5] **11.12**

Whilst the affirmative resolution procedure does provides a check on the government's ability to extend its powers, the affirmative resolution procedure is a relatively blunt tool for legislative scrutiny. A draft regulation must either stand or fall as a whole. If Parliamentarians agree with some, but not all, aspects of a proposed regulation, they have no ability to suggest amendments. **11.13**

Although all 18 sections envisage affirmative resolution, there are distinctions **11.14**

---

[5] ss 2, 4, 5, 6, 8, 9, 10, 12, 13 (procedure set out in s 14), 15, 17, 20, 21, 26, 34, 35, 38 and 39.

between them. In three situations, not only must there be a vote affirming the Secretary of State's draft in each House of Parliament, but there must also be a prior consultation procedure.[6] In three cases, although the section requires affirmative resolution, this is a one-off requirement: on the first occasion on which a statutory instrument is made under the section, a resolution of both Houses is required, but thereafter any subsequent regulations are subject only to the weaker negative resolution procedure.[7] Under s 39, only regulations which modify a (passport-related) statute are subject to affirmative resolution (s 39(6)), but other regulations made pursuant to this section will stand unless annulled by one of the Houses of Parliament.

11.15   In November 2005 the Parliamentary Select Committee on Delegated Powers and Regulatory Reform concluded that Parliamentary scrutiny of the Identity Cards Bill needed to be enhanced. Unlike the other Parliamentary Committees which focused on the substance of the Bill,[8] this Committee examined the procedural aspects of the Bill, and analyzed whether the executive arm of government was seeking excessive powers without sufficient Parliamentary scrutiny.

11.16   At the time of the Committee's report, compulsion was to be introduced through regulations, albeit subject to the 'super-affirmative resolution' process. The Committee concluded that this procedure was, 'not an appropriate alternative to a Bill for potentially controversial measures of great public concern'.[9] (Clause 6, the compulsion clause, was subsequently removed from the Bill following repeated rejections by the House of Lords.)

11.17   The Committee also criticized what is now s 13 of the Act, the power to make public services conditional on identity checks. They stated that, 'we consider it is not appropriate to leave the application of that policy to subordinate legislation'. Rather, they argued, such a power should only be introduced following fresh primary legislation at a later stage in the national identity project.

3. Cost

11.18   During the Identity Cards Bill's passage through Parliament, the likely cost of the scheme was controversial. Estimates differed wildly, and figures relating to the running costs, cost of ID cards, and the likely fees and charges to individuals, organizations and government departments to access or modify information, constantly changed.

---

[6] ss 14 (public services), 15 (checks on the Register) and 34 (Code of Practice on Civil Penalties).
[7] ss 5(7), 10(6) and 34.
[8] See in particular Joint Committee on Human Rights, Fifth Report of Session 2004–05, *Identity Cards Bill*, 2 February 2005 (HL 35/HC 283); Home Affairs Select Committee, Fourth Report of Session 2003–04, *Identity Cards*, 30 July 2004 (HC 130-I); Select Committee on the Constitution, Third Report of Session 2005–06, *Identity Cards Bill*, 24 October 2005 (HL 44).
[9] *Hansard*, HL col 1060 (12 December 2005).

The government argued that the Bill would be 'self-financing'. Critics argued **11.19** that any shortfalls in the finances were likely to be met by increasing charges to individuals for the issue of ID cards or the notification of any errors or changes in their recorded information, or rigorously enforcing the civil penalties scheme. Lobby groups representing vulnerable groups (such as the elderly, young, poor or mentally ill) suggested that such moves would disproportionately affect the groups they represented.

Given these concerns, in January 2006 the House of Lords amended the **11.20** Bill to include a requirement that the government carry out a detailed analysis on the costs of the scheme and report to Parliament before it could be implemented.

The Lords' amendment was rejected by the House of Commons, but a com- **11.21** promise was reached: rather than conducting a pre-scheme analysis of cost, the Secretary of State would regularly report to Parliament on the existing and likely costs which the scheme was incurring. This would ensure continuing Parliamentary oversight without upsetting the Home Office's implementation timetable.

Section 37 sets out the procedure for the Secretary of State's report. The **11.22** first report must be laid before Parliament on or before 30 September 2006 (s 37(1)). It must set out his estimate of 'the public expenditure likely to be incurred on the ID cards scheme during the ten years beginning with the laying of his report'. This includes likely expenditure of the Secretary of State and designated documents authorities on three items:

(a) the establishment and maintenance of the Register (s 37(3)(a));

(b) the issue, modification, renewal, replacement, re-issue and surrender of ID cards (s 37(3)(b));

(c) the provision to persons by the Secretary of State of information recorded in individuals' entries in the Register (s 37(3)(c)).

The duty created by s 37 is a continuing one: the Secretary of State must **11.23** prepare and lay before Parliament such a report at least every six months. Each time, his report must project likely expenditure ten years from that date, rather than from the date of Royal Assent for the Act.

There are three limitations to the s 37 duty. First, it requires the Secretary of **11.24** State to detail future likely expenditure only, not expenditure already incurred. In practice, he may include this information in his report, but it is not explicitly included in s 37.

Second, the requirement relates to 'expenditure' only, and not income. Monies **11.25** obtained through fees charged to accredited organizations for use of the verification system, from bodies who have paid to access information on the Register, charges to individuals for re-issuing ID cards which the Secretary of State has recalled or cancelled, or modifying their information on the Register, will not be included within his Parliamentary report.

11.26   Third, s 37(4) provides that the Secretary of State may edit his report due to procurement reasons: if it appears to him that publication of a particular matter would be 'prejudicial to securing the best value from the use of public money', he may exclude that matter from his report. Although it is sensible that this caveat is included, it is noted that there is no requirement to indicate to Parliament that he has exercised this right of exclusion. Such a requirement would have upheld commercial confidentiality and the public interest in securing best value in procurement on the one hand, but would also have served to maximize Parliament's ability to scrutinize the finances of the scheme.

4. Impact Assessments

11.27   The Racial Equality Impact Assessments (REIAs) and the Regulatory Impact Assessment (RIA) published alongside the Identity Cards Bill were necessarily partial only, as the full impact of the scheme which the Bill was to establish could not be assessed in the absence of further detail. In these circumstances, it is arguable that statutory instruments implementing key aspects of the scheme should be accompanied by REIAs or RIAs, as appropriate, in order to facilitate meaningful Parliamentary scrutiny. The government has indicated that there a series of impact assessments will be made at various stages in secondary legislation as operational detail emerges.

11.28   The three sections which require a consultation to be carried out prior to statutory instruments being laid before Parliament (related to identity checks for public services (ss 13 and 14), checks on the Register (s 15), and civil penalties (s 34)) would benefit from detailed impact assessments about how the measures will affect businesses and vulnerable minorities in particular.[10]

11.29   The Commission for Racial Equality (CRE) was highly critical of both the substance and the form of the REIAs produced by the Home Office to accompany the Identity Cards Bill, considering them to be inadequate and out of keeping with CRE guidelines.[11] They extrapolated from statistics on police use of stop and search powers that the Bill would lead to differential treatment in service provision. Foreign nationals, refugees, ethnic minorities, gypsies and travellers would be stigmatized and face difficulty in accessing public services, they argued.

11.30   The CRE recommended that full Parliamentary scrutiny was required at each stage of implementation, and that consideration should be given to alternative policies which might achieve the government's aims, or options which would mitigate adverse impacts on particular racial, ethnic, religious or national groups. It is suggested that these concerns should be borne in mind by Parliamentarians, particularly when considering regulations which will implement the power under

---

[10] Under the Cabinet Office's Code of Practice on Consultation (January 2004), such impact assessments may be required in these circumstances (see in particular principle (vi)).

[11] CRE Briefing, *Identity Cards Bill: House of Lords Report Stage*, 16 January 2006, 1.

s 13 to make services provided by the public and private sector dependent on identity checks.

5. 'Function Creep' and Parliament's Role

As many of the definitions contained in the Act are potentially broad, and **11.31** assurances were made in Parliament by Home Office ministers that they would be sensibly or narrowly implemented, Parliamentarians should be alert to the possibility of 'function creep' in exercising their oversight powers.

C. THE NATIONAL IDENTITY SCHEME COMMISSIONER

1. Overview

Section 22 establishes a National Identity Scheme Commissioner to oversee **11.32** the operation of the ID cards scheme and the National Identity Register. The Commissioner has certain powers, set out in s 22, and reporting duties, set out in s 23.

Although the Commissioner's role has been strengthened significantly since **11.33** the 2005–06 Identity Cards Bill began its passage through Parliament, and the position no longer suffers from what a House of Commons research paper termed 'regulatory impotence',[12] it is far from the full, robust and independent watchdog of the scheme which many critics called for. The Commissioner's functions are strictly limited; he or she is explicitly excluded from reviewing crucial aspects of the Act; staffing levels, resources and appointment terms for the Commissioner are to be determined by the Secretary of State; and, even if the Commissioner discovers misuse or abuse in the operation of the scheme, there is no provision to require him or her to bring this to the attention of the individual affected or to provide any remedy.

2. Appointment

The National Identity Scheme Commissioner is to be appointed by the Crown, **11.34** on the recommendation of the Secretary of State (s 22(1)).

The UK has a range of different statutory commissioners, some appointed by **11.35** the Queen, some by the Prime Minister, and some by the Secretary of State. Certain commissioners appointed by the Queen nevertheless report to the Secretary of State, such as HM Inspectors of Constabulary and HM Inspector of Prisons. In the case of the Information Commissioner, he is appointed by the Queen by Letters Patent, is a corporation sole, and reports directly to Parliament.

---

[12] *The Identity Cards Bill, Bill 9 of 2005–06*, House of Commons Research Paper 05/43 (13 June 2005) 49.

11.36   In the draft Bill published by the Home Office in April 2004, clause 25(1) provided that the Commissioner must be appointed by the Prime Minister. However, the original Bill presented to Parliament in July 2005 instead provided that the Secretary of State, not the Prime Minister, would be responsible for appointment (clause 24(1)). This proved controversial in the House of Lords in particular.[13] The government dismissed concern over the appointment mechanism, indicating that it was only an 'issue of presentation' and would have no practical impact.[14]

11.37   Whether the Commissioner's appointment is to be made by the Secretary of State, the Prime Minister or the Queen on their recommendation is important in relation to his or her independence. The practical import of the appointment system is two-fold. First, the process of an appointment by the Queen or Prime Minister rather than the relevant Secretary of State will mean that the appointment (or dismissal) of the Commissioner will be at some distance from the department that is subject to the oversight. If the responsibility for appointment is that of the Secretary of State for the very department being reviewed, then if the office holder is critical of the department, decisions as to his or her re-appointment or dismissal might be tainted. This would be less likely to arise were the appointment process more distant from the department subject to the oversight. Second, although there is rarely likely to be a conflict of interest in practice, the appointment process is still important in terms of the perception of the independence of the appointee, and his or her ability to act as a check and balance on the Secretary of State and his department's use of their powers.

11.38   There is another aspect of the provisions governing the Commissioner's office which arguably has the potential to undermine his or her independence, and the perception of independence. The Act provides no detail on the terms of the Commissioner's appointment. Section 22(6) simply provides that 'the Commissioner is to hold office in accordance with the terms of his appointment'. There is no statutory security of tenure, as no term of office is set out in the Act. Nor is provision made for the circumstances in which the Commissioner may be dismissed.

11.39   This statutory silence may be contrasted with other statutes governing office holders. The Criminal Appeal Act 1995, for example, which created the Criminal Cases Review Commission, indicates the term of appointment for office holders (fixed term of up to five years),[15] whether the office holder will be eligible for re-appointment at the end of that term (he or she will, provided he or she does not serve a continuous term of office in excess of ten years),[16] and the circumstances giving rise to dismissal.[17] Similar provisions are set out in the governing statutes

---

[13] See in particular the debate concerning Lord Phillips of Sudbury's proposed Amendment 76A: *Hansard*, HL col 37 (30 January 2006).
[14] ibid.   [15] Criminal Appeal Act 1995, Sch 1, para 2(3).   [16] ibid, Sch 1, para 2(4) and (5).
[17] ibid, Sch 1, para 2(7).

for the Commission for Equality and Human Rights[18] and the Independent Police Complaints Commission.[19] The Regulation of Investigatory Powers Act 2000 (RIPA) details the terms of appointment linked to offices it creates.[20] The Data Protection Act 1998 also sets out the rules relating to the Information Commissioner's retirement.[21]

3. Staffing

Staff numbers will not be determined until after the Commissioner has been appointed, as s 22(7) provides that the Secretary of State must first consult with the Commissioner and obtain Treasury approval before providing such staff as he (the Secretary of State) considers necessary for the carrying out of the Commissioner's functions. **11.40**

4. Functions of the Commissioner

The Commissioner's functions are set out in s 22(2), (3) and (4). He or she has four specific functions, set out in s 22(2)(a)–(d). These functions all involve oversight of the operation of the national ID scheme. This is an exhaustive list and the Commissioner has no additional implied functions. Seven matters are explicitly excluded from the Commissioner's remit by s 22(4)(a)–(g). **11.41**

During the final stages of the Identity Cards Bill's passage through Parliament in 2006, there was a late amendment to what is now s 22 moved by the government.[22] This amendment was designed, Home Office Minister Baroness Scotland told the House, to address concerns expressed by the Lords during Committee stage. It provided clarification of the Commissioner's functions as set out in s 22(2)(a)–(d), and confirmed that two matters were included within those functions despite doubts which had been expressed. **11.42**

First, she noted that the Lords had been 'particularly concerned' about the handling of complaints, but that, 'as the amendment clarifies, the Commissioner will have oversight of the complaints handling procedures and, no doubt, will include in his report any concerns that he or she might have about the way in which the agency is handling any complaints that it receives'.[23] Second, she stated: 'I was most attentive to the concerns raised by noble Lords in Committee, in particular those about the security and integrity of the information held on the register. It is clear from this amendment that the commissioner must have regard to that and will report on it.'[24] **11.43**

---

[18] Equality Act 2006, Sch 1. The tenure of Commissioners, reappointment and dismissal are set out in para 3.

[19] Police Reform Act 2002, Sch 2. Commissioners are appointed for fixed terms of up to five years (paras 1(3) and 2(4)). Reasons for and method of dismissal from the IPCC are set out in para 2(6).

[20] Office-holders under RIPA have three-year terms with the possibility of reappointment.

[21] Data Protection Act 1998, Sch 5, Pt II, para 12(3).   [22] House of Lords, Amendment 77.

[23] *Hansard*, HL col 43 (30 January 2006).   [24] ibid.

11.44   The government's amendment was agreed to and now forms s 22(3) of the Act. It does not add to the four functions of the Commissioner as set out in s 22(2), but it does clarify the scope of the first three functions.

11.45   The first function is to keep under review 'the arrangements for the time being maintained' by the Secretary of State for the purposes of his functions under the Act or associated regulations (s 22(2)(a)). The second function is a mirror provision relating to designated documents authorities: to keep under review their arrangements for the purposes of their functions under the Act or associated regulations (s 22(2)(b)).

11.46   The Commissioner's third function is to review the arrangements made for obtaining, recording and using information under the Act by 'persons to whom information may be provided' (s 22(2)(c)).

11.47   The fourth and final function of the Commissioner is to review the uses to which ID cards are being put. Performance of this function will be heavily reliant on the staffing and funding made available to the Commissioner by the Treasury pursuant to s 22(6). One of the concerns relating to the Commissioner which arose in Parliament was that of resources. Provision is not made for specific funding in this legislation, nor could it easily be. As with any non-departmental office, the Treasury holds the purse strings. However, as likely expenditure under s 22(6) must be included in the Secretary of State's six-monthly expenditure report to Parliament (s 37), it is suggested that any under-funding may be noticed by Parliament, and this may have an impact on resourcing decisions.

11.48   Section 22(4) provides that the matters to be kept under review by the Commissioner do not include seven issues, listed as (a) to (g). The Explanatory Notes to the Act set out the matters which will not be part of the Commissioner's functions,[25] such as appeals against civil penalties (which will be dealt with by the civil courts), criminal offences (which will be dealt with by the criminal courts), and the verification powers for passports under s 38. The provision of information to the intelligence and security agencies also falls outside the remit of the National Identity Scheme Commissioner, but is subject to oversight by the Intelligence Services Commissioner (s 24).

5. Duty to Provide Information to the Commissioner

11.49 It is the duty of every Home Office official to provide the Commissioner with 'all such information (including information recorded in the Register) as he may require for the purpose of carrying out his functions under this Act' (s 22(5)). Provision of such information is lawful under s 27.

11.50   This duty is specific to the Home Office. There is no similar statutory duty placed on others, such as employees or officials of designated document

---

[25] Explanatory Notes, para 142.

authorities. As the duty relates to 'all such information' the Commissioner 'may' require to carry out his or her 'functions' under the Act, it is suggested that the duty relates not only to the s 2(2)(a) function, but to all four functions.

6. Freedom of Information

The new Commissioner will be a public authority for the purposes of the   **11.51**
Freedom of Information Act 2000 (s 22(8)).

7. Reports by the Commissioner

Under s 23, the Commissioner must lay an annual report before Parliament   **11.52**
about the carrying out of his or her functions.

The previous incarnations of this duty in clause 25 of the draft Bill and the   **11.53**
2004–05 Identity Cards Bill provided that the Commissioner's report would be
made to the Secretary of State, not Parliament. The new provision allows for
stronger oversight. There is a 'vetting' right for the Secretary of State under
s 23(4), however. If it appears to the Secretary of State, after consultation with
the Commissioner, that publication of a particular matter in a report would be
prejudicial to national security or the prevention and detection of crime, it may
be removed from the report laid before Parliament. In those circumstances, the
Secretary of State would need to lay a statement before Parliament that a matter
had been excluded (s 23(5)).

8. Limitations

Many of the concerns raised relating to the Commissioner at pre-legislative   **11.54**
stage and during the Bill's passage through Parliament have been dealt with in
the final Act: the Commissioner now reports directly to Parliament and the
functions extend beyond those originally included in the Home Office's draft
Bill. Criticisms remain, particularly in relation to the limits on the Commissioner's powers and his or her ability to assist individuals affected by the new
identity infrastructure.

The Information Commissioner welcomed the expansion of the new Com-   **11.55**
missioner's role in the 2004–05 Bill which eventually became the Identity Cards
Act 2006, but he stated that this did not go far enough:

The powers stop short of providing sanctions against those who transgress, save for
reporting this to the Secretary of State or Parliament. There are also no formal duties in
relation to complaints from aggrieved individuals who may be suffering detriment as a
result of administrative or other failings. The Information Commissioner's own powers
under the Data Protection Act to undertake audits should be extended to cover the
Identity Card scheme—a power similar to that enjoyed by other European Data Protection

Commissioners. An audit should not have to depend upon the consent of the Agency running the scheme.[26]

11.56 During a debate in the House of Lords on the Bill (on a proposed amendment relating to the method of appointment), an indication of how the government may perceive the Commissioner's likely role was provided by a Labour Peer:

> The noble Lord is not, I think, advocating complete independence, such as the Information Commissioner has. The Information Commissioner has the power to serve enforcement and information notices on data controllers, Secretary of State data controllers included. He also has the power to bring prosecutions. Total independence is therefore entirely appropriate in such a case. The National Identity Scheme Commissioner, by contrast, has a rather different role—that of reviewing and reporting—so that both the Secretary of State and Parliament benefit from his overseeing the scheme.[27]

D. THE INTELLIGENCE SERVICES COMMISSIONER AND TRIBUNAL

1. Overview

11.57 Section 24 amends the RIPA 2000. RIPA sets out the functions of the Intelligence Services Commissioner and the Investigatory Powers Tribunal, and s 24 adds to their functions oversight of the provision of information held on the Register to the intelligence and security agencies as defined in that Act.

2. Intelligence Services Commissioner

11.58 RIPA defines the Intelligence Services Commissioner's role. Essentially, his or her function is oversight of the Intelligence Services (except interception practices),[28] and the Secretary of State, Ministry of Defence and the army in relation to their exercise of powers under RIPA, the Intelligence Services Act 1994, and the Security Service Act 1989. This function is now expanded by s 24 of the Identity Cards Act 2006.

11.59 The Intelligence Services Commissioner is empowered to carry out bi-annual visits to the Intelligence Services, departments of the relevant Secretaries of State and the Ministry of Defence. All members of the Intelligence Services, the armed forces and officials of the Secretary of State's department are required to provide any information and assistance necessary to enable the Commissioner to carry out his functions.

11.60 All breaches of legislation or codes of practice are reported to the Commissioner and included in the Commissioner's annual report to the Prime Minister,

---

[26] *The Identity Cards Bill: the Information Commissioner's Perspective*, December 2004, 4.

[27] *Hansard*, HL col 39 (30 January 2006) (Lord Bassam).

[28] Oversight of interception is carried out by the Interception of Communications Commissioner.

which also documents his or her findings on the work of the Intelligence Services throughout the previous year. The Prime Minister then lays a copy of the report before each house of Parliament. The report is divided into a publishable section and a confidential annexe. The publishable section should contain as much information as possible without compromising the work of the Intelligence Services.

3. Investigatory Powers Tribunal

The Investigatory Powers Tribunal provides oversight by reacting to complaints made by members of the public. The potential for the Tribunal to provide remedies in individual cases concerning the national identity scheme is examined in chapter 12.

11.61

E. OFFICE OF SURVEILLANCE COMMISSIONERS

Finally, the Office of Surveillance Commissioners (OSC) may have a limited oversight role in relation to the operation of the Identity Cards Act 2006. The OSC is responsible for oversight of property interference under Pt III of the Police Act 1997, and surveillance and the use of 'covert human intelligence sources' by all organizations bound by RIPA, other than the intelligence services.

11.62

12

REMEDIES

A. INTRODUCTION

Aside from the general oversight provisions within the Identity Cards Act 2006   **12.01**
itself, there are a number of other ways that an individual who is aggrieved can
seek redress. Such remedies include resort to the Information Commissioner,
the civil courts (via the Human Rights Act 1998 (HRA) or otherwise), the
Parliamentary Ombudsmen, and other sector-specific oversight bodies.

B. INFORMATION COMMISSIONER

The Information Commissioner's Office is an independent body responsible   **12.02**
in part for safeguarding personal information by regulating and enforcing the
Data Protection Act 1998 (DPA). As a guardian of personal privacy rights, it
is anticipated that the Information Commissioner will have a large role in super-
vising the National Identity Scheme alongside the National Identity Scheme
Commissioner. Indeed, the government made it clear during the Parliamentary
debates that 'the Information Commissioner's powers relating to data protection and freedom of information will apply to the operation of the national
identity register'.[1]

For the purposes of the DPA, the Secretary of State is considered to be a 'data   **12.03**
controller' and therefore must adhere to the data protection principles spelled

---

[1] *Hansard*, HL col 1518 (19 December 2005).

out in the DPA.[2] There are eight data protection principles which can be found in Sch 1 to the DPA:

(i)   personal data shall be processed fairly and lawfully;

(ii)   personal data shall be obtained only for one or more specified and lawful purposes, and shall not be further processed in any manner incompatible with that purpose or those purposes;

(iii) personal data shall be adequate, relevant and not excessive in relation to the purpose or purposes for which they are processed;

(iv) personal data processed for any purpose or purposes shall not be kept for longer than is necessary for that purpose or those purposes;

(v)   personal data shall be processed in accordance with the rights of data subjects under the DPA;

(vi) appropriate technical and organizational measures shall be taken against unauthorized or unlawful processing of personal data and against accidental loss or destruction of, or damage to, personal data;

(vii) personal data shall not be transferred to a country or territory outside the European Economic Area unless that country or territory ensures an adequate level of protection for the rights and freedoms of data subjects in relation to the processing of personal data.

12.04   The application of the DPA to the identity cards scheme and the corresponding status of the Secretary of State as a 'data controller' opens up a number of potential legal avenues for redress. For example, individuals are entitled to apply to the Information Commissioner under s 42 of the DPA for an assessment of whether a data controller is processing information in accordance with the DPA.

12.05   Individuals are also entitled to apply to see what personal information is held about them on the Register by making a subject access request under s 7 of the DPA. Requests should be made in writing and sent by recorded delivery to avoid any dispute about whether the request was received. The request should state that an individual is requesting personal information about him or herself pursuant to the DPA. The data controller is entitled to request a fee in order to process the information, which is usually £10,[3] but can be more depending on the nature of the information requested. The data controller should provide access to the information within 40 days. If an individual is unhappy with the outcome of a subject access request, he or she can ultimately complain to the Information Commissioner.

12.06   If there is an error in the information contained about an individual on the Register, that individual can apply to have the information removed or corrected

---

[2] As accepted by Baroness Scotland: *Hansard*, HL col 1519 (19 December 2005).

[3] Correct as of 22 April 2006: http://www.ico.gov.uk/eventual.aspx?id=6787&expmovie=1.

under the DPA.[4] If the Secretary of State refuses to amend the information, an individual can apply to the Information Commissioner for assistance, and ultimately to the courts under s 14 of the DPA. Section 14 states that a court may order the data controller to rectify, block, erase or destroy the data where the data being held is inaccurate. The Information Commissioner will want to be assured that the Secretary of State has adequate systems in place to ensure that the information contained within it is accurate, rather than leaving audit responsibilities solely to the individual concerned.[5]

The Information Commissioner is empowered by s 40 of the DPA to issue enforcement notices where a data controller is contravening any of the data protection principles. Failure to comply with such an order attracts criminal sanctions, thus the Secretary of State could be found liable for refusing to amend inaccurate information or for retaining personal information longer than is necessary for the purposes for which it was processed. This latter point might be difficult to prove, given that the statutory purposes as set out in s 1(3) of the Identity Cards Act 2006 are so broad.[6]   **12.07**

This raises a question about the way in which the DPA and the Identity Cards Act 2006 interact for the purposes of oversight. While the DPA undoubtedly applies to the National Identity Scheme, the way in which the scheme will be governed in practice remains to be seen. It is unclear whether the Identity Cards Act 2006 can be said to supersede the auditing requirements imposed by the DPA, thereby absolving the Secretary of State of certain DPA obligations. However, Richard Thomas, the current Information Commissioner, envisages his role as one of broad statutory oversight: **12.08**

The Government I am not sure is contemplating an independent body. I am just throwing this idea out for debate and discussion but, if there were to be such a body, then I would see it as being a dedicated body with wider concerns and purely the data protection ones, but I would then be a longstop responsible for a wide range of activities. I am not a dedicated sector-specific regulator but I would be a sort of longstop looking at the data protection aspects.[7]

---

[4] The government has indicated that this will not be necessary as it plans to make an individual's Register entry available to be checked securely online: *Hansard*, HL col 1521 (19 December 2005).

[5] For further information, see chapter 6.

[6] See the first supplementary memorandum submitted to the Home Affairs Select Committee by Dr C Pounder and S Cullen, eds, *Data Protection and Privacy Practice* (May 2004).

[7] Richard Thomas, evidence to the Home Affairs Select Committee, 3 February 2004, Q217.

C. CIVIL COURTS

1. Appealing Civil Penalties

12.09 Within the Identity Cards Act 2006, there is provision for an individual to access the civil courts in objecting to a civil penalty that is being imposed by the Secretary of State.[8]

2. Judicial Review

12.10 However, if an individual is aggrieved by any decision of the Secretary of State or the National Identity Scheme Commissioner within the context of the Identity Cards Act 2006, there is also an avenue of redress to the High Court by way of judicial review. Judicial review is a means by which an improper exercise of power can be remedied. The grounds for such cases are broadly that the body has acted illegally or irrationally, in bad faith, or disproportionately, or that the decision was reached unfairly because of a defect in the procedure which led to the decision.

12.11 The high threshold underlying judicial review applications make them difficult avenues by which to obtain redress. In general, an individual also cannot seek judicial review if alternative remedies are available. In any event, an application for leave to bring an application must be launched within three months of the grounds for judicial review having arisen.

3. The Human Rights Act 1998

(a) *Overview*

12.12 There has been much debate and discussion during the Identity Cards Bill's tumultuous passages through Parliament about the impact of the HRA on the National Identity Scheme. Lobby and opposition groups have consistently argued that parts of the legislation infringe the Articles of the European Convention on Human Rights, which was incorporated into domestic law by the HRA with effect from October 2000. Many of the claims made about the incompatibility of the National Identity Scheme as a whole with the HRA are overblown and will likely fail. However, it may well be that there will be successful HRA challenges which will arise out of the specific circumstances. This section examines the provisions of the Act that are likely to be prone to HRA criticism, and provides a framework for launching such a claim in the courts.

12.13 The main potential human rights challenges under the Identity Cards Act 2006 include challenges under Article 8 (right to respect for private and family

---

[8] For further information, see chapter 10.

life), Article 10 (freedom of expression), and Article 14 (prohibition against discrimination).

(b) *Challenging the Identity Cards Act 2006 in Practice*

Before examining each Article in turn, there is a question about whether the **12.14** Identity Cards Act 2006 as a whole will stand up to HRA scrutiny. Notably, Articles 8 and 10 contain qualified rights meaning that the rights can be restricted in certain limited circumstances. In particular, a public authority can restrict the rights under Articles 8 and 10 where such restriction is in accordance with the law, and necessary in a democratic society for the pursuit of a legitimate aim. The legitimate aims justifying restrictions on Articles 8 and 10 rights are national security, public safety or the economic well-being of the country, the prevention of disorder or crime, the protection of health or morals, or the protection of the rights and freedoms of others and, additionally in the context of Article 10, territorial integrity, the protection of the reputation of others, preventing the disclosure of information received in confidence, or maintaining the authority and impartiality of the judiciary.

Virtually all of the alleged interferences with privacy rights or the right to **12.15** freedom of expression under the Identity Cards Act 2006 will be considered to be 'in accordance with law' (ie because they are in accordance with the Identity Cards Act 2006 itself). The question of the Act's compliance with the remaining requirements of Articles 8(2) and 10(2) remains to be decided—whether the aims of the Identity Cards Act 2006 are legitimate and whether the provisions of the Act are proportionate to achieving such aims.

A restriction on the right to respect for private life or freedom of expression **12.16** will only be lawful if it is implemented for one of the legitimate aims set out in Articles 8(2) or 10(2), respectively. An issue under Articles 8 or 10 might arise under the Identity Cards Act 2006 if the statutory purposes as set out in s 1(3) and (4) are considered to be broader than the permissible legitimate aim restrictions in Articles 8(2) or 10(2). Indeed, the Identity Cards Act 2006 provides that the Register is to be established and maintained only for the statutory purposes, which are to facilitate the provision of a convenient method for individuals to prove their identity, and for registrable facts about an individual to be checked wherever it is necessary in the public interest. Public interest is defined extremely broadly, encompassing not only national security, prevention or detection of crime but also the enforcement of immigration controls, the enforcement of prohibitions on unauthorized working or employment, and for securing the efficient and effective provision of public services.[9] However, the scope of the 'public interest' definition is even broader than it appears at first blush, as the definition of 'public services' goes on to demonstrate. The 'provision of a public service' is defined in s 42(2) and (3) and includes the 'provision of any service to an

---

[9] For further information, see chapter 5.

individual by a public authority', including where an individual is stopped and searched by the police.[10] As such, the aims enshrined in the Identity Cards Act 2006 might not stand up to HRA challenge.[11] Again, any challenge based on the compatibility of the National Identity Scheme as a whole with the HRA is likely doomed to fail, whilst individual claims will be taken on their merits.

(c) *The Right to Privacy*

12.17 The privacy issues raised by the National Identity Scheme surfaced as the Bill worked its way through Parliament. Article 8(1) of the Convention protects an individual's right to respect for private and family life, home and correspondence from interference by public authorities. The scope of protection under Article 8 is broad: it protects not just an individual's right to privacy, but also a multitude of personal concerns including one's bodily integrity, personal identity and lifestyle, including sexuality and sexual orientation, and reputation.

12.18 As expounded above, the right to respect for private and family life under Article 8 is not absolute. Under Article 8(2), a public authority can restrict the rights under Article 8 where such restriction is in accordance with the law, for a legitimate aim and necessary in a democratic society in the interests of national security, public safety or the economic well-being of the country, for the prevention of disorder or crime, for the protection of health or morals, or for the protection of the rights and freedoms of others.

12.19 Virtually all of the alleged interferences with privacy rights under the Identity Cards Act 2006 will be considered to be 'in accordance with law' (ie because they are in accordance with the Identity Cards Act 2006 itself). There are outstanding Article 8(2) compliance issues—whether the aims of the Identity Cards Act 2006 are legitimate and whether the provisions of the Act are proportionate to achieving such aims. As stated above in para 12.12, challenges to the Act as a whole are overblown, but individual claims based on particular facts might succeed. Similarly, many of the information sharing powers in the Act allow an individual's personal information as contained on the Register to be shared without his or her consent in the interests of national security, the prevention or detection of crime or, most notably, 'other purposes specified by Order made by the Secretary of State'.[12]

12.20 Finally, even where a restriction on the right to privacy is in accordance with law and for a legitimate aim, the restriction must be necessary in a democratic society, which means that it must be proportionate and minimally intrusive.

(d) *Freedom of Expression*

12.21 Article 10 protects an individual's right to freedom of expression, which includes the freedom to hold opinions and to receive and impart information and ideas

---

[10] For further information, see chapter 7.
[11] For further analysis, see the discussion of s 17(7) in chapter 8.
[12] For further information, see the discussion of s 17(3) in chapter 8.

without interference by public authorities. Article 10 issues might arise in the context of ss 25(5) and 27, as discussed earlier.[13]

(e) *Prohibition Against Discrimination*

12.22 The government attempted to address allegations of unlawful discrimination under the National Identity Scheme by publishing a Race Equality Impact Assessment. The Assessment was described by the Commission for Racial Equality (CRE) as inadequate to the task of ensuring that the Identity Cards Act 2006 does not create, perpetuate and worsen adverse impacts on ethnic minority groups.[14] As the Act itself is enabling legislation, its actual impact on vulnerable groups remains to be seen.

12.23 Article 14 of the Convention is the anti-discrimination provision. Article 14 is not a freestanding guarantee of equal treatment; rather, it protects discrimination only in relation to the enjoyment of the rights and freedoms set out in the Convention. Article 14 prohibits discrimination on grounds of sex, race, colour, language, religion, political or other opinion, national or social origin, association with a national minority, property, birth or other status. The latter ground indicates that the list is not exhaustive, and indeed other analogous grounds of discrimination have been recognized, including sexual orientation and marital status.

12.24 Many provisions of the Identity Cards Act 2006 raise concerns about potential unlawful discrimination. For example, ethnic minorities are more likely to be stopped by the police and required to verify their identities, thereby negatively impacting on race relations in the community.[15] Patterns of differential treatment can also be found in service provision and recruitment procedures.[16]

12.25 Further, the government has indicated that the National Identity Scheme will apply first to foreign nationals. This could raise issues under police stop and search powers and the provision of public services,[17] as well as introducing a scheme of civil and criminal penalties to foreign nationals before extending the scheme more widely.

4. Launching a Human Rights Act 1998 Claim

12.26 An individual who would like to bring an action in the civil courts for a breach of his or her human rights under the HRA must launch such a claim within one year of the decision complained of. Alternatively, an individual may launch a judicial review application which alleges human rights violations as part of a claim that a decision is procedurally improper, irrational or illegal.[18] Of course,

---

[13] For more information, see chapter 9.

[14] CRE Briefing, *Identity Cards Bill: House of Lords Report Stage*, 16 January 2006.

[15] ibid, para 7, referencing Beck and Broadhurst, 'Policing the community: impact of national identity cards in the European Union' (1998) 24 *Journal of Ethnic and Migration Studies* 413–431.

[16] ibid, para 8.   [17] ibid, para 10.   [18] See para 12.10 above.

a judicial review application must be launched within three months of the decision complained of.

12.27　Ultimately, if an individual has exhausted his or her domestic remedies, an application may lie to the European Court of Human Rights in Strasbourg on the basis of an alleged Convention breach. Any application should be launched within six months of the final decision of a UK authority.

D. PARLIAMENTARY OMBUDSMAN

12.28　An individual who is aggrieved by the Identity Cards Act 2006 can also launch a complaint indirectly to the Parliamentary Ombudsman (more formally known as the Parliamentary Commissioner for Administration) about any agency issuing ID cards, via his or her MP. The Parliamentary Ombudsman investigates complaints concerning injustice as a result of maladministration within central government departments. The government noted during the Parliamentary debates that:

> The office of the Parliamentary Commissioner for Administration would be able to review any complaints about the agency issuing identity cards, brought to it through a Member of Parliament, in exactly the same way as it currently does for complaints about the UK Passport Service or other government departments and agencies.[19]

12.29　The Ombudsman has the power to correct mistakes arising out of such maladministration as well as ordering compensation. Any complaint to the Ombudsman should be launched within one year of the alleged injustice.

E. SECTOR-SPECIFIC OVERSIGHT BODIES

12.30　Of course, the power to oversee the National Identity Scheme will also be down to sector-specific oversight bodies. For example, individuals who are concerned about the actions of the police have a means of redress through the Independent Police Complaints Commission or the Police Ombudsman in Northern Ireland.

12.31　Individuals who are concerned about the actions of the National Health Service can complain to the Healthcare Commission and then to the Health Service Ombudsman.

12.32　Individuals who are concerned about potential breaches of the Regulation of Investigatory Powers Act 2000 by law enforcement agencies using surveillance powers, can complain to the Investigatory Powers Tribunal.

---

[19] *Hansard*, HL col 1518 (19 December 2005).

APPENDIX 1

Identity Cards Act 2006

CONTENTS

Identity Cards Act 2006

Registration

1 The National Identity Register

(1)   It shall be the duty of the Secretary of State to establish and maintain a register of individuals (to be known as 'the National Identity Register').

(2)   The purposes for which the Register is to be established and maintained are confined to the statutory purposes.

(3)   The statutory purposes are to facilitate, by the maintenance of a secure and reliable record of registrable facts about individuals in the United Kingdom –

    (a)   the provision of a convenient method for such individuals to prove registrable facts about themselves to others who reasonably require proof; and

    (b)   the provision of a secure and reliable method for registrable facts about such individuals to be ascertained or verified wherever that is necessary in the public interest.

(4)   For the purposes of this Act something is necessary in the public interest if, and only if, it is –

    (a)   in the interests of national security;

    (b)   for the purposes of the prevention or detection of crime;

    (c)   for the purposes of the enforcement of immigration controls;

    (d)   for the purposes of the enforcement of prohibitions on unauthorised working or employment; or

    (e)   for the purpose of securing the efficient and effective provision of public services.

(5)   In this Act 'registrable fact', in relation to an individual, means –

    (a)   his identity;

    (b)   the address of his principal place of residence in the United Kingdom;

    (c)   the address of every other place in the United Kingdom or elsewhere where he has a place of residence;

    (d)   where in the United Kingdom and elsewhere he has previously been resident;

    (e)   the times at which he was resident at different places in the United Kingdom or elsewhere;

    (f)   his current residential status;

    (g)   residential statuses previously held by him;

    (h)   information about numbers allocated to him for identification purposes and about the documents to which they relate;

    (i)   information about occasions on which information recorded about him in the Register has been provided to any person; and

    (j)   information recorded in the Register at his request.

(6)   But the registrable facts falling within subsection (5)(h) do not include any sensitive

personal data (within the meaning of the Data Protection Act 1998 (c. 29)) or anything the disclosure of which would tend to reveal such data.

(7) In this section references to an individual's identity are references to –
  (a) his full name;
  (b) other names by which he is or has previously been known;
  (c) his gender;
  (d) his date and place of birth and, if he has died, the date of his death; and
  (e) external characteristics of his that are capable of being used for identifying him.

(8) In this section 'residential status', in relation to an individual, means –
  (a) his nationality;
  (b) his entitlement to remain in the United Kingdom; and
  (c) where that entitlement derives from a grant of leave to enter or remain in the United Kingdom, the terms and conditions of that leave.

2 Individuals entered in Register

(1) An entry must be made in the Register for every individual who –
  (a) is entitled to be entered in it; and
  (b) applies to be entered in it.

(2) The individuals entitled to be entered in the Register are –
  (a) every individual who has attained the age of 16 and, without being excluded under subsection (3) from an entitlement to be registered, is residing at a place in the United Kingdom; and
  (b) every individual of a prescribed description who has resided in the United Kingdom or who is proposing to enter the United Kingdom.

(3) Regulations made by the Secretary of State may provide that an individual residing in the United Kingdom is excluded from an entitlement to be registered if –
  (a) he is residing in the United Kingdom in exercise of an entitlement to remain there that will end less than the prescribed period after it was acquired;
  (b) he is an individual of a prescribed description who has not yet been resident in the United Kingdom for the prescribed period; or
  (c) he is residing in the United Kingdom despite having no entitlement to remain there.

(4) An entry for an individual may be made in the Register (whether or not he has applied to be, or is entitled to be, entered in it) if –
  (a) information capable of being recorded in an entry for him is otherwise available to be recorded; and
  (b) the Secretary of State considers that the addition of the entry to the Register would be consistent with the statutory purposes.

(5) An entry in the Register consisting of all the information recorded about an individual must be given a unique number, to be known as his National Identity Registration Number; and that number must comply with the prescribed requirements.

(6) The Secretary of State may by order modify the age for the time being specified in subsection (2)(a).

(7) The Secretary of State must not make an order containing (with or without other provision) any provision that he is authorised to make by subsection (6) unless a

draft of the order has been laid before Parliament and approved by a resolution of each House.

3 Information recorded in Register

(1) Information –
   (a) may be entered in the Register, and
   (b) once entered, may continue to be recorded there, only if and for so long as it is consistent with the statutory purposes for it to be recorded in the Register.

(2) Information may not be recorded in the Register unless it is –
   (a) information the inclusion of which in an individual's entry is authorised by Schedule 1;
   (b) information of a technical nature for use in connection with the administration of the Register;
   (c) information of a technical nature for use in connection with the administration of arrangements made for purposes connected with the issue or cancellation of ID cards; or
   (d) information that must be recorded in the Register in accordance with subsection (3).

(3) Information about an individual must be recorded in his entry in the Register (whether or not it is authorised by Schedule 1) if –
   (a) he has made an application to the Secretary of State requesting the recording of the information as part of his entry;
   (b) the information is of a description identified in regulations made by the Secretary of State as a description of information that may be made the subject of such a request; and
   (c) the Secretary of State considers that it is both practicable and appropriate for it to be recorded in accordance with the applicant's request.

(4) An individual's entry in the Register must include any information falling within paragraph 9 of Schedule 1 that relates to an occasion on which information contained in his entry has been provided to a person without the individual's consent.

(5) Where –
   (a) the Secretary of State and an individual have agreed on what is to be recorded about a matter in that individual's entry in the Register, and
   (b) the Secretary of State has given, and not withdrawn, a direction that is to be recorded in that individual's case about that matter is to e determined by the agreement, there is to be a conclusive presumption for the purposes of this Act that the information to which the direction relates is accurate and complete information about that matter.

(6) The Secretary of State may by order modify the information for the time being set out in Schedule 1.

(7) The Secretary of State must not make an order containing (with or without other provision) any provision for adding information to the information that may be recorded in the Register unless a draft of the order has been laid before Parliament and approved by a resolution of each House.

(8) A statutory instrument containing an order which –
   (a) contains provisions that the Secretary of State is authorised to make by this section, and
   (b) is not an order a draft of which is required to have been laid before Parliament

and approved by a resolution of each House, shall be subject to annulment in pursuance of a resolution of either House of Parliament.

4 Designation of documents for purposes of registration etc.

(1) The Secretary of State may by order designate a description of documents for the purposes of this Act.

(2) The only documents that may be the subject of an order designating a description of documents for the purposes of this Act are documents which any of the persons mentioned in subsection (3) is authorised or required to issue, whether by or under an enactment or otherwise.

(3) Those persons are –
   (a) a Minister of the Crown;
   (b) a government department;
   (c) a Northern Ireland department;
   (d) the National Assembly for Wales;
   (e) any other person who carries out functions conferred by or under any enactment that fall to be carried out on behalf of the Crown.

(4) The Secretary of State must not make an order containing (with or without other provision) any provision that he is authorised to make by this section unless a draft of the order has been laid before Parliament and approved by a resolution of each House.

5 Applications relating to entries in Register

(1) An application by an individual to be entered in the Register may be made either –
   (a) by being included in the prescribed manner in an application for a designated document; or
   (b) by being submitted in the prescribed manner directly to the Secretary of State.

(2) Where an application to be issued with a designated document is made by an individual, the application must do one of the following –
   (a) include an application by that individual to be entered in the Register;
   (b) state that the individual is already entered in the Register and confirm the contents of his entry;
   (c) state that the individual is entered in the Register and confirm the contents of his entry subject to the changes notified in the application.

(3) Where an individual makes –
   (a) an application to be entered in the Register, or
   (b) an application which for the purposes of this Act confirms (with or without changes) the contents of his entry in the Register, the application must be accompanied by the prescribed information.

(4) Where an individual has made an application falling within subsection (3)(a) or (b), the Secretary of State may require him to do such one or more of the things specified in subsection (5) as the Secretary of State thinks fit for the purpose of –
   (a) verifying information that may be entered in the Register about that individual in consequence of that application; or

      (b) otherwise ensuring that there is a complete, up-to-date and accurate entry about that individual in the Register.

(5) The things that an individual may be required to do under subsection (4) are –

      (a) to attend at an agreed place and time or (in the absence of agreement) at a specified place and time;

      (b) to allow his fingerprints, and other biometric information about himself, to be taken and recorded;

      (c) to allow himself to be photographed;

      (d) otherwise to provide such information as may be required by the Secretary of State.

(6) Regulations under this section must not require an individual to provide information to another person unless it is information required by the Secretary of State for the statutory purposes.

(7) The power of the Secretary of State to make regulations containing (with or without other provision) any provision that he is authorised to make by this section is exercisable, on the first occasion on which regulations are made under this section, only if a draft of the regulations has been laid before Parliament and approved by a resolution of each House.

ID cards

6 Issue etc. of ID cards

(1) For the purposes of this Act an ID card is a card which –

      (a) is issued to an individual by the Secretary of State, or as part of or together with a designated document; and

      (b) does, as respects that individual, both of the things specified in subsection (2).

(2) Those things are –

      (a) recording registrable facts about the individual that are already recorded as part of his entry in the Register;

      (b) carrying data enabling the card to be used for facilitating the making of applications for information recorded in a prescribed part of the individual's entry in the Register, or for otherwise facilitating the provision of that information to a person entitled to be provided with it.

(3) An ID card issued to an individual –

      (a) must record only the prescribed information;

      (b) must record prescribed parts of it in an encrypted form;

      (c) is valid only for the prescribed period; and

      (d) remains the property of the person issuing it.

(4) Except in prescribed cases, an ID card must be issued to an individual if he –

      (a) is entitled to be entered in the Register or is subject to compulsory registration; and

      (b) is an individual about whom the prescribed registrable facts are recorded in the Register; but this subsection does not require an ID card to be issued as part of or together with a designated document issued on an application made in a case falling within subsection (7)(a) to (c).

(5) In prescribed cases an ID card may be issued to an individual who –

      (a) is not required to be issued with one; but

      (b) is an individual about whom the prescribed registrable facts are recorded in the Register.

(6)   An ID card relating to an individual is not to be issued except on an application made by him which either –

    (a) accompanies an application made by him to be entered in the Register; or

    (b) in the prescribed manner confirms (with or without changes) the contents of an entry already made in the Register for that individual.

(7)   Where an individual who is not already the holder of an ID card makes an application to be issued with a designated document, his application must, in the prescribed manner, include an application by him to be issued with such a card unless –

    (a) it is being made before 1st January 2010;

    (b) the designated document applied for is a United Kingdom passport (within the meaning of the Immigration Act 1971 (c. 77)); and

    (c) the application for that document contains a declaration by that individual that he does not wish to be issued with such a card.

(8)   Other applications for the issue of an ID card –

    (a) may be made only in the prescribed manner;

    (b) may be made to the Secretary of State or, in prescribed cases, to a designated documents authority; and

    (c) must be accompanied by the prescribed information;

and regulations for the purposes of paragraph (b) may authorise an application to be made to a designated documents authority irrespective of whether an application is made to that authority for the issue of a designated document.

(9)   The Secretary of State must not make regulations containing (with or without other provision) any provision for prescribing –

    (a) the information to be recorded in or on an ID card,

    (b) the form in which information is to be recorded in or on such a card, or

    (c) the registrable facts which are to be relevant for the purposes of subsection (4)(b),

unless a draft of the regulations has been laid before Parliament and approved by a resolution of each House.

7 ID cards for those compulsorily registered

(1)   This section applies where an individual –

    (a) is subject to compulsory registration; and

    (b) is entered in the Register.

(2)   If the individual –

    (a) holds a valid ID card that is due to expire within the prescribed period, or

    (b) does not hold a valid ID card, he must apply for one within the prescribed period.

(3)   Where an individual applies for an ID card in pursuance of this section, the Secretary of State may require him to do such one or more of the things specified in subsection (4) as the Secretary of State thinks fit for the purpose of –

    (a) verifying information provided for the purposes of the application; or

    (b) otherwise ensuring that there is a complete, up-to-date and accurate entry about that individual in the Register.

(4)   The things that an individual may be required to do under subsection (3) are –

    (a) to attend at an agreed place and time or (in the absence of agreement) at a specified place and time;

(b) to allow his fingerprints, and other biometric information about himself, to be taken and recorded;

(c) to allow himself to be photographed;

(d) otherwise to provide such information as may be required by the Secretary of State.

(5) An individual who contravenes –

(a) a requirement imposed by subsection (2), or

(b) a requirement imposed under subsection (3), shall be liable to a civil penalty not exceeding £1,000.

8 Functions of persons issuing designated documents

(1) A designated documents authority may issue a designated document to an individual only if –

(a) it is satisfied that the requirements imposed by or under this Act in relation to the application for the issue of that document to that individual have been complied with;

(b) it is satisfied that the Secretary of State has considered and disposed of so much of that application as relates to the making of an entry in the Register or the confirmation (with or without changes) of the contents of such an entry; and

(c) it has ascertained whether the individual already holds a valid ID card.

(2) A designated documents authority which issues a designated document to an individual in a case in which –

(a) the individual does not already hold a valid ID card, and

(b) the designated document is being issued otherwise than on an application made in a case falling within section 6(7)(a) to (c), must ensure that the document is issued together with an ID card satisfying the prescribed requirements.

(3) Regulations made by the Secretary of State may impose requirements regulating how designated documents authorities handle –

(a) applications to be entered in the Register that are made to them;

(b) applications to be issued with ID cards that are made to them (whether or not as part of an application for a designated document); and

(c) applications made to them that confirm (with or without changes) the contents of an individual's entry in the Register.

(4) Regulations made by the Secretary of State may also require designated documents authorities to notify the Secretary of State where a designated document that was issued together with an ID card –

(a) is modified, suspended or revoked; or

(b) is required to be surrendered.

(5) The Secretary of State must not make regulations containing (with or without other provision) any provision prescribing requirements for the purposes of subsection (2) unless a draft of the regulations has been laid before Parliament and approved by a resolution of each House.

Maintaining accuracy of Register etc.

9 Power to require information for validating Register

(1) Where it appears to the Secretary of State that a person on whom a requirement may be imposed under this section may have information in his possession which could be used for verifying –

    (a) something recorded in the Register about an individual,

    (b) something provided to the Secretary of State or a designated documents authority for the purpose of being recorded in an individual's entry in the Register, or

    (c) something otherwise available to the Secretary of State to be recorded about an individual in the Register, the Secretary of State may require that person to provide him with the information.

(2) Where it appears to a designated documents authority that a person on whom a requirement may be imposed under this section may have information in his possession which could be used for verifying –

    (a) something that is recorded in the Register about an individual who has applied to the authority for the issue or modification of a designated document or of an ID card, or

    (b) something that has been provided to that authority for the purpose of being recorded in the entry of such an individual in the Register, the authority may require that person to provide it with the information.

(3) It shall be the duty of a person who –

    (a) is required to provide information under this section, and

    (b) has the information in his possession, to comply with the requirement within whatever period is specified in the requirement.

(4) A requirement may be imposed under this section on any person specified for the purposes of this section in an order made by the Secretary of State.

(5) The persons who may be specified in such an order include –

    (a) Ministers of the Crown;

    (b) government departments;

    (c) a Northern Ireland department;

    (d) the National Assembly for Wales;

    (e) any other person who carries out functions conferred by or under an enactment that fall to be carried out on behalf of the Crown.

(6) The power of the Secretary of State to make an order specifying a person as a person on whom a requirement may be imposed under this section includes power to provide –

    (a) that his duty to provide the information that he is required to provide is owed to the person imposing it; and

    (b) that the duty is enforceable in civil proceedings –

        (i) for an injunction;

        (ii) for specific performance of a statutory duty under section 45 of the Court of Session Act 1988 (c. 36); or

        (iii) for any other appropriate remedy or relief.

(7) The Secretary of State may, in such cases (if any) as he thinks fit, make payments to a person providing information in accordance with this section in respect of the provision of the information.

(8) The Secretary of State must not make an order containing (with or without other provision) any provision that he is authorised to make by this section unless a draft of the order has been laid before Parliament and approved by a resolution of each House.

10 Notification of changes affecting accuracy of Register

(1) An individual to whom an ID card has been issued must notify the Secretary of State about –
  (a) every prescribed change of circumstances affecting the information recorded about him in the Register; and
  (b) every error in that information of which he is aware.

(2) A notification for the purposes of this section must be given –
  (a) in the prescribed manner; and
  (b) within the prescribed period after the change of circumstances occurs or the individual in question becomes aware of the error.

(3) Where an individual has given a notification for the purposes of this section, the Secretary of State may require him to do such one or more of the things falling within subsection (4) as the Secretary of State thinks fit for the purpose of –
  (a) verifying the information that may be entered in the Register about that individual in consequence of the notified change or for the purpose of correcting the error; or
  (b) otherwise ensuring that there is a complete, up-to-date and accurate entry about that individual in the Register.

(4) The things that an individual may be required to do under subsection (3) are –
  (a) to attend at an agreed place and time or (in the absence of agreement) at a specified place and time;
  (b) to allow his fingerprints, and other biometric information about himself, to be taken and recorded;
  (c) to allow himself to be photographed;
  (d) otherwise to provide such information as may be required by the Secretary of State.

(5) Regulations under this section must not require an individual to provide information to another person unless it is information required by the Secretary of State for the statutory purposes.

(6) The power of the Secretary of State to make regulations containing (with or without other provision) any provision that he is authorised to make by this section is exercisable, on the first occasion on which regulations are made under this section, only if a draft of the regulations has been laid before Parliament and approved by a resolution of each House.

(7) An individual who contravenes a requirement imposed on him by or under this section shall be liable to a civil penalty not exceeding £1,000.

11 Invalidity and surrender of ID cards

(1) Regulations may require an individual to whom an ID card has been issued to notify the Secretary of State, and such other persons as may be prescribed, if he knows or has reason to suspect that the card has been –
  (a) lost;
  (b) stolen;
  (c) damaged;
  (d) tampered with; or
  (e) destroyed.

(2) The Secretary of State may cancel an ID card if it appears to him –
  (a) that the card was issued in reliance on inaccurate or incomplete information;

(b) that the card has been lost, stolen, damaged, tampered with or destroyed;

(c) that there has been a modification of information recorded in the entry in the Register of the holder of the card;

(d) that another change of circumstances requires a modification of information recorded in or on the card; or

(e) that it is an ID card of a description of cards that the Secretary of State has decided should be re-issued.

(3) A person who is knowingly in possession of an ID card without either –

(a) the lawful authority of the individual to whom it was issued, or

(b) the permission of the Secretary of State, must surrender the card as soon as it is practicable to do so.

(4) Where it appears to the Secretary of State that a person is in possession of –

(a) an ID card issued to another,

(b) an ID card that has expired or been cancelled or is otherwise invalid,

(c) an ID card that has not yet been cancelled but is of a description of cards that the Secretary of State has decided should be re-issued, or

(d) an ID card that is in that person's possession in consequence of a contravention of a relevant requirement, the Secretary of State may require that person to surrender the card within such period as he may specify.

(5) Where an ID card has to be surrendered under subsection (3) or (4), it must be surrendered –

(a) to the Secretary of State; or

(b) in the case of a card issued by a designated documents authority, either to the Secretary of State or to that authority.

(6) A person who contravenes a requirement imposed by or under –

(a) any regulations under subsection (1), or

(b) subsection (3) or (4), shall be liable to a civil penalty not exceeding £1,000.

(7) In this section –

(a) references to a card having been damaged include references to anything in or on it being, or having become, unreadable or otherwise unusable; and

(b) references to a card having been tampered with include references to information in or on it having been modified for an unlawful purpose, or copied or otherwise extracted for such a purpose.

(8) In this section 'relevant requirement' means a requirement to surrender or otherwise to deliver an ID card to the Secretary of State, or to another, which is imposed –

(a) by virtue of any order under section 39, or

(b) by any enactment relating to the surrender of any other document.

Provision of information from Register for verification purposes etc.

12 Provision of information for verification or otherwise with consent

(1) The Secretary of State may provide a person with information recorded in an individual's entry in the Register if –

(a) an application for the provision of the information to that person is made by or with the authority of that individual; or

(b) that individual otherwise consents to the provision of that information to that person.

(2) The only information about an individual that may be provided to a person under this section is –

(a) information about the individual falling within paragraph 1, 3 or 4 of Schedule 1 (name, date and place of birth, gender and addresses, residential status, identifying numbers and validity of identifying documents);

(b) the information contained in any photograph of the individual recorded in the Register;

(c) the information about the individual's signature that is so recorded;

(d) information about whether an ID card issued to the individual is in force and, if not, why not;

(e) information which, by virtue of section 3(3), is recorded in the Register at the individual's request;

(f) the questions recorded by virtue of paragraph 8 of Schedule 1 for use for the purposes of applications for information about the individual;

(g) information confined to the grant or refusal of confirmation that information falling within subsection (3) that has been submitted to the Secretary of State coincides with information so falling that is recorded in the individual's entry in the Register; and

(h) information confined to the grant or refusal of confirmation that the individual's entry in the Register does not contain information of a particular description falling within that subsection.

(3) The information falling within this subsection is –

(a) information comprised in a fingerprint;

(b) other biometric information;

(c) the number to be used for the purposes of applications for information about the individual in question;

(d) the password or other code to be so used; and

(e) the answers to the questions to be so used.

(4) The Secretary of State may –

(a) by order modify subsections (2) and (3); and

(b) by regulations impose restrictions in addition to those contained in this section on the information that may be provided to a person under this section.

(5) The power of the Secretary of State by order to modify subsections (2) and (3) does not include –

(a) power to omit subsection (2); or

(b) power to add information falling within paragraph 9 of Schedule 1 to either of those subsections.

(6) The Secretary of State may also by regulations make provision as to –

(a) how an authority or consent for the purposes of subsection (1) is to be given;

(b) the persons by whom, and the circumstances in which, an application for those purposes may be made; and

(c) how such an application is to be made.

(7) The Secretary of State may by regulations make it a condition of the provision of information under this section –

(a) that the person to whom it is provided has registered prescribed particulars about himself with the Secretary of State;

(b) that that person and the applicant for the information (where different) are for the time being approved by the Secretary of State in the prescribed manner; and

(c) that apparatus used for the purposes of the application, and apparatus that it is proposed to use for the receipt and storage of the information, is for the time being approved in the prescribed manner by the person specified in or determined under the regulations.

(8) The power of the Secretary of State under this section to provide information about an individual to another person is exercisable only where the provision of the information is subject to the satisfaction in relation to that other person of conditions imposed under subsection (7)(a) and (b).

(9) The Secretary of State must not make an order containing (with or without other provision) any provision that he is authorised to make by subsection (4)(a) unless a draft of the order has been laid before Parliament and approved by a resolution of each House.

(10) The restrictions imposed by or under this section on the information that may be provided to a person do not affect any right apart from this Act for an individual to be provided with information about the contents of his entry in the Register.

Required identity check

13 Power to make public services conditional on identity checks

(1) Regulations may make provision allowing or requiring a person who provides a public service to make it a condition of providing the service to an individual that the individual produces –

(a) an ID card;

(b) other evidence of registrable facts about himself; or

(c) both.

(2) Regulations under this section may not allow or require the imposition of a condition on –

(a) the entitlement of an individual to receive a payment under or in accordance with any enactment, or

(b) the provision of any public service that has to be provided free of charge, except in cases where the individual is of a description of individuals who are subject to compulsory registration.

(3) Nothing in this section authorises the making of regulations the effect of which would be to require an individual –

(a) to carry an ID card with him at all times; or

(b) to produce such a card otherwise than for purposes connected with an application by him for the provision of a public service, or with the provision of a public service for which he has applied.

14 Procedure for regulations under s. 13

(1) The power to make regulations under section 13 shall be exercisable –

(a) in relation to the provision of Welsh public services, by the National Assembly for Wales;

(b) in relation to the provision of Northern Ireland public services, by a Northern Ireland department designated for the purpose by order made by the Office of the First Minister and deputy First Minister; and

(c) so far as not exercisable by any other person under paragraph (a) or (b), by the Secretary of State.

(2) In subsection (1) –

(a) the reference to the provision of Welsh public services is a reference to the provision of public services in Wales, so far as their provision is a matter in relation to which the National Assembly for Wales has functions; and

(b) the reference to the provision of Northern Ireland public services is a reference to the provision of public services in Northern Ireland, so far as their provision is a transferred matter (within the meaning of section 4(1) of the Northern Ireland Act 1998 (c. 47)).

(3) Regulations containing (with or without other provision) any provision the making of which is authorised by section 13 must not be made by the Secretary of State or a Northern Ireland department unless a draft of the regulations –

(a) in the case of regulations made by the Secretary of State, has been laid before Parliament and approved by a resolution of each House; and

(b) in the case of regulations made by a Northern Ireland department, has been laid before and approved by the Northern Ireland Assembly.

(4) Before –

(a) draft regulations under section 13 are laid before either House of Parliament or the Northern Ireland Assembly, or

(b) regulations under that section are made by the National Assembly for Wales, the person proposing to make the regulations must take such steps as that person thinks fit for securing that members of the public likely to be affected by the regulations are informed about the matters mentioned in subsection (5), and for consulting them about the proposal.

(5) Those matters are –

(a) the reasons for the making of the regulations; and

(b) why reliance is not being placed on powers conferred otherwise than by this Act.

(6) Where –

(a) a power to impose conditions for the provision of a public service is exercisable under an enactment not contained in this Act, and

(b) that power is exercisable only after consultation with such persons as may be specified or described in that enactment, the power under section 13 to impose a condition for the provision of that service or to make provision in relation to such a condition is to be exercisable only after consultation with the persons so specified or described.

15 Power to provide for checks on the Register

(1) The Secretary of State may by regulations make provision authorising a person providing a public service in respect of which –

(a) a condition is imposed under section 13, or

(b) a condition for the production of an ID card, or of evidence of registrable facts, or both, is imposed by or under any other enactment, to be provided with information recorded in the Register that he requires for the purpose of ascertaining or verifying registrable facts about an individual who has applied for the provision of the service.

(2) Regulations under this section may not authorise the provision to any person of information falling within paragraph 9 of Schedule 1.

(3) The Secretary of State may by regulations make provision as to –

(a) the manner in which applications for the provision of information under this section must be made;

(b) the persons by whom, and the circumstances in which, such an application may be made; and

(c) the information that may be provided in response to such an application and the manner in which it may be provided.

(4) The Secretary of State may by regulations make it a condition of the provision of information under this section –

(a) that the person to whom it is provided has registered prescribed particulars about himself with the Secretary of State;

(b) that that person and the applicant for the information (where different) are for the time being approved by the Secretary of State in the prescribed manner; and

(c) that apparatus used for the purposes of the application, and apparatus that it is proposed to use for the receipt and storage of the information, is for the time being approved in the prescribed manner by the person specified in or determined under the regulations.

(5) The power of the Secretary of State under this section to provide information about an individual to another person is exercisable only where the provision of the information is subject to the satisfaction in relation to that other person of conditions imposed under subsection (4)(a) and (b).

(6) The Secretary of State must not make regulations containing (with or without other provision) any provision that he is authorised to make by this section unless a draft of the regulations has been laid before Parliament and approved by a resolution of each House.

(7) Before draft regulations under this section are laid before either House of Parliament, the Secretary of State must take such steps as he thinks fit for securing that –

(a) members of the public in the United Kingdom are informed about the reasons for the proposal to make the regulations; and

(b) for consulting them about it.

(8) In this section 'enactment' includes an enactment comprised in an Act of the Scottish Parliament.

16 Prohibition on requirements to produce identity cards

(1) It shall be unlawful to make it a condition of doing anything in relation to an individual that the individual –

(a) makes an application under section 12(1) for the provision to him of information recorded in his entry in the Register;

(b) exercises the right conferred by section 7 of the Data Protection Act 1998 (c. 29) to obtain information recorded in his entry in the Register; or

(c) provides a person with information about what is recorded in his entry in the Register.

(2) It shall also be unlawful in cases not falling within subsection (3) for any person –

(a) to make it a condition of doing anything in relation to an individual that the individual makes an application, or gives an authority or consent, for the purposes of section 12(1) in order to secure the provision to another person of information recorded in the individual's entry in the Register;

(b) to make it a condition of doing anything in relation to an individual that the individual establishes his identity by the production of an ID card; or

(c) otherwise to impose a requirement on an individual to produce such a card.

(3) Each of the following is a case in which a condition or requirement referred to in subsection (2) may be imposed in relation to or on an individual –

(a) where the condition or requirement is imposed in accordance with regulations under section 13, or in accordance with provision made by or under any other enactment;

(b) where provision is made allowing the individual to satisfy the condition or other requirement using reasonable alternative methods of establishing his identity;

(c) where the individual is of a description of individuals who are subject to compulsory registration.

(4) The obligation of a person by virtue of this section not to impose a condition or requirement in relation to or on an individual is a duty owed to that individual and is enforceable by him in civil proceedings –

(a) for an injunction or interdict; or

(b) for any other appropriate remedy or relief.

(5) In this section 'enactment' includes an enactment comprised in an Act of the Scottish Parliament.

Other purposes for which registered information can be provided

17 Public authorities etc.

(1) The Secretary of State may, without the individual's consent, provide a person with information recorded in an individual's entry in the Register if –

(a) the provision of the information is authorised by this section; and

(b) there is compliance with any requirements imposed by or under section 21 in relation to the provision of the information.

(2) The provision of information is authorised by this section where it is –

(a) the provision of information to the Director-General of the Security Service for purposes connected with the carrying out of any of that Service's functions;

(b) the provision of information to the Chief of the Secret Intelligence Service for purposes connected with the carrying out of any of that Service's functions;

(c) the provision of information to the Director of the Government Communications Headquarters for purposes connected with the carrying out of any of the functions of GCHQ; or

(d) the provision of information to the Director General of the Serious Organised Crime Agency for purposes connected with the carrying out of any of that Agency's functions.

(3) The provision of information not falling within paragraph 9 of Schedule 1 is authorised by this section where the information is provided to a chief officer of police –

(a) in the interests of national security;

(b) for purposes connected with the prevention or detection of crime; or

(c) for other purposes specified by order made by the Secretary of State.

(4) The provision of information not falling within paragraph 9 of Schedule 1 is

authorised by this section where the information is provided to the Commissioners for Her Majesty's Revenue and Customs –

(a) in the interests of national security;

(b) for purposes connected with the prevention or detection of crime;

(c) for purposes connected with the prevention, detection or investigation of conduct in respect of which the Commissioners have power to impose penalties, or with the imposition of such penalties;

(d) for the purpose of facilitating the checking of information provided to the Commissioners in connection with anything under their care and management, or with any other matter in relation to which the Commissioners have duties under any enactment;

(e) for purposes connected with any of the functions of the Commissioners in relation to national insurance contributions or national insurance numbers; or

(f) for other purposes specified by order made by the Secretary of State.

(5) The provision of information not falling within paragraph 9 of Schedule 1 is authorised by this section where the information is provided –

(a) to a prescribed government department, or

(b) to a prescribed Northern Ireland department, for purposes connected with the carrying out of any prescribed functions of that department or of a Minister in charge of it.

(6) The provision of information to a designated documents authority is authorised by this section where the information is provided for purposes connected with the exercise or performance by the authority of –

(a) any of its powers or duties by virtue of this Act; or

(b) any of its other powers or duties in relation to the issue or modification of designated documents.

(7) The powers of the Secretary of State by virtue of this section to make an order or regulations authorising the provision of information to a person are exercisable for the purposes only of authorising the provision of information in circumstances in which its provision to the person in question is necessary in the public interest.

(8) The Secretary of State must not make an order or regulations containing (with or without other provision) any provision that he is authorised to make under this section unless a draft of the order or regulations has been laid before Parliament and approved by a resolution of each House.

(9) In this section –

'chief officer of police' means –

(a) the chief officer of police of a police force maintained for a police area in England and Wales;

(b) the chief constable of a police force maintained under the Police (Scotland) Act 1967 (c. 77);

(c) the Chief Constable of the Police Service of Northern Ireland;

(d) the Chief Constable of the Ministry of Defence Police;

(e) the Chief Constable of the Civil Nuclear Constabulary;

(f) the Chief Constable of the British Transport Police;

(g) the chief officer of the States of Jersey Police Force;

(h) the chief officer of the salaried police force of the Island of Guernsey; or

(i)   the Chief Constable of the Isle of Man Constabulary; 'GCHQ' has the same meaning as in the Intelligence Services Act 1994 (c. 13).

(10) Nothing in this section is to be construed as restricting any power to disclose information that exists apart from this section.

18 Prevention and detection of crime

(1)   The Secretary of State may, without the individual's consent, provide a person with information recorded in an individual's entry in the Register if –
  (a) the provision of the information is authorised by this section; and
  (b) there is compliance with any requirements imposed by or under section 21 in relation to the provision of the information.

(2)   The provision to a person of information not falling within paragraph 9 of Schedule 1 is authorised by this section (so far as it is not otherwise authorised by section 17) if the information is provided for any of the purposes specified in section 17(2)(a) to (d) of the Anti-terrorism, Crime and Security Act 2001 (c. 24) (criminal proceedings and investigations).

(3)   Section 18 of the Anti-terrorism, Crime and Security Act 2001 (restriction on disclosure of information for overseas purposes) shall have effect in relation to the provision to a person of information by virtue of subsection (2) as it applies in relation to a disclosure of information in exercise of a power to which section 17 of that Act applies.

(4)   The provision of information falling within paragraph 9 of Schedule 1 is authorised by this section if it is provided –
  (a) to a person to whom information may be provided by virtue of any of subsections (3) to (5) of section 17 or is made as mentioned in subsection (2) of this section; and
  (b) for purposes connected with the prevention or detection of serious crime.

19 Correcting inaccurate or incomplete information

(1)   This section applies where –
  (a) information about an individual has been provided for verification purposes to the Secretary of State or to a designated documents authority; and
  (b) it appears to the Secretary of State that the information was inaccurate or incomplete in one or more particulars.

(2)   The Secretary of State may, without the individual's consent, provide the person who provided the inaccurate or incomplete information with information about –
  (a) the respects in which it is inaccurate or incomplete; and
  (b) what is in fact recorded in that individual's entry in respect of the matters to which the inaccurate or incomplete information related.

(3)   The provision of information to a person under this section is subject to compliance with any requirements imposed by or under section 21 in relation to its provision.

(4)   The reference in this section to providing information about an individual for verification purposes is a reference to providing information about that individual which is required (whether under section 9 or otherwise) or intended to be used by the Secretary of State or a designated documents authority for verifying –
  (a) something recorded in that individual's entry in the Register,

(b) something provided to the Secretary of State or a designated documents authority for the purpose of being recorded in an entry about that individual in the
Register, or

(c) something otherwise available to the Secretary of State to be so recorded.

20 Power to authorise provision of information in other circumstances

(1) In a case where there is no authorisation under sections 17 to 19 for the provision of
information, the Secretary of State may nevertheless, without the individual's consent, provide a public authority with information recorded in an individual's entry
in the Register if –

(a) the information is not information falling within paragraph 9 of Schedule 1;

(b) the information is of a description specified or described in an order made by
the Secretary of State;

(c) the information is provided to a public authority so specified or described;

(d) the information is provided for the purposes so specified or described; and

(e) there is compliance with any requirements imposed by or under section 21 in
relation to the provision of the information.

(2) The power of the Secretary of State by virtue of this section to make an order
authorising the provision of information to a public authority is exercisable for the
purpose only of authorising the provision of information in circumstances in which
its provision to the authority in question is necessary in the public interest.

(3) The Secretary of State must not make an order containing (with or without other
provision) any provision that he is authorised to make by this section unless a draft
of the order has been laid before Parliament and approved by a resolution of each
House.

21 Rules for providing information without individual's consent

(1) Under sections 17 to 20 the Secretary of State may provide a person with information within paragraph 2 of Schedule 1 only if he is satisfied that it would not have
been reasonably practicable for the person to whom the information is provided to
have obtained the information by other means.

(2) The Secretary of State may by regulations make provision –

(a) imposing requirements that must be satisfied before information is provided
under any of sections 17 to 20; and

(b) restricting the persons who may be authorised to act on his behalf for or in
connection with the provision of information under any of those sections.

(3) Those regulations may include –

(a) provision requiring a person to be provided with information only where an
application for it has been made by or on behalf of that person;

(b) provision specifying or describing the persons who are entitled to make
applications for the provision of information to a person; and

(c) provision imposing other requirements as to the manner in which such
applications must be made.

(4) The Secretary of State may by regulations make it a condition of providing
information to a person –

(a) that that person (where not specified in sections 17 to 20) and the applicant
for the information (where different) are for the time being approved by the
Secretary of State in the prescribed manner; and

(b) that apparatus used for the purposes of the application, and apparatus that it is proposed to use for the receipt and storage of the information, is for the time being approved in the prescribed manner by the person specified in or determined under the regulations.

(5) The Secretary of State may also by regulations provide that information that may be provided to a person under any of sections 17 to 20 may be provided instead to another person who –

(a) is authorised by that person to be a recipient of information provided under that section;

(b) holds such office, rank or position as may be specified in the regulations; and

(c) is under the direction or control of that person, or is otherwise answerable or subordinate to him, in respect of any of his duties as a person holding that office, rank or position.

(6) A power of the Secretary of State under any of sections 17 to 20 to provide information about an individual to another person is exercisable only where the provision of the information is subject to the satisfaction in relation to that other person of conditions imposed under subsection 4)(a).

(7) The Secretary of State must not make regulations containing (with or without other provision) any provision that he is authorised to make by this section unless a draft of the regulations has been laid before Parliament and approved by a resolution of each House.

Supervision of operation of Act

22 Appointment of National Identity Scheme Commissioner

(1) The Secretary of State must appoint a Commissioner to be known as the National Identity Scheme Commissioner.

(2) It shall be the function of the Commissioner (subject to subsection (4)) to keep under review –

(a) the arrangements for the time being maintained by the Secretary of State for the purposes of his functions under this Act or the subordinate legislation made under it;

(b) the arrangements for the time being maintained by designated documents authorities for the purposes of their functions under this Act or that subordinate legislation;

(c) the arrangements made, by persons to whom information may be provided, for obtaining the information available to them under this Act or that subordinate legislation and for recording and using it; and

(d) the uses to which ID cards are being put.

(3) Where the Commissioner reviews any arrangements in accordance with subsection (2), his review must include, in particular, a review of the extent to which the arrangements make appropriate provision –

(a) for securing the confidentiality and integrity of information recorded in the Register; and

(b) for dealing with complaints made to the Secretary of State or a designated documents authority about the carrying out of the functions mentioned in that subsection.

(4) The matters to be kept under review by the Commissioner do not include –

(a) the exercise of powers which under this Act are exercisable by statutory instrument or by statutory rule for the purposes of the Statutory Rules (Northern Ireland) Order 1979 (S.I. 1979/1573 (N.I. 12));

(b) appeals against civil penalties;

(c) the operation of so much of this Act or of any subordinate legislation as imposes or relates to criminal offences;

(d) the provision of information to the Director-General of the Security Service, the Chief of the Secret Intelligence Service or the Director of the Government Communications Headquarters;

(e) the provision to another member of the intelligence services, in accordance with regulations under section 21(5), of information that may be provided to that Director-General, Chief or Director;

(f) the exercise by the Secretary of State of his powers under section 38; or

(g) arrangements made for the purposes of anything mentioned in paragraphs (a) to (f).

(5) It shall be the duty of every official of the Secretary of State's department to provide the Commissioner with all such information (including information recorded in the Register) as he may require for the purpose of carrying out his functions under this Act.

(6) The Commissioner is to hold office in accordance with the terms of his appointment; and there shall be paid to him out of money provided by Parliament such allowances as the Treasury may determine.

(7) The Secretary of State –

(a) after consultation with the Commissioner, and

(b) subject to the approval of the Treasury as to numbers, must provide the Commissioner with such staff as the Secretary of State considers necessary for the carrying out of the Commissioner's functions.

(8) In Part 6 of Schedule 1 to the Freedom of Information Act 2000 (c. 36) (public authorities for the purposes of that Act), at the appropriate place, insert – 'The National Identity Scheme Commissioner.'

(9) In this section 'intelligence service' has the same meaning as in the Regulation of Investigatory Powers Act 2000 (c. 23).

23 Reports by Commissioner

(1) As soon as practicable after the end of each calendar year, the Commissioner must make a report to the Secretary of State about the carrying out of the Commissioner's functions.

(2) The Commissioner may also, at any other time, make such report to the Secretary of State on any matter relating to the carrying out of those functions as the Commissioner thinks fit.

(3) The Secretary of State must lay before Parliament a copy of every report made to him under this section.

(4) If it appears to the Secretary of State, after consultation with the Commissioner, that the publication of a particular matter contained in a report under this section would be prejudicial to –

(a) national security, or

(b) the prevention or detection of crime, the Secretary of State may exclude that matter from the copy of the report that he lays before Parliament.

(5) Where a matter is excluded under subsection (4) from a copy of a report laid before

Parliament, the Secretary of State must, when he lays that copy of the report, also lay before Parliament a statement that a matter has been excluded from the report under that subsection.

24 Jurisdiction of Intelligence Services Commissioner and Tribunal

(1) The Regulation of Investigatory Powers Act 2000 (c. 23) is amended as follows.

(2) In section 59 (functions of Intelligence Services Commissioner), after subsection (2) insert –

'(2A) The Intelligence Services Commissioner shall also keep under review –

(a) the acquisition, storage and use by the intelligence services of information recorded in the National Identity Register;

(b) the provision of such information to members of the intelligence services in accordance with any provision made by or under the Identity Cards Act 2006;

(c) arrangements made by the Secretary of State or any of the intelligence services for the purposes of anything mentioned in paragraph (a) or (b).'

(3) In section 65(2)(b) (complaints in relation to which Tribunal has jurisdiction), after 'subsection (4)' insert 'or (4A)'.

(4) In section 65(3) (proceedings in relation to which the Tribunal has jurisdiction), for the 'or' at the end of paragraph (c) substitute –

'(ca) they are proceedings relating to the provision to a member of any of the intelligence services of information recorded in an individual's entry in the National Identity Register;

(cb) they are proceedings relating to the acquisition, storage or use of such information by any of the intelligence services; or'.

(5) After section 65(4) insert –

'(4A) The Tribunal is also the appropriate forum for a complaint if it is a complaint by an individual about what he believes to be –

(a) the provision to a member of any of the intelligence services of information recorded in that individual's entry in the National Identity Register; or

(b) the acquisition, storage or use of such information by any of the intelligence services.'

Offences

25 Possession of false identity documents etc.

(1) It is an offence for a person with the requisite intention to have in his possession or under his control –

(a) an identity document that is false and that he knows or believes to be false;

(b) an identity document that was improperly obtained and that he knows or believes to have been improperly obtained; or

(c) an identity document that relates to someone else.

(2) The requisite intention for the purposes of subsection (1) is –

(a) the intention of using the document for establishing registrable facts about himself; or

(b) the intention of allowing or inducing another to use it for establishing, ascertaining or verifying registrable facts about himself or about any other person (with the exception, in the case of a document within paragraph (c) of that subsection, of the individual to whom it relates).

(3) It is an offence for a person with the requisite intention to make, or to have in his possession or under his control –

   (a) any apparatus which, to his knowledge, is or has been specially designed or adapted for the making of false identity documents; or

   (b) any article or material which, to his knowledge, is or has been specially designed or adapted to be used in the making of false identity documents.

(4) The requisite intention for the purposes of subsection (3) is the intention –

   (a) that he or another will make a false identity document; and

   (b) that the document will be used by somebody for establishing, ascertaining or verifying registrable facts about a person.

(5) It is an offence for a person to have in his possession or under his control, without reasonable excuse –

   (a) an identity document that is false;

   (b) an identity document that was improperly obtained;

   (c) an identity document that relates to someone else; or

   (d) any apparatus, article or material which, to his knowledge, is or has been specially designed or adapted for the making of false identity documents or to be used in the making of such documents.

(6) A person guilty of an offence under subsection (1) or (3) shall be liable, on conviction on indictment, to imprisonment for a term not exceeding ten years or to a fine, or to both.

(7) A person guilty of an offence under subsection (5) shall be liable –

   (a) on conviction on indictment, to imprisonment for a term not exceeding two years or to a fine, or to both;

   (b) on summary conviction in England and Wales, to imprisonment for a term not exceeding twelve months or to a fine not exceeding the statutory maximum, or to both;

   (c) on summary conviction in Scotland or Northern Ireland, to imprisonment for a term not exceeding six months or to a fine not exceeding the statutory maximum, or to both; but, in relation to an offence committed before the commencement of section 154(1) of the Criminal Justice Act 2003 (c. 44), the reference in paragraph (b) to twelve months is to be read as a reference to six months.

(8) For the purposes of this section –

   (a) an identity document is false only if it is false within the meaning of Part 1 of the Forgery and Counterfeiting Act 1981 (c. 45) (see section 9(1) of that Act); and

   (b) an identity document was improperly obtained if false information was provided, in or in connection with the application for its issue or an application for its modification, to the person who issued it or (as the case may be) to a person entitled to modify it; and references to the making of a false identity document include references to the modification of an identity document so that it becomes false.

(9) Subsection (8)(a) does not apply in the application of this section to Scotland.

(10) In this section 'identity document' has the meaning given by section 26.

26 Identity documents for the purposes of s. 25

(1) In section 25 'identity document' means any document that is, or purports to be –

   (a) an ID card;

214

(b) a designated document;

(c) an immigration document;

(d) a United Kingdom passport (within the meaning of the Immigration Act 1971 (c. 77));

(e) a passport issued by or on behalf of the authorities of a country or territory outside the United Kingdom or by or on behalf of an international organisation;

(f) a document that can be used (in some or all circumstances) instead of a passport;

(g) a UK driving licence; or

(h) a driving licence issued by or on behalf of the authorities of a country or territory outside the United Kingdom.

(2) In subsection (1) 'immigration document' means –

(a) a document used for confirming the right of a person under the Community Treaties in respect of entry or residence in the United Kingdom;

(b) a document which is given in exercise of immigration functions and records information about leave granted to a person to enter or to remain in the United Kingdom; or

(c) a registration card (within the meaning of section 26A of the Immigration Act 1971);

and in paragraph (b) 'immigration functions' means functions under the Immigration Acts (within the meaning of the Asylum and Immigration (Treatment of Claimants, etc.) Act 2004 (c. 19)).

(3) In that subsection 'UK driving licence' means –

(a) a licence to drive a motor vehicle granted under Part 3 of the Road Traffic Act 1988 (c. 52); or

(b) a licence to drive a motor vehicle granted under Part 2 of the Road Traffic (Northern Ireland) Order 1981 (S.I. 1981/154 (N.I. 1)).

(4) The Secretary of State may by order modify the list of documents in subsection (1).

(5) The Secretary of State must not make an order containing (with or without other provision) any provision that he is authorised to make by subsection (4) unless a draft of the order has been laid before Parliament and approved by a resolution of each House.

27 Unauthorised disclosure of information

(1) A person is guilty of an offence if, without lawful authority –

(a) he provides any person with information that he is required to keep confidential; or

(b) he otherwise makes a disclosure of any such information.

(2) For the purposes of this section a person is required to keep information confidential if it is information that is or has become available to him by reason of his holding an office or employment the duties of which relate, in whole or in part, to –

(a) the establishment or maintenance of the Register;

(b) the issue, manufacture, modification, cancellation or surrender of ID cards; or

(c) the carrying out of the Commissioner's functions.

(3) For the purposes of this section information is provided or otherwise disclosed with lawful authority if, and only if the provision or other disclosure of the information –

(a) is authorised by or under this Act or another enactment;

(b) is in pursuance of an order or direction of a court or of a tribunal established by or under any enactment;

(c) is in pursuance of a Community obligation; or

(d) is for the purposes of the performance of the duties of an office or employment of the sort mentioned in subsection (2).

(4) It is a defence for a person charged with an offence under this section to show that, at the time of the alleged offence, he believed, on reasonable grounds, that he had lawful authority to provide the information or to make the other disclosure in question.

(5) A person guilty of an offence under this section shall be liable, on conviction on indictment, to imprisonment for a term not exceeding two years or to a fine, or to both.

28 Providing false information

(1) A person is guilty of an offence if, in circumstances falling within subsection (2), he provides false information to any person –

(a) for the purpose of securing the making or modification of an entry in the Register;

(b) in confirming (with or without changes) the contents of an entry in the Register; or

(c) for the purpose of obtaining for himself or another the issue or modification of an ID card.

(2) Those circumstances are that, at the time of the provision of the information he –

(a) knows or believes the information to be false; or

(b) is reckless as to whether or not it is false.

(3) A person guilty of an offence under this section shall be liable –

(a) on conviction on indictment, to imprisonment for a term not exceeding two years or to a fine, or to both;

(b) on summary conviction in England and Wales, to imprisonment for a term not exceeding twelve months or to a fine not exceeding the statutory maximum, or to both;

(c) on summary conviction in Scotland or Northern Ireland, to imprisonment for a term not exceeding six months or to a fine not exceeding the statutory maximum, or to both; but, in relation to an offence committed before the commencement of section 154(1) of the Criminal Justice Act 2003 (c. 44), the reference in paragraph (b) to twelve months is to be read as a reference to six months.

29 Tampering with the Register etc.

(1) A person is guilty of an offence under this section if –

(a) he engages in any conduct that causes an unauthorised modification of information recorded in the Register; and

(b) at the time when he engages in the conduct, he has the requisite intent.

(2) For the purposes of this section a person has the requisite intent if he –

(a) intends to cause a modification of information recorded in the Register; or

(b) is reckless as to whether or not his conduct will cause such a modification.

(3) For the purposes of this section the cases in which conduct causes a modification of information recorded in the Register include –

(a) where it contributes to a modification of such information; and

(b) where it makes it more difficult or impossible for such information to be retrieved in a legible form from a computer on which it is stored by the Secretary of State, or contributes to making that more difficult or impossible.

(4) It is immaterial for the purposes of this section –

    (a) whether the conduct constituting the offence, or any of it, took place in the United Kingdom; or

    (b) in the case of conduct outside the United Kingdom, whether it is conduct of a British citizen.

(5) For the purposes of this section a modification is unauthorised, in relation to the person whose conduct causes it, if –

    (a) he is not himself entitled to determine if the modification may be made; and

    (b) he does not have a consent to the modification from a person who is so entitled.

(6) In proceedings against a person for an offence under this section in respect of conduct causing a modification of information recorded in the Register it is to be a defence for that person to show that, at the time of the conduct, he believed, on reasonable grounds –

    (a) that he was a person entitled to determine if that modification might be made; or

    (b) that consent to the modification had been given by a person so entitled.

(7) A person guilty of an offence under this section shall be liable –

    (a) on conviction on indictment, to imprisonment for a term not exceeding ten years or to a fine, or to both;

    (b) on summary conviction in England and Wales, to imprisonment for a term not exceeding twelve months or to a fine not exceeding the statutory maximum, or to both;

    (c) on summary conviction in Scotland or Northern Ireland, to imprisonment for a term not exceeding six months or to a fine not exceeding the statutory maximum, or to both; but, in relation to an offence committed before the commencement of section 154(1) of the Criminal Justice Act 2003 (c. 44), the reference in paragraph (b) to twelve months is to be read as a reference to six months.

(8) In the case of an offence by virtue of this section in respect of conduct wholly or partly outside the United Kingdom –

    (a) proceedings for the offence may be taken at any place in the United Kingdom; and

    (b) the offence may for all incidental purposes be treated as having been committed at any such place.

(9) In this section –

'conduct' includes acts and omissions; and

'modification' includes a temporary modification.

30 Amendments relating to offences

(1) In section 1(2) of the Criminal Justice Act 1993 (c. 36) (Group A offences in respect of which jurisdiction is extended for some purposes in relation to conduct outside England and Wales), after paragraph (c) insert –

'(ca) an offence under section 25 of the Identity Cards Act 2006;'.

(2) In section 31 of the Immigration and Asylum Act 1999 (defences based on Article 31(1) of the Refugee Convention) –

    (a) in subsection (3) (offences in England and Wales and Northern Ireland to which section applies), after paragraph (a) insert –

'(aa) section 25(1) or (5) of the Identity Cards Act 2006;'

(b) in subsection (4) (offences in Scotland to which section applies), after paragraph (b) insert –

'(ba) under section 25(1) or (5) of the Identity Cards Act 2006;'.

(3) In section 14(2) of the Asylum and Immigration (Treatment of Claimants, etc.) Act 2004 (c. 19) (powers of arrest for immigration officers), after paragraph (p) insert –

'(q) an offence under section 25 of the Identity Cards Act 2006.'

(4) In Article 26(2) of the Police and Criminal Evidence (Northern Ireland) Order 1989 (S.I. 1989/1341 (N.I. 12)) (offences for which an arrest may be made without a warrant), at the end insert –

'(q) an offence under –

(i) section 25(5) of the Identity Cards Act 2006 (possession of false document etc.);

(ii) section 27 of that Act (disclosure of information on National Identity Register); or

(iii) section 28 of that Act (providing false information).'

(5) In Article 38(2) of the Criminal Justice (Northern Ireland) Order 1996 (S.I. 1996/ 3160 (N.I. 24)) (which makes provision in relation to conduct outside Northern Ireland corresponding to that made by section 1(2) of the Criminal Justice Act 1993 (c. 36)), after sub-paragraph (c) insert –

'(ca) an offence under section 25 of the Identity Cards Act 2006;'.

Civil penalties

31 Imposition of civil penalties

(1) This section applies where the Secretary of State is satisfied that a person ('the defaulter') is a person who is liable under this Act to a civil penalty not exceeding a specified amount.

(2) The Secretary of State may, by a notice given to the defaulter in the prescribed manner, impose on him a penalty of such amount, not exceeding the specified amount, as the Secretary of State thinks fit.

(3) A notice imposing such a penalty must –

(a) set out the Secretary of State's reasons for deciding that the defaulter is liable to a penalty;

(b) state the amount of the penalty that is being imposed;

(c) specify a date before which the penalty must be paid to the Secretary of State;

(d) describe how payment may be made;

(e) explain the steps that the defaulter may take if he objects to the penalty; and

(f) set out and explain the powers of the Secretary of State to enforce the penalty.

(4) The date for the payment of a penalty must be not less than 14 days after the giving of the notice imposing it.

(5) A penalty imposed in accordance with this section –

(a) must be paid to the Secretary of State in a manner described in the notice imposing it; and

(b) if not so paid by the specified date, is to be recoverable by him accordingly.

(6) In proceedings for recovery of a penalty so imposed no question may be raised as to –

(a) whether the defaulter was liable to the penalty;

(b) whether the imposition of the penalty was unreasonable; or

(c) the amount of the penalty.

(7) Sums received by the Secretary of State in respect of penalties imposed in accordance with this section must be paid into the Consolidated Fund.

32 Objection to penalty

(1) A person to whom a notice under section 31 has been given may give notice to the Secretary of State that he objects to the penalty on one or more of the following grounds –

    (a) that he is not liable to it;

    (b) that the circumstances of the contravention in respect of which he is liable make the imposition of a penalty unreasonable;

    (c) that the amount of the penalty is too high.

(2) The notice of objection –

    (a) must set out the grounds of the objection and the objector's reasons for objecting on those grounds; and

    (b) must be given to the Secretary of State in the prescribed manner and within the prescribed period after the giving of the notice imposing the penalty.

(3) The Secretary of State must consider a notice of objection given in accordance with this section and may then –

    (a) cancel the penalty;

    (b) reduce it;

    (c) increase it; or

    (d) confirm it.

(4) The Secretary of State must not enforce a penalty in respect of which he has received a notice of objection before he has notified the objector of the outcome of his consideration of the objection.

(5) That notification of the outcome of his consideration must be given, in the prescribed manner –

    (a) before the end of the prescribed period; or

    (b) within such longer period as he may agree with the objector.

(6) Where, on consideration of an objection, the Secretary of State increases the penalty, he must give the objector a new penalty notice under section 31; and, where he reduces it, he must notify the objector of the reduced amount.

33 Appeals against penalties

(1) A person on whom a penalty has been imposed under section 31 may appeal to the court on one or more of the following grounds –

    (a) that he is not liable to it;

    (b) that the circumstances of the contravention in respect of which he is liable make the imposition of a penalty unreasonable;

    (c) that the amount of the penalty is too high.

(2) An appeal under this section must be brought within such period after the giving of the notice imposing the penalty to which it relates as may be specified by rules of court.

(3) On an appeal under this section, the court may –

    (a) allow the appeal and cancel the penalty;

    (b) allow the appeal and reduce the penalty; or

    (c) dismiss the appeal.

(4)   An appeal under this section shall be by way of a rehearing of the Secretary of State's decision to impose the penalty.

(5)   The matters to which the court may have regard when determining an appeal under this section include all matters that the court considers relevant, including –

(a) matters of which the Secretary of State was unaware when he made his decision; and

(b) matters which (apart from this subsection) the court would be prevented from having regard to by virtue of rules of court.

(6)   An appeal under this section may be brought in relation to a penalty irrespective of whether a notice of objection under section 32 has been given in respect of that penalty and of whether there has been an increase or reduction under that section.

(7)   In this section 'the court' means –

(a) in England and Wales or Northern Ireland, a county court; and

(b) in Scotland, the sheriff.

34 Code of practice on penalties

(1)   The Secretary of State must issue a code of practice setting out the matters that must be considered when determining –

(a) whether a civil penalty should be imposed under this Act; and

(b) the amount of such a penalty.

(2)   The Secretary of State must have regard to the code when –

(a) imposing a civil penalty under this Act; or

(b) considering a notice of objection under section 32.

(3)   The court must have regard to the code when determining any appeal under section 33.

(4)   Before issuing the code, the Secretary of State must lay a draft of it before Parliament.

(5)   Before a draft code under this section is laid before Parliament, the Secretary of State must take such steps as he thinks fit –

(a) for securing that members of the public in the United Kingdom are informed about the proposed code; and

(b) for consulting them about it.

(6)   The code issued under this section does not come into force until the time specified by order made by the Secretary of State.

(7)   The Secretary of State may from time to time –

(a) revise the whole or a part of the code; and

(b) issue the revised code.

(8)   Subsections (4) to (6) apply to a revised code as they apply to the code first issued under this section.

(9)   The power of the Secretary of State to make an order containing (with or without other provision) a provision authorised by this section is exercisable, on the first occasion on which an order is made under this section, only if a draft of the order has been laid before Parliament and approved by a resolution of each House.

(10) A statutory instrument containing an order which –

(a) contains provisions that the Secretary of State is authorised to make by this section, and

(b) is not an order a draft of which is required to have been laid before Parliament and approved by a resolution of each House, shall be subject to annulment in pursuance of a resolution of either House of Parliament.

Fees and charges

35 Fees in respect of functions carried out under Act

(1) The Secretary of State may by regulations impose fees, of such amounts as he thinks fit, to be paid to him in respect of any one or more of the following –

    (a) applications to him for entries to be made in the Register, for the modification of entries or for the issue of ID cards;

    (b) the making or modification of entries in the Register;

    (c) the issue of ID cards;

    (d) applications for the provision of information contained in entries in the Register;

    (e) the provision of such information;

    (f) applications for confirmation that information supplied coincides with information recorded in the Register;

    (g) the issue or refusal of such confirmations;

    (h) applications for the approval of a person or of apparatus in accordance with any regulations under this Act;

    (i) the grant of such approvals.

(2) The provision that may be made by regulations under this section includes –

    (a) provision for the payment of fees by instalments; and

    (b) provision establishing arrangements under which instalments may be paid in anticipation of a fee becoming due.

(3) In prescribing a fee under this section in respect of anything mentioned in a particular paragraph of subsection (1), the Secretary of State may take into account –

    (a) expenses that will be or have been incurred by him in respect of that thing, both in the circumstances in relation to which the fee is prescribed and in other circumstances;

    (b) expenses that will be or have been incurred by him in respect of such other things mentioned in that subsection as he thinks fit;

    (c) other expenses that will be or have been incurred by him in connection with any provision made by or under this Act;

    (d) expenses that will be or have been incurred by any person in connection with applications for, and the issue of, designated documents (whether or not together with ID cards);

    (e) expenses that will be or have been incurred in the provision of consular services (within the meaning of section 1 of the Consular Fees Act 1980 (c. 23)); and

    (f) such differences between different persons by or in relation to whom that thing may be done as he thinks fit.

(4) The consent of the Treasury is required for the making of regulations under subsection (1).

(5) Every power conferred by or under an enactment to fix or impose fees in respect of –

    (a) applications for a designated document, or

    (b) the issue of designated documents, includes power to fix or impose fees in respect of things done by virtue of this Act in connection with such applications, or with the issue of such documents.

(6) References in this section to expenses that will be incurred for any purpose include

references to expenses that the Secretary of State considers are likely to be incurred for that purpose over such period as he thinks appropriate, including expenses that will be incurred only after the commencement of particular provisions of this Act.

(7) The power of the Secretary of State to make regulations containing (with or without other provision) a provision that he is authorised to make by subsection (1) is exercisable –

(a) on the first occasion on which regulations are made under this section, and

(b) on every subsequent occasion on which it appears to the Secretary of State that the power is being exercised for purposes that are not confined to the modification of existing fees to take account of changes in the value of money, only if a draft of the regulations has been laid before Parliament and approved by a resolution of each House.

(8) Fees received by the Secretary of State by virtue of this section must be paid into the Consolidated Fund.

36 Amendment of Consular Fees Act 1980

In section 1 of the Consular Fees Act 1980 (power to impose fees in respect of the carrying out of consular functions), after subsection (4) insert –

'(4A) In prescribing a fee under subsection (1) for the doing of a particular thing, Her Majesty in Council may take into account –

(a) the expenses that will be or have been incurred in doing that thing, both in the circumstances in relation to which the fee is prescribed and in other circumstances;

(b) the expenses that will be or have been incurred in doing such other things in the exercise of functions mentioned in that subsection as She thinks fit;

(c) expenses that will be or have been incurred by the Secretary of State in connection with arrangements made for purposes connected with both the exercise of such functions and provision made by or under the Identity Cards Act 2006; and

(d) such differences between different persons in relation to whom things may be or have been done as She thinks fit.

(4B) The power of Her Majesty in Council under subsection (1) to prescribe fees and the power of the Secretary of State under subsection (3) to make regulations each includes power –

(a) to make different provision for different cases;

(b) to make provision subject to such exemptions and exceptions as the person exercising the power thinks fit; and

(c) to make such incidental, supplemental, consequential and transitional provision as that person thinks fit.

(4C) References in this section to expenses that will be incurred for any purpose include references to expenses that Her Majesty in Council considers are likely to be incurred for that purpose over such period as She thinks appropriate, including expenses that will only be incurred after the commencement of a particular enactment.'

37 Report to Parliament about likely costs of ID cards scheme

(1) Before the end of the six months beginning with the day on which this Act is passed, the Secretary of State must prepare and lay before Parliament a report setting out his estimate of the public expenditure likely to be incurred on the ID cards scheme during the ten years beginning with the laying of the report.

(2) Before the end of every six months beginning with the laying of a report under this section, the Secretary of State must prepare and lay before Parliament a further report setting out his estimate of the public expenditure likely to be incurred on the ID cards scheme during the ten years beginning with the end of those six months.

(3) References in this section, in relation to any period of ten years, to the public expenditure likely to be incurred on the ID cards scheme are references to the expenditure likely to be incurred over that period by the Secretary of State and designated documents authorities on –

(a) the establishment and maintenance of the Register;

(b) the issue, modification, renewal, replacement, re-issue and surrender of ID cards;

(c) the provision to persons by the Secretary of State of information recorded in individuals' entries in the Register.

(4) If it appears to the Secretary of State that it would be prejudicial to securing the best value from the use of public money to publish any matter by including it in his next report under this section, he may exclude that matter from that report.

Provisions relating to passports

38 Verifying information provided with passport applications etc.

(1) Where it appears to the Secretary of State that a person on whom a requirement may be imposed under this section may have information in his possession which could be used –

(a) for verifying information provided to the Secretary of State for the purposes of, or in connection with, an application for the issue of a passport, or

(b) for determining whether to withdraw an individual's passport, the Secretary of State may require that person to provide him with the information.

(2) It shall be the duty of a person who –

(a) is required to provide information under this section, and

(b) has the information in his possession, to comply with the requirement within whatever period is specified in the requirement.

(3) A requirement may be imposed under this section on –

(a) a Minister of the Crown;

(b) a government department;

(c) a Northern Ireland department;

(d) the National Assembly for Wales; or

(e) any person not falling within paragraph (a) to (d) who is specified for the purposes of this section in an order made by the Secretary of State.

(4) The persons who may be specified in an order under subsection (3)(e) include any person who carries out functions conferred by or under an enactment that fall to be carried out on behalf of the Crown.

(5) The power of the Secretary of State to make an order specifying a person as a person on whom a requirement may be imposed under this section includes power to provide –

(a) that his duty to provide the information that he is required to provide is owed to the person imposing it; and

(b) that the duty is enforceable in civil proceedings –

(i) for an injunction;

      (ii) for specific performance of a statutory duty under section 45 of the Court of Session Act 1988 (c. 36); or

      (iii) for any other appropriate remedy or relief.

(6)   The Secretary of State may, in such cases (if any) as he thinks fit, make payments to a person providing information in accordance with this section in respect of the provision of the information.

(7)   The Secretary of State must not make an order containing (with or without other provision) any provision that he is authorised to make by this section unless a draft of the order has been laid before Parliament and approved by a resolution of each House.

39 Amendments of legislation relating to passports

(1)   In sections 14E, 19, 21B and 21C of the Football Spectators Act 1989 (c. 37) (enforcement of banning orders etc.), for 'passport', wherever occurring, substitute 'travel authorisation'.

(2)   In section 22A(1) of that Act (interpretation), after the definition of 'prescribed' insert –

' "travel authorisation", in relation to a person, means one or both of the following –

      (a) any UK passport (within the meaning of the Immigration Act 1971) that has been issued to him;

      (b) any ID card issued to him under the Identity Cards Act 2006 which records that he is a British citizen.'

(3)   In sections 33, 35 and 36 of the Criminal Justice and Police Act 2001 (c. 16) (travel restriction orders), for 'passport', wherever occurring, substitute 'travel authorisation'.

(4)   For section 33(8) of that Act substitute –

'(8) In this section "UK travel authorisation", in relation to a person, means one or both of the following –

      (a) any UK passport (within the meaning of the Immigration Act 1971) that has been issued to him;

      (b) any ID card issued to him under the Identity Cards Act 2006 which records that he is a British citizen.'

(5)   The Secretary of State may by order modify –

      (a) any enactment (including an enactment amended by this section), or

      (b) a provision of any subordinate legislation, for the purpose of including a reference to an ID card, or to an ID card of a description not already mentioned in that enactment or provision, in any reference (however worded) to a passport.

(6)   The Secretary of State must not make an order containing (with or without other provision) any provision that he is authorised to make by this section for modifying an enactment unless a draft of the order has been laid before Parliament and approved by a resolution of each House.

(7)   A statutory instrument containing an order which –

      (a) contains provisions that the Secretary of State is authorised to make by this section, and

      (b) is not an order a draft of which is required to have been laid before Parliament and approved by a resolution of each House, shall be subject to annulment in pursuance of a resolution of either House of Parliament.

Supplemental

40 Orders and regulations

(1) Every power conferred by this Act on the Secretary of State or the National Assembly for Wales to make an order or regulations is a power exercisable by statutory instrument.

(2) The following powers are powers exercisable by statutory rule for the purposes of the Statutory Rules (Northern Ireland) Order 1979 (S.I. 1979/1573 (N.I. 12)) –

  (a) the power of a Northern Ireland department to make regulations under section 13; and

  (b) the power of the Office of the First Minister and deputy First Minister to make an order under section 14(1)(b) designating a Northern Ireland department for the purposes of the power to make such regulations.

(3) A statutory instrument containing regulations which –

  (a) contain provisions that the Secretary of State is authorised to make by this Act, and

  (b) are not regulations a draft of which is required to have been laid before Parliament and approved by a resolution of each House, shall be subject to annulment in pursuance of a resolution of either House of Parliament.

(4) Every power conferred by this Act on a person to make an order or regulations (other than the power of the Secretary of State to make an order under section 44(3)) includes power –

  (a) to make different provision for different cases;

  (b) to make provision subject to such exemptions and exceptions as that person thinks fit; and

  (c) to make such incidental, supplemental, consequential and transitional provision as that person thinks fit.

(5) The power under subsection (4) to make incidental, supplemental and consequential provision in connection with so much of any order or regulations as authorises or requires anything to be done by or in relation to an individual under the age of 16 includes power to provide –

  (a) for the designation of a person to act on that individual's behalf for the purposes of this Act;

  (b) for that individual's obligations and liabilities by virtue of this Act to fall, in the manner and to the extent specified, on the person designated; and

  (c) for section 10 to have effect (even where that individual is not issued with an ID card) as if obligations arising under that section where an ID card has been issued fell to be discharged in relation to that individual by the person designated.

(6) The power of the Secretary of State under subsection (4) to make supplemental and consequential provision in connection with a modification of Schedule 1 made by an order under section 3(6) includes power –

  (a) to make modifications of any reference in this Act to a paragraph of that Schedule; and

  (b) in connection with that modification, to amend section 12(2) and (3) in such manner as he thinks fit.

(7) Any power to make provision by regulations under this Act for the approval of a person or of apparatus includes power to provide –

(a) for the grant of an approval subject to prescribed conditions;

(b) for the modification of such conditions in the prescribed manner; and

(c) for the suspension or withdrawal of an approval.

41 Expenses of Secretary of State

There shall be paid out of money provided by Parliament –

(a) any sums authorised or required to be paid by the Secretary of State for or in connection with the carrying out of his functions under this Act; and

(b) any increase attributable to this Act in the sums which are payable out of money so provided under any other Act.

42 General interpretation

(1) In this Act –

'apparatus' includes any equipment, machinery or device and any wire or cable, together with any software used with it;

'biometric information', in relation to an individual, means data about his external characteristics, including, in particular, the features of an iris or of any other part of the eye;

'card' includes a document or other article, or a combination of a document and an article, in or on which information is or may be recorded;

'the Commissioner' means the National Identity Scheme Commissioner appointed under section 22;

'confirm', in relation to the contents of an individual's entry in the Register, is to be construed in accordance with subsection (4);

'contravention' includes a failure to comply, and cognate expressions are to be construed accordingly;

'crime' means a crime within the meaning of the Regulation of Investigatory Powers Act 2000 (c. 23) (see section 81(2) of that Act);

'designated document' means a document of a description designated for the purposes of this Act by an order under section 4;

'designated documents authority' means a person with the power or duty to issue a designated document;

'detection', in relation to crime or serious crime, is to be construed in accordance with subsection (9);

'document' includes a stamp or label;

'enactment' includes –

(a) a provision of Northern Ireland legislation; and

(b) enactments passed or made after the passing of this Act;

'false', in relation to information, includes containing any inaccuracy or omission that results in a tendency to mislead (and is to be construed subject to section 3(5));

'fingerprint', in relation to an individual, means a record (in any form and produced by any method) of the skin pattern and other physical characteristics or features of any of his fingers;

'ID card' is to be construed in accordance with section 6(1);

'information' includes documents and records;

'issue', in relation to a document or card, and cognate expressions are to be construed in accordance with subsection (5);

'modification' includes omission, addition or alteration, and cognate expressions are to be construed accordingly;

'necessary in the public interest' is to be construed in accordance with section 1(4);

'place of residence' and 'resides' and cognate expressions are to be construed subject to any regulations under subsection (10);

'prescribed' means prescribed by regulations made by the Secretary of State;

'public authority' has the same meaning as in section 6 of the Human Rights Act 1998 (c. 42);

'public service' is to be construed in accordance with subsection (2);

'the Register' means the National Identity Register established and maintained under section 1;

'registrable fact' has the meaning given by section 1(5) and (6);

'serious crime' means crime that is serious crime within the meaning of the Regulation of Investigatory Powers Act 2000 (c. 23) (see section 81(2) and (3) of that Act);

'statutory purposes' means the purposes specified in section 1(3);

'subject to compulsory registration' means required to be entered in the Register in accordance with an obligation imposed by an Act of Parliament passed after the passing of this Act;

'subordinate legislation' has the same meaning as in the Interpretation Act 1978 (c. 30).

(2) References in this Act to the provision of a public service are references to –

  (a) the provision of any service to an individual by a public authority;

  (b) the exercise or performance in relation to an individual of any power or duty of a Minister of the Crown, the Treasury or a Northern Ireland department;

  (c) the doing by any other person of anything in relation to an individual which that other person is authorised or required to do for purposes connected with the carrying out of any function conferred by or under an enactment;

  (d) the provision of any service to an individual under arrangements made (directly or indirectly) between the person providing the service and a public authority who, for purposes connected with the carrying out of a function so conferred on that authority, bears the whole or a part of the expense of providing the service to that individual; or

  (e) the acceptance or acknowledgment of the conduct of an individual as compliance by that individual with a requirement imposed on him by or under an enactment, or the receipt of any notification or information provided by an individual for the purpose of complying with such a requirement.

(3) References in this Act to an application for the provision of a public service include references to any claim, request or requirement for the provision of the service.

(4) References in this Act to an individual confirming the contents of his entry in the Register are references to his confirming that entry to the extent only that it consists of information falling within paragraphs 1 to 5 of Schedule 1 or section 3(3).

(5) References in this Act to the issue of a document or card include references to its renewal, replacement or re-issue (with or without modifications).

(6) References in this Act to a designated document being issued together with an ID card include references to the ID card and the designated document being comprised in the same card.

(7) References in this Act to providing a person with information recorded in an

individual's entry in the Register include references to confirming or otherwise disclosing to him –

(a) that the information is recorded in that entry; or

(b) that particular information is not recorded in that entry.

(8) References in this Act to information recorded in an individual's entry in the Register include references to a password or code generated by a method so recorded.

(9) Section 81(5) of the Regulation of Investigatory Powers Act 2000 (c. 23) (which defines detection) applies for the purposes of this Act as it applies for the purposes of the provisions of that Act that are not in Chapter 1 of Part 1 of that Act.

(10) The Secretary of State may by regulations make provision for the purposes of this Act as to the circumstances in which a place is to be regarded, in relation to an individual –

(a) as a place where he resides; or

(b) as his principal place of residence in the United Kingdom.

43 Scotland

(1) The use in or as regards Scotland of the Register or of a card issued in accordance with this Act is authorised, and is capable of being authorised, only –

(a) in relation to a matter, or for purposes, outside the legislative competence of the Scottish Parliament; or

(b) in accordance with an Act of that Parliament.

(2) Regulations under section 13 may not allow or require the imposition of a condition in or as regards Scotland on the provision of a public service except where the provision of that service is outside the legislative competence of the Scottish Parliament.

(3) Nothing in this section restricts –

(a) the effect of any provision of this Act authorising information recorded in the Register to be provided to a person;

(b) any power under this Act to make provision authorising such information to be provided to a person; or

(c) any power under this Act to make provision (including provision about the use of ID cards) for purposes connected with the authorisation by virtue of this Act of the provision of such information to a person.

44 Short title, repeals, commencement, transitory provision and extent

(1) This Act may be cited as the Identity Cards Act 2006.

(2) The enactments in Schedule 2 are repealed to the extent shown in the second column of that Schedule.

(3) This Act (apart from this section and sections 36 and 38) shall come into force on such day as the Secretary of State may by order appoint; and different days may be appointed for different purposes.

(4) The power to bring provisions of this Act into force on different days for different purposes includes power –

(a) to bring provisions into force on different days in relation to different areas or descriptions of persons;

(b) to bring provisions into force in relation to a specified area or a specified descrip-tion of persons for the purpose of conducting a trial of the arrangements under which the provisions will have effect when brought into force in relation to other areas or descriptions of persons; and

(c) power to make transitional provision in connection with the bringing into force of any provision of this Act following the conduct of such a trial.

(5) Sections 36 and 38 come into force at the end of the period of two months beginning with the day on which this Act is passed.

(6) Her Majesty may by Order in Council provide for provisions of this Act to extend with such modifications (if any) as She thinks fit to any of the Channel Islands or to the Isle of Man.

(7) Section 40(4) applies to the power of Her Majesty in Council to make an Order in Council under subsection (6) as it applies to the power of any other person to make an order under this Act.

(8) This Act extends to Northern Ireland.

SCHEDULES

SCHEDULE 1
SECTION 3
INFORMATION THAT MAY BE RECORDED IN REGISTER

Personal information

1   The following may be recorded in an individual's entry in the Register –
   (a) his full name;
   (b) other names by which he is or has been known;
   (c) his date of birth;
   (d) his place of birth;
   (e) his gender;
   (f) the address of his principal place of residence in the United Kingdom;
   (g) the address of every other place in the United Kingdom or elsewhere where he has a place of residence.

Identifying information

2   The following may be recorded in an individual's entry in the Register –
   (a) a photograph of his head and shoulders (showing the features of the face);
   (b) his signature;
   (c) his fingerprints;
   (d) other biometric information about him.

Residential status

3   The following may be recorded in an individual's entry in the Register –
   (a) his nationality;
   (b) his entitlement to remain in the United Kingdom;
   (c) where that entitlement derives from a grant of leave to enter or remain in the United Kingdom, the terms and conditions of that leave.

Personal reference numbers etc.

4 (1) The following may be recorded in an individual's entry in the Register –
   (a) his National Identity Registration Number;
   (b) the number of any ID card issued to him;

(c) any national insurance number allocated to him;

(d) the number of any immigration document relating to him;

(e) the number of any United Kingdom passport (within the meaning of the Immigration Act 1971 (c. 77)) that has been issued to him;

(f) the number of any passport issued to him by or on behalf of the authorities of a country or territory outside the United Kingdom or by or on behalf of an international organisation;

(g) the number of any document that can be used by him (in some or all circumstances) instead of a passport;

(h) the number of any identity card issued to him by the authorities of a country or territory outside the United Kingdom;

(i) any reference number allocated to him by the Secretary of State in connection with an application made by him for permission to enter or to remain in the United Kingdom;

(j) the number of any work permit (within the meaning of the Immigration Act 1971) relating to him;

(k) any driver number given to him by a driving licence;

(l) the number of any designated document which is held by him and is a document the number of which does not fall within any of the preceding sub-paragraphs;

(m) the date of expiry or period of validity of a document the number of which is recorded by virtue of this paragraph.

(2) In this paragraph 'immigration document' means –

(a) a document used for confirming the right of a person under the Community Treaties in respect of entry or residence in the United Kingdom;

(b) a document which is given in exercise of immigration functions and records information about leave granted to a person to enter or to remain in the United Kingdom; or

(c) a registration card (within the meaning of section 26A of the Immigration Act 1971);

and in paragraph (b) 'immigration functions' means functions under the Immigration Acts (within the meaning of the Asylum and Immigration (Treatment of Claimants, etc.) Act 2004 (c. 19)).

(3) In this paragraph 'driving licence' means –

(a) a licence to drive a motor vehicle granted under Part 3 of the Road Traffic Act 1988 (c. 52); or

(b) a licence to drive a motor vehicle granted under Part 2 of the Road Traffic (Northern Ireland) Order 1981 (S.I. 1981/154 (N.I. 1)).

Record history

5 The following may be recorded in an individual's entry in the Register –

(a) information falling within the preceding paragraphs that has previously been recorded about him in the Register;

(b) particulars of changes affecting that information and of changes made to his entry in the Register;

(c) his date of death.

Registration and ID card history

6   The following may be recorded in an individual's entry in the Register –

    (a) the date of every application for registration made by him;

    (b) the date of every application by him for a modification of the contents of his entry;

    (c) the date of every application by him confirming the contents of his entry (with or without changes);

    (d) the reason for any omission from the information recorded in his entry;

    (e) particulars (in addition to its number) of every ID card issued to him;

    (f) whether each such card is in force and, if not, why not;

    (g) particulars of every person who has countersigned an application by him for an ID card or a designated document, so far as those particulars were included on the application;

    (h) particulars of every notification given by him for the purposes of regulations under section 11(1) (lost, stolen and damaged ID cards etc.);

    (i) particulars of every requirement by the Secretary of State for the individual to surrender an ID card issued to him.

Validation information

7   The following may be recorded in the entry in the Register for an individual –

    (a) the information provided in connection with every application by him to be entered in the Register, for a modification of the contents of his entry or for the issue of an ID card;

    (b) the information provided in connection with every application by him confirming his entry in the Register (with or without changes);

    (c) particulars of the steps taken, in connection with an application mentioned in paragraph (a) or (b) or otherwise, for identifying the applicant or for verifying the information provided in connection with the application;

    (d) particulars of any other steps taken or information obtained (otherwise than in connection with an application mentioned in paragraph (a) or (b)) for ensuring that there is a complete, up-to-date and accurate entry about that individual in the Register;

    (e) particulars of every notification given by that individual for the purposes of section 10.

Security information

8   The following may be recorded in the entry in the Register for an individual –

    (a) a personal identification number to be used for facilitating the making of applications for information recorded in his entry, and for facilitating the provision of the information;

    (b) a password or other code to be used for that purpose or particulars of a method of generating such a password or code;

    (c) questions and answers to be used for identifying a person seeking to make such an application or to apply for or to make a modification of that entry.

Records of provision of information

9   The following may be recorded in the entry in the Register for an individual –

(a) particulars of every occasion on which information contained in the individual's entry has been provided to a person;

(b) particulars of every person to whom such information has been provided on such an occasion;

(c) other particulars, in relation to each such occasion, of the provision of the information.

SCHEDULE 2

SECTION 44

REPEALS

Short title and chapter	Extent of repeal
Forgery and Counterfeiting Act 1981 (c. 45)	In section 5 – (a) subsection (5)(f) and (fa); and (b) subsections (9) to (11).
Asylum and Immigration (Treatment of Claimants, etc.) Act 2004 (c. 19)	Section 3. In section 14(2), the word 'and' at the end of paragraph (o).

APPENDIX 2

Parliamentary Progress Timetable

Stage	Date	Hansard reference	Issues	Result
Commons First Reading	25 May 2005	HC col 706; HC Bill 9	Bill introduced in the Commons	
Commons Second Reading	28 June 2005	HC col 1151	General and wide-ranging debate on effectiveness/necessity Audit trail; identity theft; civil liberties; access of private companies to the database; police powers; costs; sharing information with other governments; issues for Irish citizens; terrorism; IT problems; function creep; effect on minorities; security; compulsion; alienation	Second reading of the Bill agreed to (314:283) Bill committed to a Standing Committee Programming of Proceedings agreed to (313:286) Identity Cards Bill [Money] agreed to (311:219) Identity Cards Bill [Ways and Means] agreed to
Standing Committee D 1st Sitting	5 July 2005	Standing Committee D col 3	Discussion of clauses 1–3 Access to the register should only be allowed to those who 'reasonably require' it Insertion of a clause defining public interest and explaining the necessity of the Bill	
Standing Committee D 2nd Sitting	6 July 2005	Standing Committee D col 43	Insertion of a clause defining public interest and explaining the necessity of the Bill Registration of addresses Registration of convictions/medical records Registration of death Relationship between the Bill and the Data Protection Act 1988	Clause 1 'The National Identity Register' as amended by this sitting, ordered to stand as part of the Bill (10:6) (continued)

233

Stage	Date	Hansard reference	Issues	Result
Standing Committee D 3rd Sitting	7 July 2005 am	Standing Committee D col 75	Age from which cards should be carried (16 or 18) Effect on the elderly Effect on tourists Should registration happen at birth or 16 years old Usefulness of the card against terrorism	
Standing Committee D 4th Sitting	7 July 2005 pm	Standing Committee D col 101	Status of visitors to the UK Whether the issue of a card should come with registration Maintenance of information on failed asylum seekers	Clause 2 'Individuals Entered in Register' as amended by this sitting, ordered to stand as part of the Bill
Standing Committee D 5th Sitting	12 July 2005 am	Standing Committee D col 147	Who can access information on the database/how long information on it can be recorded/whether security services can browse for information or demand to see an identity card Which documents are 'designated' Compulsion Reliability/necessity of biometric data	Clauses 3 'Information Recorded in Register', Clause 4 'Designation of Documents for Purpose of Registration etc' as amended by this sitting ordered to stand as part of the Bill Schedule 1 agreed to
Standing Committee D 6th Sitting	12 July 2005 pm	Standing Committee D col 191	Reasonable excuses for failure to register Penalties for failure to register Orders under s 6 should be primary legislation Funding/charging Whether cards can contain other voluntary information Ownership of the cards and information held on them Connection between issuing of card and registration	Clause 5 Applications Relating to Entries in this Register', Clause 6 'Powers of the Secretary of State to Require Registration', Clause 7 'Procedure for Orders Under s.6', Clause 8 'Issue etc of ID Cards, Clause 9 'Renewal of ID Cards for Those Compulsorily Registered', Clause 10 'Functions of Persons Issuing Designated Documents' as amended in this sitting, ordered to stand as part of the Bill

Sitting	Date	Reference	Issues discussed	Clauses
Standing Committee D 7th Sitting	14 July 2005 am	Standing Committee D col 267	Which documents are designated and who can decide this Whether requests for information must be 'reasonable' Width of definition of registrable information and list of specified persons Sharing of information between governments of Scotland, Wales and Northern Ireland Compensation for people if extra information causes inconvenience	
Standing Committee D 8th Sitting	14 July 2005 pm	Standing Committee D col 287	Regulations on which individuals' information can be provided (on consent) Checks to avoid system abuse Free access of individuals to data held about themselves Linkage of identity cards and other forms of identification with public service provision (including EU citizens) Requirement to carry identity cards at all times Discrimination Grounds for passing information from the register to government agencies	Clause 11 'Power to Require Information for Validating Register', Clause 12 'Notification of Changes Affecting Accuracy of Register', Clause 13 'Invalidity and Surrender of ID Cards', Clause 14 'Use of Information for Verification or Otherwise with Consent', Clause 15 'Power to Make Public Services Conditional on Identity Checks', Clause 16 'Procedures for Regulations Under s 15', Clause 17 'Power to Provide for Checks on the Register', Clause 18 'Prohibition on Requirements to Produce Identity Cards' as amended in this sitting, ordered to stand as part of the Bill
Standing Committee D 9th Sitting	19 July 2005 am	Standing Committee D col 335	Breadth of powers of the Secretary of State Provision of information for crime prevention Vagueness Effective provision of public services	Clause 19 'Public Authorities etc', Clause 20 'Prevention and Detection of Crime', Clause 21 'Correcting Inaccurate or Incomplete Information', (continued)

Stage	Date	Hansard reference	Issues	Result
			Outsourcing to private companies	Clause 22 'Power to Authorise Provision of Information in other Circumstances',
			Security	Clause 23 'Rules for Providing Information Without Individual's Consent'
			Parliamentary scrutiny of the use of information	as amended in this sitting, ordered to stand as part of the Bill
			Notification to individuals about correction of inaccuracies	
			Authorization of other uses of information	
			Role of the Commissioner	
Standing Committee D 10th Sitting	19 July 2005 pm	Standing Committee D col 379	Role and function of the Commissioner including to whom he is accountable	Clause 24 'Appointment of National Identity Scheme Commissioner',
			Reasonable reason for possession of another person's identity card	Clause 25 'Reports by Commissioner',
			Penalties	Clause 26, Jurisdiction of Intelligence Services Commissioner and Tribunal
			Identity documents	Clause 27, 'Possession of False Identity Documents'
			Whether accidental leakage of information should be punishable	Clause 28, 'Identity Documents for the Purposes of s 27'
			Protection for 'whistleblowers'	Clause 29 'Unauthorised Disclosure of Information',
				Clause 30 'Providing False Information' as amended in this sitting, ordered to stand as part of the Bill
Standing Committee D 11th Sitting	21 July 2005	Standing Committee D col 423	'Dangers of hacking'	Clause 31 'Tampering with Register etc',
			Information in the possession of third parties	Clause 32, 'Consequential Amendments Relating to Offences',
			Penalties	Clause 33 'Imposition of Civil Penalties',
			Creation of regulations	Clause 34 'Objection to Penalty',
				Clause 35 'Appeals Against Penalties',
				Clause 36 'Codes of Practice on Penalties',
				Clause 37 'Fees in Respect of Functions Carried Out in the Act',

Stage	Date	Reference	Description
Commons remaining stages including Third Reading	18 October 2005	HC col 708	Clause 38 'Amendment of Consular Fees Act', Clause 39 'Verifying Information Provided with Passports etc', Clause 40 'Amendments of Legislation Relating to Passports', Clause 41 'Orders and Regulations', Clause 42, Clause 43 'General Interpretation', Clause 44 'Scotland', Clause 45 'Short Title, Repeals, Commencement, Transitory Provision and Extent' as amended in this sitting, ordered to stand as part of the Bill
Lords First Reading	19 October 2005	HL Bill 28; HL col 751	Bill is introduced in the Lords
Lords Second Reading	31 October 2005	HL col 12	Second reading of the Bill
			Salisbury convention
			Purpose of the cards
			Security
			Civil liberties
			Cost
			Identity theft/crime generally/benefit fraud
			Whether the system would be unique
			Identity cards for those under 18 years old
			Opposition of major NGOs to the bill
			Racism
			Terrorism
			Effect on ethnic minorities

(continued)

Stage	Date	Hansard reference	Issues	Result
Lords Committee 1st Day	15 November 2005	HL col 958; 1042	Annual review Cost Title of the Bill IT difficulties Security Popularity Civil liberties Future uses of the identity card Compulsion Identity cards in Scotland Making the register independent from government Parliamentary scrutiny Reliability of biometrics Penalties Amendments 1, 2, 3, 4, 5, 8 considered	
Lords Committee 2nd Day	16 November 2005	HL col 1073; 1157	Verification of identity should be reasonably required Civil liberties Limitation of access to the register for crimes to those 'triable on indictment' Limitation of access for prevention of crime to 'serious crime' Purpose and definition of the Bill Identity cards as a source of independence for women Illegal working Definition of efficiency in provision of a public service Costs	Amendment 9 (Verification of identity by an individual should be to 'others who reasonably require proof') agreed to (141:126)

Stage	Date	Reference	Issues discussed	Clauses
Lords Committee 3rd Day	23 November 2005	HL col 1625; 1698	What information may be recorded on the register Security/unauthorised access/data protection Range of registrable facts Amendments 9, 11, 13, 15, 16, 17, 18, 21, 22, 24, 36 considered Clarity Names that should be on the register Whether those under 18 years old should be included on the register and be issued with an identity card Whether those above 70 years old should be on the register and be issued with an identity card Whether gender should be a registrable fact Whether the card should apply to UK citizens only Whether DNA should be on the register Registration of facts without consent Civil liberties Provision of details on entry on register to individual concerned Registration of death Whether Secretary of State should be able to decide what voluntary information is held Witness protection schemes Liability of the state for inaccurate information Length of time information should be recorded for Amendments 38A, 39, 40, 41, 43, 44, 46, 48, 49, 50, 53, 55, 67, 69, 70, 73 discussed	Clause 1 'The National Identity Register', Clause 2 'Individuals Entered in Register', Clause 3 'Information Recorded in Register' All agreed to
Lords Committee 4th Day	12 December 2005	HL col 971; 1048	Compulsion; whether compulsion should come through primary legislation The use of passport format for names Limitation of designated documents to passports	Clause 4 'Designation of Documents for Purposes of Registration', Clause 5 'Applications Relating to Entries in Register',

Stage	Date	Hansard reference	Issues	Result
			Whether photographs should be full-face Parliamentary review before compulsion Reliability of biometrics Regularisation of foreign nationals What biometrics may be included Civil liberties Personal identity numbers Preventing penalties for failure to have ID cards (pre-compulsion) When/whether individuals must notify government of changes to registrable facts/reimbursement of costs to individual Audit trails Penalties (intentionality) Type/necessity of fingerprinting Whether databases may be shared with other states Amendments 80B, 86, 90, 92, 96A, 101, 105, 106, 112, 114, 115, 117A, 121, 124, 138, 138A discussed	Clause 6 'Powers of the Secretary of State to Require Registration', Clause 7 'Procedure for Orders Under Section 6' All agreed to Schedule 1 'Information that May Be Recorded in the Register' agreed to
Lords Committee 5th Day	14 December 2005	HL col 1257; 1333	Storing information unknown to individuals Tendering of contracts Whether the state should give free replacements where individuals are not at fault for loss Linkage of ID cards and public service provision Details of authorisations should be kept Costs Individuals should be notified of mistakes/changes to their profiles	Clause 8 'Issues etc of ID Cards', Clause 9 'ID Cards for Those Compulsorily Registered', Clause 10 'Functions of Persons Issuing Designated Documents, Clause 11 'Power to Require Information for Validating Register, Clause 12 'Notification of Changes Affecting Accuracy of Register, Clause 13 'Invalidity and Surrender of ID Cards, (continued)

Clause 14 'Provision of Information for Verification or Otherwise with Consent,
Clause 15 'Power to Make Public Services Conditional on Identity Checks,
Clause 16 'Procedure for Regulations under s. 15',
Clause 17 'Power to Provide for Checks on the Register',
Clause 18 'Prohibition on Requirements to Produce Identity Cards',
Clause 19 'Public Authorities etc',
Clause 20 'Prevention and Detection of Crime',
Clause 21 'Correcting Inaccurate or Incomplete Information',
Clause 22 'Power to Authorise Provision of Information in other Circumstances',
Clause 23 'Rules for Providing Information Without Individual's Consent'
All agreed to.

Disclosure of information to individuals to prevent crime/terrorism
Information on the register should only be accessed if necessary (or prevention of serious crime/terrorism)
Discrimination
Whether individuals are required to keep identity cards issued to them
Vagueness of information that may be used for verification purposes
Audit trail
Consent for provision of information; that it should be express
Use of register for research
Data sharing
Role of the Commissioner
Status of police forces in Jersey, Guernsey and Isle of Man
Amendments 141, 150A, 151, 162, 165, 178, 181, 192, 195, 201, 202, 205A, 210, 210ZA, 216A considered

Clauses 24 'Appointment of National Identity Scheme Commissioner',
Clause 25 'Reports by Commissioner',
Clause 26, Jurisdiction of Intelligence Services Commissioner and Tribunal
Clause 27, 'Possession of False Identity Documents'
Clause 28, 'Identity Documents for the Purposes of s 27'
Clause 29 'Unauthorised Disclosure of Information',
Clause 30 'Providing False Information', (continued)

Independent oversight
Role of the Commissioner
Complaints
Penalties (warning beforehand)
Costs
Amendments 221, 228, 255A, 259A considered

Lords Committee 6th Day

19 December 2005

HL col 1511

Stage	Date	Hansard reference	Issues	Result
				Clause 31 'Tampering with Register etc', Clause 32, 'Consequential Amendments Relating to Offences', Clause 33 'Imposition of Civil Penalties', Clause 34 'Objection to Penalty', Clause 35 'Appeals Against Penalties, Clause 36 'Codes of Practice on Penalties', Clause 37 'Fees in Respect of Functions Carried Out in the Act', Clause 38 'Amendment of Consular Fees Act', Clause 39 'Verifying Information Provided with Passports etc', Clause 40 'Amendments of Legislation Relating to Passports', Clause 41 'Orders and Regulations', Clause 42, 'Expenses of Secretary of State' Clause 43 'General Interpretation', Clause 44 'Scotland', Clause 45 'Short Title, Repeals, Commencement, Transitory Provision and Extent' All agreed to. Schedule 2 'Repeals' agreed to. Long Title agreed to.
Lords Report Stage 1st Day	16 January 2006	HL col 427; 511	Amendment 1 to Clause 1: costs—estimates (agreed to 237:156) Amendment 4 to Clause 1: security (agreed to 206:144) Amendment 5 to Clause 1: seriousness of crimes leading to access to the register for police (withdrawn) Amendment 6 to Clause 1: access to public services (agreed to 194:141)	Amendments 1, 4, 6, 7, 17, 18, 21–24, 29 all agreed to.

242

| Lords Report Stage 2nd Day | 23 January 2006 | HL col 955; 1040 | Amendment 7 to Clause 1: residence (agreed to)
 Amendment 9 to Clause 1: other identity cards (withdrawn)
 Amendment 11 to Clause 1: technical (withdrawn)
 Amendment 14A to Clause 2: raise age from 16 to 18 years old (withdrawn)
 Amendment 17 to Clause 2: technical (agreed to)
 Amendment 18 to Clause 3: statutory purposes of the register (agreed to)
 Amendments 21–24 to Clause 3: technical (agreed to)
 Amendment 27 to Schedule 1: location (agreed to)
 Amendment 29 to Schedule 1: photographs of face (agreed to)
 Amendment 32A to Schedule 1: encryption (withdrawn)
 Amendment 33 to Schedule 1: audit trail (withdrawn)

 Amendment 35 to Clause 4: designated documents (agreed to)
 Amendment 36 to Clause 4: authorization by Secretary of State (agreed to)
 Amendment 38 to Clause 5: compulsion (agreed to 186:142)
 Amendment 39 to Clause 5: enrolment centres (agreed to)
 Amendment 43 to Clause 5: draft resolution approved by each House (agreed to)
 Amendment 46 to Clause 6: requiring primary legislation for compulsion (agreed to 198:140)
 Amendment 52 to Clause 7: technical (consequential on Amendment 46) (agreed to)
 Amendment 52A to Clause 8: separation of identity cards from designated documents (withdrawn) | Amendments 35, 38, 39, 46, 52, 52H, 54, 54A, 55, 56, 58, 59, 60, 61, 63, 64 all agreed to |

(continued)

Stage	Date	Hansard reference	Issues	Result
			Amendment 52B to Clause 8: breaking link between identity cards and register (withdrawn)	
			Amendment 52C to Clause 8: limit identity cards for anything beyond identification (withdrawn)	
			Amendment 52D to Clause 8: number of identity cards (withdrawn)	
			Amendment 52F to Clause 8: prescribed period of validity of ID card (withdrawn)	
			Amendment 52G to Clause 8: ownership of cards (withdrawn)	
			Amendment 52H to Clause 8: technical (agreed to)	
			Amendment 53 to Clause 8: compulsion (withdrawn)	
			Amendment 54 to Clause 8: compulsion (agreed to)	
			Amendment 54A to Clause 8: technical (agreed to)	
			Amendment 54B to Clause 8: technical (withdrawn)	
			Amendment 55 to Clause 8: technical (agreed to)	
			Amendment 55A to Clause 9: technical (withdrawn)	
			Amendment 56 to Clause 9: technical (agreed to)	
			Amendment 58 to Clause 10: draft resolution approved by each house (agreed to)	
			Amendment 58A after Clause 10: proposed new clause on surrender of documents (withdrawn)	
			Amendment 59 to Clause 11: technical (agreed to)	
			Amendments 60–61 to Clause 12: draft regulations to be approved by each House (agreed to)	

244

(continued)

			Amendment 62B to Clause 13: authority of Secretary of State (withdrawn)
			Amendment 62E to Clause 14: technical (withdrawn)
			Amendments 63–64 to Clause 14: technical (agreed to)
			Amendment 64A to Clause 15: access to services (withdrawn)
			Amendment 64E to Clause 15: consultation with minority groups (withdrawn)
Lords Report Stage 3rd Day	30 January 2006	HL col 11	Amendments 65–66 to Clause 17: technical (agreed to)
			Amendment 66A to Clause 17: requiring individuals to produce cards pre-compulsion (withdrawn)
			Amendment 68 to Clause 19: regulations and parliamentary scrutiny (agreed to)
			Amendments 69–70 to Clause 20: technical (agreed to)
			Amendment 72 to Clause 21: technical (agreed to)
			Amendment 72D to Clause 23: provision of information (withdrawn)
			Amendment 73–74 to Clause 23: provision of information (agreed to)
			Amendment 74A to Clause 23: data protection (withdrawn)
			Amendment 75 to Clause 23: technical (agreed to)
			Amendment 76 after Clause 23: functions of the Secretary of State and disclosure of information (disagreed to 155:155)
			Amendment 76A of Clause 24: independence of Commissioner (agreed to 155:138)
			Amendments 65, 66, 68, 69, 70, 72, 73, 74, 75, 76A, 77, 85, 85A, 106–110, 112–114, 115, 117, 118, 120, 121, 122, 123 all agreed to

245

Stage	Date	Hansard reference	Issues	Result
			Amendment 77 of Clause 24: role of Commissioner (agreed to)	
			Amendment 78 of Clause 24: amendment of amendment 77 (withdrawn)	
			Amendment 85 to Clause 25: role of Commissioner (agreed to 154:139)	
			Amendment 85A to Clause 25: reports of the Commissioner (agreed to)	
			Amendment 93 after Clause 26: Technical Advisory Board (withdrawn)	
			Amendment 98 to Clause 29: penalties for intentional disclosure (withdrawn)	
			Amendment 101A to Clause 33: warnings and penalties (withdrawn)	
			Amendment 106 to Clause 36: technical (agreed to)	
			Amendments 107–110 to Clause 37: technical (agreed to)	
			Amendment 111 after Clause 40: proof of identity (withdrawn)	
			Amendment 111A before Clause 41: parliamentary oversight/Europe (withdrawn)	
			Amendments 112–114 to Clause 41: technical (agreed to)	
			Amendment 114A to Clause 41: disability (withdrawn)	
			Amendment 115 to Clause 41: technical (agreed to)	
			Amendment 116A to Clause 43: definition of consent (withdrawn)	
			Amendments 117, 118 to Clause 43: technical (agreed to)	

Stage	Date	Reference	Proceedings	Notes
			Amendment 120 to Clause 43: compliance with requirements (agreed to) Amendment 120A to Clause 45: change to Title of the Bill (disagreed to 57:71) Amendment 121 to Clause 45: technical (agreed to) Amendment 121A to Clause 45: EU technical standards (withdrawn) Amendment 122 to Clause 45: technical (agreed to) Amendment 123 after Clause 45: Report on Costs and Benefits (agreed to)	Third reading of the Bill Amendments 2, 3, 5, 6, 7, 8, 9, 10, 11, 12, 14, 15 all agreed to Returned to Commons with Amendments
Lords Third Reading	6 February 2006	HL col 425	Identity fraud Amendment 1 to Clause 1: compulsion (rejected) Amendment 2 to Clause 1: physical characteristics (agreed to) Amendment 3 to Clause 3: audit trail (agreed to) Amendment 4 to Clause 4: designated documents (withdrawn) Amendment 5 to Clause 12: provision of information without consent (agreed to) Amendment 6 to Clause 12: consent (agreed to) Amendment 7 to Clause 16: compulsion to carry ID card (agreed to) Amendments 8–10 to Clause 16: technical (agreed to) Amendment 11 to Clause 22: Identity Scheme Commissioner (agreed to) Amendment 12 to Clause 22: technical (agreed to) Amendment 13 to Clause 23: cost review (agreed to) Amendment 14 to Clause 34: penalties (withdrawn) Amendment 14 to Clause 34: penalties (agreed to)	

(continued)

Stage	Date	Hansard reference	Issues	Result
			Amendment 15 to Clause 34: informing people about the Act (agreed to) Amendments 16–18 to Clause 34: technical (agreed to) Amendment 19 to Clause 35: individuals checking accuracy of the register (withdrawn) Amendment 21 before Clause 39: Parliamentary control (withdrawn)	
Commons Consideration of Lords amendments	13 February 2006	HC col 1145	Lords Amendments 20, 22, 22, 23, and 68–70 discussed.	Lords Amendment 21 disagreed to. Government Amendment (a) in lieu of Lords amendment 21 agreed to. Lords Amendments 20 and 23 agreed to Lords Amendment 16 disagreed to (310:279) Lords Amendment 22 disagreed to (310:259) Lords Amendment 1 disagreed to Lords Amendments 68 to 70 disagreed to (314:261).
Lords consideration of Commons amendments	6 March 2006	HL col 533	Motion A: Costs: whether to accept Government's Amendment 70A in lieu of Amendments 1, 68, 69, 70 Motion B: Reliability of registration: whether to accept Commons Amendment 3A in lieu of Lords Amendment 3 Motion C: Lords technical Amendment 4 Motion D and D1: Compulsion: whether to insist on Amendments 16 and 22 removing link between application for passports and identity card and addition to the register Motion E: Compulsory registration, whether to accept Commons Amendment 21A in lieu of Amendment 21	Amendment 70A agreed to Amendment 3A agreed to Lords agree not to insist on Amendment 4 Lords insist on Amendments 16 and 22 (227:166) Amendment 21A agreed to

Stage	Date	Column	Description	Outcome
			Motion F: Role of the Commissioner, whether to accept Commons Amendment 47A in lieu of Amendment 47, Amendment 48A in lieu of Amendment 48, Amendment 50A in lieu of Amendment 50 and Amendment 51A in lieu of Amendment 51A	Amendments 47A, 48A, 50A and 51A agreed to
Commons consideration of Lords amendments	13 March 2006		Compulsion: whether to insist on disagreeing with Lords Amendments 16 and 22 that seek to remove requirement for anyone obtaining a designated document such as a passport to register and be issued with an identity card.	Commons insists on disagreement with the Lords over Amendments 16 and 22 (310:277). Amendment (a) agreed to in lieu. Bill is returned to the Lords.
Lords consideration of Commons amendments	15 March 2006	HL col 1223	Motion A and A1: Compulsion: whether to insist on Amendments 16 and 22. Lords insisting on their amendments to remove requirement for anyone obtaining a designated document such as a passport to register and be issued with an identity card.	Motion A rejected and Motion A1 agreed to. Lords insist on Amendments 16 and 22 and disagree with the Commons Amendment 22C in lieu (218:183). Bill is returned to the Commons.
Commons consideration of Lords reply	16 March 2006	HC col 1641	Lords reasons 16C and 22D discussed. Government insists on its disagreements with Lords over Amendments 16 and 22 and proposes Amendments (a) and (b) in lieu thereof. Government does not insist on its Amendment 22C	Lords Amendments 16C and 22D rejected (292:241). Bill returned to the Lords
Lords consideration of Commons amendments	20 March 2006	HL col 21	Commons Amendments 22E and 22F discussed and rejected. Lords Amendments 22G and 22H proposed to amend Motion A of this sitting which would delay the proposed automatic linkage between designated documents and identity cards so that it would apply only to applications made after 31 December 2011	Motion A1 agreed to. Commons' Amendments 22E and 22F rejected, Lord Phillips' amendments (22G and 22H) agreed to (211:175)

(continued)

Stage	Date	Hansard reference	Issues	Result
Commons consideration of Lords amendments	21 March 2006	HC col 181	Lords reasons 22G and 22H discussed. Discussion of Amendments as to compulsion; to delay compulsory linkage of designated documents to ID cards and placement on the Register until 2012. Debate essentially about the timing for implementing the requirement for people applying for a designated document, such as a passport, to register and obtain an identity card, rather than the principle of so doing.	Lords Amendments 22G and 22H rejected (284:241). Bill returned to Lords.
Lords consideration of Commons amendments	28 March 2006	HL col 644	Discussion of amendments as to compulsion on Register entry; having an opt-out clause for the register (Lords Amendments 22J and 22K) to break the link between the application for a passport and the application to be entered on to the national identity register	Amendments 22J and 22K proposed (219:191). Bill returned to Commons.
Commons consideration of Lords message	29 March 2006	HC col 875	Discussion of Lords Amendments 22J and 22K to prevent linkage of certain documents with identity cards through an opt-out system. Decided that it would not be possible for the Government to accept a complete opt-out for people who apply for documents designated under the Bill from the requirement to be entered on the national identity register and issued with an identity card. Right to opt out will expire on 1 January 2010.	Amendments 22J and 22K rejected (305:251). Bill returned to Lords.

Lords consideration of Commons message	29 March 2006	HL col 796	Discussion of Government's objections (22JA and 22L). Lords Amendments 22M, 22N, 22O—that ID cards not be compulsory with passports until 1 January 2010, nor will it be compulsory to those who 'opt-out' to inform the Government of changes of address, though all applicants will be included on the register	Motion A1 Amendments 22M, 22N, 22O agreed to (287:60). Bill returned to Commons.
Commons consideration of Lords message	29 March 2006 9.36pm	HC col 999	Lords Amendments 22M, 22N and 22O discussed.	Lords Amendments 22M, 22N, 22O accepted by Commons (301:84).
Royal Assent	30 March 2006 11.37am	HL col 861	Bill is enacted	Identity Cards Act 2006

APPENDIX 3

The Identity Cards Act 2006

Code of Practice on Civil Penalties

DRAFT

This document is an indicative draft only. It has no legal effect and is subject to consultation and alteration

1. THE BASIS FOR THIS CODE OF PRACTICE

1.1 This code is issued under section 36 of the Identity Cards Act 2006 ("the Act"). The purpose of the code is to set out the matters which the Secretary of State and civil courts should consider when determining the amount to be imposed in any case by way of a civil penalty under the Act.

1.2 The civil penalty scheme is not intended to be punitive or revenue-raising. It is intended to establish a mechanism which delivers a proportionate means of ensuring compliance with the terms of the Act. If there is good reason for failure to comply or in cases where the requirements of the Act have been complied with at the time when an objection or appeal is considered, it will normally be appropriate to waive any penalty. The amounts of the penalty specified in the Act are maximum penalties only. The actual amount imposed will be determined on a case by case basis having regard to the principles set out in this code and all the circumstances of the case.

1.3 In accordance with the Act, regard must be had to this code –

- By the Secretary of State when imposing a civil penalty under the Act;
- By the Secretary of State when considering an objection under section 34 of
- the Act; and
- By the court when determining an appeal under section 35 of the Act.

2. LIABILITY FOR CIVIL PENALTIES

2.1 Under the Act the Secretary of State may impose a penalty where he is <u>satisfied</u> that a person is liable to a penalty. Liability may arise in the following situations under the following sections:

Section 6: Compulsory Registration

2.2 **Section 6(4)(a)** <u>Failure to comply with an obligation to register imposed by way of an order made under section 6: maximum penalty £2,500.</u> An order made under section 6 will set out the categories of person to whom it applies and the date by which an application by them to be entered on the Register must be made. In considering liability, the Secretary of State will need to be satisfied that an individual is within the categories of person covered by an order; that the time within which he is required to apply has passed; and that no application was made by him within

253

that time. For example, if the order only applies to persons under a specified age, the Secretary of State will need to be satisfied that the individual concerned is under that age. If the order only applies to persons of particular nationalities, the Secretary of State will need to be satisfied as to the individual's nationality.

2.3 Section 6(4)(b) Failure to comply with a requirement imposed in connection with an obligation to register: maximum penalty £2,500. The requirements which may be imposed on a person to verify his identity in connection with the application are set out in sections 5(4) and (5). They are:

- To attend at a specified place and time;
- To allow his fingerprints and other biometric information such as facial biometrics or iris scans to be recorded;
- To allow himself to be photographed;
- Otherwise to provide such information as may be required by the Secretary of State. This may include for example requests to provide relevant documents such as immigration documents, birth or marriage certificates.

In considering liability, the Secretary of State will need to be satisfied that the person concerned is an individual required by the order to register; that he has been required to do one or more of the things referred to in this paragraph; and that he has failed to do so.

2.4 Section 6(5) Failure to comply with a listed requirement which is imposed otherwise than in connection with an application to be registered: maximum penalty £1,000. A person who is required to register and does so, may subsequently be required to comply with a requirement to do one of the things set out in paragraph 2.3 to ensure that the information on the Register is accurate and up to date. In considering liability, the Secretary of State will need to be satisfied that the individual concerned is required by an order under section 6 to register and has done so; and that he has been subsequently required to do one or more of the things referred to in paragraph 2.3 but has failed to do so.

2.5 Section 6(6) Further failures to register: maximum penalty £2,500. A person on whom a penalty has already been imposed under section 6(4) for failing to comply with an obligation to register is liable to a further penalty on any subsequent occasion on which he fails to comply with a notice given by the Secretary of State requiring him to apply to be entered on the Register within a specified period. In considering liability, the Secretary of State will need to be satisfied that the individual concerned is required by an order under section 6 to register and has failed to do so; that a penalty for that failure has already been imposed; that a further notice has been given to him requiring him to register within a specified period; and that he has failed to do so.

Section 9: ID Cards for those compulsorily registered

2.4* Section 9(5)(a) Failure by a person subject to compulsory registration who is already entered on the Register to apply for an ID Card, if he does not hold a valid one or the one he holds is due to expire within the prescribed period: maximum penalty £1,000. In considering liability, the Secretary of State will need to be satisfied that the individual concerned is required by an order under section 6 to register; that he is entered in the Register; and that he has failed to apply for an ID card or to renew his existing ID card within the period set by regulations under clause 9 [SI xxxx].

* This error in numbering reproduces that given in the original draft.

254

2.5 **Section 9(5)(b)** <u>Failure to comply with a requirement imposed in connection with an obligation, under section 9, to apply for an ID Card: maximum penalty £1,000.</u> In considering liability, the Secretary of State will need to be satisfied that the person concerned is required by an order under section 6 to register; that he is entered in the Register; that he has been required to do one of the things referred to in paragraph 2.3 but has failed to do so.

Section 12: Notification of changes affecting the accuracy of the Register

2.6 **Section 12(6)** <u>Failure to notify the Secretary of State of prescribed changes of circumstances which affect the information held on the Register, or of errors in that information of which the cardholder is aware: maximum penalty £1,000.</u> In considering liability in relation to changes of circumstances, the Secretary of State will need to be satisfied that the person concerned has been issued with an ID card; that there has been a relevant change of circumstances as set out in regulations under section 12 [SI xxxx]; and that the person concerned has not notified the Secretary of State within the relevant period set out in those regulations. For example, regulation [x] provides that a change of permanent address for a period of 3 months or more or a change of name should be notified within 3 months of the change taking place.

2.7 In relation to errors in the information in the Register, the Secretary of State will need to be satisfied that there was an error in the entry relating to that individual and that he was aware of it. Deliberate or reckless provision of false information is a criminal offence under section 30 of the Act with a maximum penalty of 2 years imprisonment. Where there are grounds to believe that an offence under that section may have been committed, the matter should be referred to the police to consider in conjunction with the Crown Prosecution Service whether a prosecution would be appropriate.

2.8 **Section 12(6)** <u>Failure to comply with a requirement which is imposed in connection with a notification given under section 12: maximum penalty £1,000.</u> Where a notification of a change is made, the Secretary of State may require the person concerned to do one or more of the things referred to in paragraph 2.3 in order to ensure the accuracy of the Register. In considering liability, the Secretary of State will need to be satisfied that a change has been notified; that the person concerned has been required to do one or more of the things referred to in paragraph 2.3 but has failed to do so.

Section 13: Invalidity and Surrender of ID Cards

2.9 **Section 13(6)(a)** <u>Failure on the part of a cardholder to notify the Secretary of State, where he (the cardholder) knows or has reason to suspect that the card has been lost, stolen, damaged, tampered with, or destroyed. Maximum penalty £1,000.</u> Regulations under section 13 [SI xxxx] require a cardholder to notify the Secretary of State within one month if he knows or suspects his card has been lost, stolen, damaged, tampered with or destroyed. In considering liability, the Secretary of State will need to be satisfied that one of those things has occurred; that the cardholder must have been aware of that fact; and that he failed to notify the Secretary of State within the prescribed period.

2.10 **Section 13(6)(b)** <u>Failure on the part of a person who is knowingly in possession of an ID Card without the lawful authority of the individual to whom it was issued, or</u>

the permission of the Secretary of State, to surrender it as soon as it is practicable to do so: maximum penalty £1,000.

2.11 Section 13(6)(b) Failure, by a person in possession of an ID Card, to comply with a requirement imposed by the Secretary of State to surrender it within a specified period: maximum penalty £1,000. The Secretary of State may impose such a requirement where it appears to him that:

- The ID Card is issued to another;
- The ID Card has expired or been cancelled or is otherwise invalid;
- The ID Card has not yet been cancelled but is of a description of cards that he has decided should be re-issued;
- The ID Card is in the person's possession in contravention of a relevant requirement.

2.12 In considering liability, the Secretary of State will need to satisfied either that the person concerned had a card belonging to someone else in his possession in circumstances where he must have known he was not authorised to do so or that a specific requirement to surrender a card has been imposed and has not been complied with. For example, while it may be obvious that a card found in the street belonging to a stranger should be surrendered, this may not be the case in relation to a card belonging to a family member. It will not be appropriate to impose a penalty on family members of a deceased person unless a specific requirement to surrender has been made and not complied with. Possession of a card issued to another without reasonable excuse may also be a criminal offence under section 27 of the Act. Where it appears there is no innocent explanation for possession of a card or that it may have been intended to mislead, the matter should be referred to the police and Crown prosecution service to consider whether a prosecution is appropriate.

3. WARNING LETTERS AND PENALTY NOTICES

Warning Letters

3.1 Before imposing a civil penalty for non compliance with a requirement, it will normally be appropriate to send a warning letter setting out the reasons why the Secretary of State has reason to believe liability to a civil penalty has arisen and urging compliance.

3.2 If there is no response to the warning letter and continued non-compliance, consideration should be given to issuing a penalty notice. Before issuing the notice, the Secretary of State will take account of all relevant facts known to him including any response to the warning letter.

The Penalty Notice

3.3 When imposing a civil penalty the Secretary of State must issue the defaulter with a notice. The contents of the notice are set out in section 33 of the Act and [SI xxxx]. It must contain the following information:

- The reasons for deciding that the person is liable to a penalty
- The amount of the penalty
- The date before which the penalty must be paid
- A description of the ways in which payment may be made
- An explanation of the steps the defaulter must take if he wishes to object to the

penalty or appeal against it to the courts or both, including the grounds on which he may object and appeal

- An explanation of the powers of the Secretary of State to enforce the penalty.

4. Objecting to Civil Penalties

4.1 Under Section 34 of the Act, a person on whom a penalty has been imposed may object to the penalty on the following three grounds:

1. That he is not liable to the penalty;
2. That the circumstances of the contravention in respect of which he is liable make the imposition of a penalty unreasonable;
3. That the amount of the penalty is too high.

4.2 A notice of objection must set out the grounds of the objection and the objector's reasons for objecting on those grounds. It should be given in writing (either by post or electronically) and within the prescribed period set out in regulations [SI xxxx] but no other formality is required. The Secretary of State must consider a notice of objection and may then:

1. cancel the penalty
2. reduce the penalty
3. increase the penalty
4. confirm the penalty

4.3 Where the Secretary of State increases a penalty he must issue the objector with a new penalty notice. If he reduces, cancels or confirms the penalty he must inform the objector in writing.

4.4 Section 6 below deals with the factors which the Secretary of State will take into account in considering an objection.

5. Appealing against Civil Penalties

5.1 A person on whom a penalty has been imposed may appeal in England, Wales or Northern Ireland to the county court, or in Scotland to the sheriff. The grounds of appeal are the same as the ones on which an objection may be made, namely,

1. That he is not liable to the penalty;
2. That the circumstances of the contravention in respect of which he is liable make the imposition of a penalty unreasonable;
3. That the amount of the penalty is too high.

5.2 An appeal may be brought regardless of whether a person has made an objection to the Secretary of State. In practice if a person appeals whilst his objection is pending, the court will delay consideration until the outcome of the objection has been notified to the objector.

5.3 An appeal will be a re-hearing of the Secretary of State's decision to impose a penalty, and any subsequent decision made after consideration of an objection. There are no statutory limitations on the evidence which may be brought before the court, including evidence which was not before the Secretary of State when he made his decision.

5.4 On consideration of an appeal the court may:

1. allow the appeal and cancel the penalty
2. allow the appeal and reduce the penalty
3. dismiss the appeal

5.5 The court has no power to increase the penalty. The purpose of the appeal is to guarantee the right of access to the courts for those on whom penalties are imposed; it is not intended to be punitive. Section 6 below gives some guidance as to the matters which a court should take into account on appeal.

6. GROUNDS OF OBJECTION AND APPEAL

6.1 The three grounds on which a person may object and appeal to a penalty are:
1. That he is not liable to the penalty;
2. That the circumstances of the contravention in respect of which he is liable make the imposition of a penalty unreasonable;
3. That the amount of the penalty is too high.

This section provides guidance on how each of those grounds should affect the level of penalty imposed:

Liability

6.2 Liability turns on whether the circumstances set out in paragraphs 2.2 to 2.9 are present.

6.3 Any evidence which suggests that the circumstances which gave rise to a penalty under a particular section were not in fact present should lead to cancellation of the penalty. The following are examples for illustrative purposes only:

- A person on whom a penalty has been imposed under section 6 because he failed to comply with an order requiring persons aged over 16 who are eligible for registration to do so, produces evidence that he is 15. The penalty should be cancelled.

- A person on whom a penalty has been imposed under section 12(6) because he has failed to notify the Secretary of State of a change of address produces evidence which shows that he did not in fact move house or that he did in fact notify the Secretary of State. The penalty should be cancelled.

- A person on whom a penalty has been imposed under section 13 for failing to notify loss of a card produces evidence that he has been abroad for 6 months and did not know his card had been stolen. The penalty should be cancelled.

The circumstances of the contravention in respect of which he is liable make the imposition of a penalty unreasonable

6.4 Even if liability is established, there may be circumstances which make the imposition of a penalty unreasonable. It is impossible to predict all the circumstances which might be raised. All relevant facts known to the Secretary of State and any representations from the person concerned should be considered at the objection stage. These may include written representations or other evidence (such as medical certificates) or representations made by telephone or e mail. At the appeal stage, the court may consider any evidence it considers relevant, whether or not the Secretary of State was aware of it when imposing the penalty or considering an objection. Some relevant factors are set out in the following paragraphs but this is not an exhaustive list. Each case should be considered on its merits.

The awareness of the person concerned of the requirement

6.5 If there is genuine doubt as to whether the person concerned was aware of the requirement, any penalty imposed should normally be cancelled. This may be because they had no notice of the requirement or because they were not able to understand it due to language difficulties, illiteracy or lack of intellectual capacity.

The significance of the contravention

6.6 A deliberate refusal to register when required to do so under section 6 is to be regarded as more serious than a failure to notify relevant changes under section 12 or to notify loss or damage to a card under section 13. This is reflected in the maximum penalty available. Although the latter contraventions are to be discouraged in order to secure the integrity of the Register, a one-off failure to notify eg a change of address should not normally be regarded as sufficiently serious to attract a penalty.

The reason for non compliance

6.7 Even if there is no doubt that there has been a relatively serious failure to comply with a requirement of which the individual concerned was aware, there may be a good reason why he has not complied. For example he may have been abroad or in hospital at the relevant time; or may have been suffering a bereavement; or there may be some other reasonable excuse.

Whether there is a history of previous contraventions

6.8 It may often be appropriate to cancel or reduce a penalty on the first occasion there is a failure to comply. However successive failures should normally attract successively higher penalties, subject to the appropriate maximum.

Whether there has been compliance since service of the penalty notice

6.9 As the purpose of the penalty scheme is to encourage compliance rather than to punish, it will usually be appropriate to cancel the penalty if the individual has complied with the relevant requirement by the time the objection or appeal is considered. Mere lateness should not generally lead to a penalty unless it is both deliberate and prolonged or repeated.

The amount of the penalty is too high

6.10 This ground overlaps to some extent with the question of reasonableness. If there are mitigating circumstances but it is still reasonable to impose a penalty, the factors in paragraphs 6.6 to 6.9 will be relevant in setting the amount of the penalty. In addition, the financial circumstances of the person concerned should be considered under this ground.

6.11 Any evidence of financial circumstances of which the Secretary of State is aware at the point of imposition of the penalty, or which is made available to him at the objection stage, or which is put before the court at the appeal stage should be taken into account.

6.12 In addition to the reductions which might be made on account of mitigating circumstances, further reductions may be made where there is evidence to suggest that the level of the penalty would cause undue financial hardship to the defaulter.

6.13 Only in the most extreme circumstances should that result in cancellation of the penalty. Rather the penalty should be reduced to an amount which is affordable.

6.14 Once the amount of a penalty is fixed, the Secretary of State or the court may agree that it should be paid by instalments in amounts and at times to be agreed.

6.15 As a general guideline, where it appears an individual is liable to a penalty and that it is reasonable in the circumstances to impose one, the Secretary of State would regard a figure of one quarter of the maximum penalty as appropriate. That figure may be further reduced if appropriate eg if there are mitigating circumstances or if there has since been a degree of compliance; or in the light of the defaulter's financial circumstances. If the contravention is particularly serious or there is a history of previous contraventions, the penalty may be increased accordingly. In considering an appeal, the civil courts will have regard to the factors in this code and any other evidence they consider relevant in deciding whether any penalty should be cancelled or reduced.

7. ENFORCEMENT OF PENALTIES

7.1 Where a person has exhausted his objection and appeal rights and has nevertheless failed to pay the penalty, the Secretary of State may enforce the penalty through the civil courts (the County Court in England and Wales and the Sheriff's Court in Scotland) as a debt due to him.

7.2 The Act places a statutory bar on the defaulter raising the grounds of objection and appeal in the enforcement proceedings. Once judgment has been obtained it may be enforced in the usual manner, such as attachment of earnings orders and warrants of execution in England and Wales or earnings arrestment or attachment in Scotland.

7.3 There is no power of imprisonment for failure to pay a civil penalty.

Index